21 世纪全国高等院校财经管理系列实用规划教材

国际商务函电

主　编　金泽虎　王桂平

北京大学出版社
PEKING UNIVERSITY PRESS

内容简介

本书系统地介绍了国际商务函电常用的英文写作基本知识，其中包括各类函电的基本格式、写作技巧、标准模板、具体案例，并且利用案例导入和案例具体分析等形式引导出丰富的国际商务专业词汇与习惯用语。在内容上，全书共分 12 章：各部分内容之间既相对独立又相互依存、彼此融合，完整、系统地反映出该门课程的主要内容。第 1 章是对国际商务函电的基本概况的介绍。第 2 章到第 11 章是本书的主干部分，其内容编排基本依据国际贸易实务流程的先后顺序展开，具体包括：建立商务关系和资信调查、询盘和报盘、合同、订单及其支付条件、信用证、包装、保险、装运、申诉与理赔、代理。第 12 章是对与函电密切相关的外贸单证进行具体的介绍。它们共同形成本书完整的体系结构。

本书适用于国际经济贸易、商务英语、国际市场营销、电子商务等应用性较强的经济贸易类和其他外向型应用性专业的学生，同时也适用于从事对外经济贸易工作的专业人员。

图书在版编目(CIP)数据

国际商务函电/金泽虎，王桂平主编. —北京：北京大学出版社，2013.5

(21 世纪全国高等院校财经管理系列实用规划教材)

ISBN 978-7-301-22388-8

Ⅰ.①国… Ⅱ.①金…②王… Ⅲ.①国际商务—英语—电报信函—写作—高等学校—教材 Ⅳ.①H315

中国版本图书馆 CIP 数据核字(2013)第 074250 号

书　　名：国际商务函电
著作责任者：金泽虎　王桂平　主编
策 划 编 辑：曹江平
责 任 编 辑：翟　源
标 准 书 号：ISBN 978-7-301-22388-8/F · 3598
出 版 发 行：北京大学出版社
地　　址：北京市海淀区成府路 205 号　100871
网　　址：http://www.pup.cn　新浪官方微博：@北京大学出版社
电 子 信 箱：pup_6@163.com
电　　话：邮购部 62752015　发行部 62750672　编辑部 62750667　出版部 62754962
印　刷　者：三河市博文印刷有限公司
经　销　者：新华书店
　　　　787 毫米×1092 毫米　16 开本　16.5 印张　377 千字
　　　　2013 年 5 月第 1 版　2015 年 5 月第 2 次印刷
定　　价：35.00 元

21世纪全国高等院校财经管理系列实用规划教材

专家编审委员会

丛 书 序

我国越来越多的高等院校设置了经济管理类学科专业，这是一个包括经济学、管理科学与工程、工商管理、公共管理、农业经济管理、图书档案学6个二级学科门类和22个专业的庞大学科体系。2006年教育部的数据表明，在全国普通高校中，经济类专业布点1518个，管理类专业布点4328个。其中除少量院校设置的经济管理专业偏重理论教学外，绝大部分属于应用型专业。经济管理类应用型专业主要着眼于培养社会主义国民经济发展所需要的德智体全面发展的高素质专门人才，要求既具有比较扎实的理论功底和良好的发展后劲，又具有较强的职业技能，并且又要求具有较好的创新精神和实践能力。

在当前开拓新型工业化道路，推进全面小康社会建设的新时期，进一步加强经济管理人才的培养，注重经济理论的系统化学习，特别是现代财经管理理论的学习，提高学生的专业理论素质和应用实践能力，培养出一大批高水平、高素质的经济管理人才，越来越成为提升我国经济竞争力、保证国民经济持续健康发展的重要前提。这就要求高等财经教育要更加注重依据国内外社会经济条件的变化，适时变革和调整教育目标和教学内容；要求经济管理学科专业更加注重应用、注重实践、注重规范、注重国际交流；要求经济管理学科专业与其他学科专业相互交融与协调发展；要求高等财经教育培养的人才具有更加丰富的社会知识和较强的人文素质及创新精神。要完成上述任务，各所高等院校需要进行深入的教学改革和创新。特别是要搞好有较高质量的教材的编写和创新工作。

出版社的领导和编辑通过对国内大学经济管理学科教材实际情况的调研，在与众多专家学者讨论的基础上，决定编写和出版一套面向经济管理学科专业的应用型系列教材，这是一项有利于促进高校教学改革发展的重要措施。

本系列教材是按照高等学校经济类和管理类学科本科专业规范、培养方案，以及课程教学大纲的要求，合理定位，由长期在教学第一线从事教学工作的教师编写，立足于21世纪经济管理类学科发展的需要，深入分析经济管理类专业本科学生现状及存在的问题，探索经济管理类专业本科学生综合素质培养的途径，以科学性、先进性、系统性和实用性为目标，其编写的特色主要体现在以下几个方面：

（1）关注经济管理学科发展的大背景，拓宽理论基础和专业知识，着眼于增强教学内容与实际的联系和应用性，突出创造能力和创新意识。

（2）体系完整、严密。系列涵盖经济类、管理类相关专业以及与经管相关的部分法律类课程，并把握相关课程之间的关系，整个系列丛书形成一套完整、严密的知识结构体系。

（3）内容新颖。借鉴国外最新的教材，融会当前有关经济管理学科的最新理论和实践经验，用最新知识充实教材内容。

（4）合作交流的成果。本系列教材是由全国上百所高校教师共同编写而成，在相互进行学术交流、经验借鉴、取长补短、集思广益的基础上，形成编写大纲。最终融合了各地特点，具有较强的适应性。

（5）案例教学。教材具备大量案例研究分析内容，让学生在学习过程中理论联系实际，特别列举了我国经济管理工作中的大量实际案例，这可大大增强学生的实际操作能力。

（6）注重能力培养。力求做到不断强化自我学习能力、思维能力、创造性解决问题的能力以及不断自我更新知识的能力，促进学生向着富有鲜明个性的方向发展。

作为高要求，财经管理类教材应在基本理论上做到以马克思主义为指导，结合我国财经工作的新实践，充分汲取中华民族优秀文化和西方科学管理思想，形成具有中国特色的创新教材。这一目标不可能一蹴而就，需要作者通过长期艰苦的学术劳动和不断地进行教材内容的更新才能达成。我希望这一系列教材的编写，将是我国拥有较高质量的高校财经管理学科应用型教材建设工程的新尝试和新起点。

我要感谢参加本系列教材编写和审稿的各位老师所付出的大量卓有成效的辛勤劳动。由于编写时间紧、相互协调难度大等原因，本系列教材肯定还存在一些不足和错漏。我相信，在各位老师的关心和帮助下，本系列教材一定能不断地改进和完善，并在我国大学经济管理类学科专业的教学改革和课程体系建设中起到应有的促进作用。

劉詩白

2007 年 8 月

刘诗白　现任西南财经大学名誉校长、教授，博士生导师，四川省社会科学联合会主席，《经济学家》杂志主编，全国高等财经院校资本论研究会会长，学术团体“新知研究院”院长。

前　　言

就国际贸易而言，改革开放头10年，中国进出口总额由1978年的206亿美元扩大到1988年的1028亿美元。此后速度不断加快，5年后的1993年发展到近2000亿美元。8年后的2001年增加到5097亿美元。加入WTO以后，对外贸易发展异常迅猛。2002年以来，进出口进入高速增长时期，连续6年实现了20%以上的增长。在2004年超过1万亿美元后，仅用3年时间就实现了从1万亿到2万亿的突破。2007年进出口总额21737亿美元，特别是2009年起出口总额超过德国，成为全球第一出口大国。2011年，我国外贸进出口总值36420.6亿美元，比2010年同期(下同)增长22.5%，外贸进出口总值刷新年度历史纪录，其中，出口总额18986亿美元，增长20.3%；进口总额17434.6亿美元，增长24.9%。贸易顺差1551.4亿美元，全球排名依次是：进出口总额世界第二，进口总额世界第二，出口总额世界第一，贸易顺差世界第一。中国国际贸易的蓬勃发展对世界、国内经济的贡献均是举足轻重的。

与此同时，我国高等教育的发展也很快，对对外经贸人才的需求更加迫切。为适应上述形势发展和变化的需要，我们组织编写了本书，本书力求体现以下3个特点。

一是内容实用，突出应用性。编写时力求结合对外经贸专业的学生特点和实际需要，在保证理论充分的同时，注重案例分析，培养独立分析问题、思考问题和解决问题的能力。

二是突出特色，注重创新。尽量借鉴优秀教材编写经验，创新教材编写理念，注重教材内容与形式的创新。形式上力求新颖活泼；内容上体现科学性、实用性与时代性的统一。既要保证内容的科学、准确与规范，又要突出实用性与时代性。力求反映出国际经济与贸易的最新成果和最新变化，充分重视国际贸易理论的前瞻性，将一般教材的滞后性压缩到尽可能低。

三是形式新颖，便于自学。编排形式尽可能新颖活泼、图文并茂，并力求文字流畅、表现生动、深入浅出、通俗易懂。每章以"案例导入"开头，各节之间穿插"相关链接"等，每章后附"本章小结"、"思考题"、"思考案例"等内容，以便于学生在掌握必要的专业知识的同时，拓展知识面、启迪智慧。

全书共分12章：各部分内容之间既相对独立又相互依存、彼此融合，完整、系统地反映出该门课程的主要内容。第1章是对国际商务函电的基本概况的介绍，第2章到第11章是本书的主干部分，其内容编排基本依据国际贸易实务流程的先后顺序展开，第12章是对与函电密切相关的外贸单证进行具体的介绍。它们共同形成本书完整的体系结构。

本书由安徽大学经济学院金泽虎、铜陵学院外语系王桂平任主编，负责全书的设计与统稿。铜陵学院李煜、吴秀群、龚春利、钱立新等老师也参与了本书的编写。各章编写分工如下：金泽虎(第10章)，王桂平(第6章、第7章、第12章)，李煜(第8章、第11章)，龚春利(第1章、第5章)，吴秀群(第2章、第3章、第4章)，钱立新(第9章)。

在本书编写的过程中，参阅了大量国内外相关著作、教材及报刊资料，在此特向这些著作及资料的原作者、原提供者表示衷心的感谢！本书不仅可以作为高等院校经济贸易和商贸英语专业本科教育的教材，而且可以供相关专业其他层次学历教育选作教材，也可以作为涉外经济贸易企业及有关管理部门管理人员的学习与参考读物。

由于编写者的水平有限，书中难免存在一些不足和错漏之处，敬请有关专家与读者批评指正。

金泽虎
2013.3

目　　录

Chapter 1　The Overview of Business Letters 1

Section One　The Structure and the Format of Business Letters 1
Section Two　Principles of Business Letter Writing 8
Section Three　Business Fax and E-mail Writing 10
Section Four　Cases in Detail 11
Section Five　Selected Sentences 15

Chapter 2　Establishing Business Relations and Status Enquiries 21

Section One　Establishing Business Relations 21
Section Two　Status Enquiries 24
Section Three　Cases in Detail 26
Section Four　Selected Sentences 32

Chapter 3　Enquiry and Offer 45

Section One　Enquiry 46
Section Two　Offer and Counter-offer 47
Section Three　Cases in detail 48
Section Four　Selected Sentences 56

Chapter 4　Contract 71

Section One　Definition and Functions of Contract 71
Section Two　Classification and Contents of Contract 72
Section Three　Cases in Detail 74
Section Four　Selected Sentences 81

Chapter 5　Orders and Terms of Payment 90

Section One　Orders and Replies 91
Section Two　Method of Payment 92
Section Three　Cases in Detail 92
Section Four　Selected Sentences 97

Chapter 6　Letter of Credit 106

Section One　Content and Classification of Letter of Credit 106
Section Two　Procedures of Letter of Credit Operations 118
Section Three　Cases in Detail 123
Section Four　Selected Sentences 129

Chapter 7　Packing 134

Section One　Forms of Packing 134
Section Two　Marking of Goods 140
Section Three　Cases in Detail 142
Section Four　Selected Sentences 149

Chapter 8　Insurance 158

Section One　Essentials of Business Letters of Insurance 159
Section Two　Cases in Detail 160
Section Three　Selected Sentences 166

Chapter 9　Shipment 177

Section One　Shipping Instruction and Shipping Advice 177
Section Two　Terms of Shipment 179
Section Three　Cases in Detail 181

Section Four Selected Sentences 192

Chapter 10 Complaints and Adjustments 198

Section One Types of Complaints 198

Section Two Adjustments 199

Section Three Cases in Detail 200

Section Four Selected Sentences 206

Chapter 11 Agency 213

Section One Essentials of Agency 214

Section Two Essentials of Business Correspondence of Agency 215

Section Three Cases in Detail 216

Section Four Selected Sentences 224

Chapter 12 Documentation in International Trade 232

Section One Types of International Trading Documents 232

Section Two Requirements of Documents Making 233

Section Three Cases in Detail 233

Section Four Selected Sentences 243

References 248

Chapter 1 The Overview of Business Letters

商务函电概况

案例导入 Case-lead-in

上海环宇工贸有限公司与荷兰 Tivoli 儿童用品公司长久以来一直有着业务来往。由于经济危机的冲击，荷兰 Tivoli 儿童用品公司破产。近年来，随着世界经济的复苏，上海环宇工贸有限公司从同行中获悉荷兰 Tivoli 儿童用品公司重新开业。得知这个消息，上海环宇工贸有限公司销售经理李小燕立即发函表示祝贺。

Section One The Structure and the Format of Business Letters 商务信函的内容与格式

The purpose of communication is to obtain complete understanding between the parties involved, and elicit the responses required. This task aims at helping students to familiarize themselves with the characteristics of business letters.

1. Parts of the Business Letter

Generally, a business letter consists of standard parts and optional parts.

Parts of a Business Letter 商务书信的组成部分	
Standard Parts 标准部分	Optional Parts 附加部分
Letterhead 信头	Attention Line 经办人姓名
Dateline 日期	Subject Line 事由或标题
Inside Address 封内地址	Reference Number 参考编号
Salutation 称呼	Enclosures 附件
Body of the Letter 正文	Carbon Copy 抄送
Complimentary Close 结尾敬语	Postscript 再启
Signature 签名	

The standard parts are essential for the business letters, while the optional parts should be chosen according to the writing need.

1) Letterhead

Letterhead designs very with business organizations and occupy the top of the first page. They may be positioned in the center or at the left margin for full block style or flush at the right margin for indented style. Most of the business firms and other organizations use stationery with a printed letterhead, which contains all or some of the following elements: the company's name, address, postcard, telephone numbers, telex, fax, e-mail address, and possibly the name of the chief executive. It may even include some picture or slogan for symbol of the company. This will be useful not only to the reader in responding to the message but also to the firm in creating a favorable impression.

2) Reference Number

3) Dateline

All business letters should have the correct date typed under the letterhead. The date records when the letter was written. It may serve as an important reference. For example, if there is a question about an order or shipment, a contract, or a reply to customer complains, you will have the dated copy of a letter in your files to verify when you wrote the message and what you said. Try to send the letter on or close to the date typed under the letterhead. The date is usually placed two line below the last line of the letterhead at the left margin for full block style or ending with the right margin for indented style. It is usual to show the date in the order day/month/year (English practice), or month/day/year(American practice). For the day, either cardinal numbers or ordinal numbers can be used. However, this is a growing tendency to omit the ordinal suffixes: −st, −nd, -rdand –th that follow the day of the month in the date line. For example: 25th March 2005; March 25th, 2005; 25 March 2005; March 25, 2005. Never give the date in figures and abbreviations of the month, for it can easily cause confusion.

4) Inside Address

The inside address consists of the name, address and zip code of the company or person to whom you are writing. It usually begins directly or on the third line below the date line. If the letter is addressed to a person, use either a courtesy title(Miss., Mr., Mrs., or Ms.), or if appropriate, rise a professional title(Dr. or Prof., for example). Do not use both kinds of titles with one name. Sometimes, the title of a person's position within the organization may be included and typed either immediately after the person's name or on the line below the person's name, whichever position results in better balance. If the letter is to a group, inside address includes the full group name and the address. Care should be taken to address the recipient as exactly as it appears on the envelop of the letter. See the examples below: Mr. Alfred McKenna, Treasurer Finance and Accounting Department Warren, Hanson & Associates 259 Third Avenue New York, New York 1007.

(1) Receiver's name known:

Mr. A. David

Sales Manager

Original Manufacturing & Trading Co.

24704 State Road

Lutz, Florida 33559

U.S.A.

(2) Receiver's name unknown:

Advertising Department or (Advertising Manager)

Kingkill Motor House Ltd.

212, D.W. Rupasinghe

Nugegoda, Srilanka

(3) Company's name known only:

Tochimoto Tenkaido Co., Ltd.

3-21, Suehiro-cho Kitaku

Osaka, Japan

5) Attention Line

It is typed two line-spacing above the salutation, underlined and, except with the fully-blocked letter-style, centered over the body of the letter.

Teah Hong & Co.

212, Beach Street

10300, Penang

Malaysia

Attention: Joe Bush

6) Salutation

The salutation is the complimentary greeting with which every letter begins. After the inside address and the reference line, the salutation is typed two lines down, flush with the left margin. The customary formal greeting in a business letter is

(1) for addressing one person :Dear Sir, Dear Madam.

(2) for addressing two or more people :Dear Sirs, Dear Madams, Gentlemen (should always be in plural form).

If the receiver is known to the writer personally, a less formal and warmer greeting is used as follows: Dear Ms. Bontoux, Dear Dr. Walter. The trend is towards "Ms." as the courtesy title for all women regardless of their marital status.

Dear <u>Mr.</u> Smith——male

Dear <u>Mrs.</u> Brown—— female, married

Dear <u>Miss</u> Jenifer——female, unmarried

Dear <u>Ms</u> David——female, marriage status unknown

Dear <u>Mason</u>—— friends or acquaintances

Use an individual's full name (Dear Leslie Lanbam) only when gender is unknown. For letters with attention lines or those addressed to organizations, the selection of an appropriate salutation has become more difficult. Formerly, "Gentlemen" was used generally for all organizations. With increasing numbers of women in business management today, however, it is problematic. Because no universally acceptable salutation has yet emerged, you'll probably be safest with Ladies and Gentlemen or Gentlemen and Ladies.

7) Subject Line

The subject heading is regarded as a part of the body of a business letter. Usually it is typed two line-spacing below the salutation, underlined, to call attention to what content the letter is about.

Dear Yuki,

Re：KH type linear ball bearings

or

Subject：Aluminium complete bottom shaft support

8) Body of the Letter

The body of the letter, which contains the messages you want to send across to the receiver, is the core of the letter. A good letter will not only get the business done but also promote good will. Thus, it should be carefully planned and messages should be stated and arranged logically. It is best, even for a short letter, to divide the body into at least two or more paragraphs, confining each paragraph to one topic. This step makes your text easier to read and presents your message more clearly.

Paragraph one—Begin with information that catches the reader's attention and refer to some need or interest of the reader, or refer to the previous correspondence if there is one. Put "you" into the letter.

Paragraph two—Bring in your involvement, or what service or information you have to offer. Put "you and I" into the letter.

Paragraph three—End the body of the letter with the action or idea that you want the reader to consider or with the results you would like to have.

9) Complimentary Close

The complimentary close is merely a polite way to end a letter. It is a part of the body of business letter. It appears in the middle of the page or flush with the left margin in fully blocked letters and two lines below the closing sentence. The expression for the complimentary close should be in accordance with the salutation. The formal business letter which begins with "Dear Sir(s)," should close with "Yours faithfully,". For the personally and less formal letter which opens with "Dear Mr. ×××" or the like, "Yours sincerely," is the usual complimentary close(the American prefer "Sincerely yours,"). "Yours truly," is a useful alternative to "Yours sincerely," when the writer wishes to be informal but has no personal acquaintance with his correspondent. For the informal letter which opens with "Dear John" or "Dear Mary", "Best Wishes" or "Best regards" can also be used.

男性(Male)	女性(Female)	结尾敬语 (Complimentary close)	备注(Remarks)
Sir Sirs	Madam Mesdames	Yours respectively Yours very respectively Respectively yours	非常正式的称呼和敬语
Dear Sir Dear Sirs	Dear Madam Mesdames	Yours faithfully Faithfully yours	英国的标准用法
Gentlemen	Ladies	Yours truly Truly yours	美国的普遍用法
Dear Mr. Smith My dear Mr. Smith	Dear Mrs. Smith Dear Miss Smith Dear Ms. Smith My dear Mrs. Smith	Yours sincerely Yours cordially Yours very sincerely Yours very cordially	用于互相熟悉的私人函，有时也用于业务函

10) Signature

The signature is the signed name of the person writing the letter. It is handwritten in ink above the typed name, the space left by the typist which appears three to five lines under either the complimentary close or the firm name. The person's name is typed beneath the signature so that the name is legible to the reader. The person's typed business title and/or the name of his or her department usually follows the typed name. For example:

Yours faithfully

per pro Edward, Brothers & Co.

Robert (handwritten)

Robert (typewritten)

Sales manager

11) Enclosure

When something is enclosed with the letter, the enclosure notation follows two lines after the signature block. If there are more than one enclosure, the number should be indicated. For example:

Encl-2

1. Price list

2. Terms and Conditions of Sale

12) Postscript

To include a brief message unrelated to the letter, a postscript may be added below everything else typed on the page. However, if you forget to include an important idea in the letter body, it is usually better to retype the letter than to add the information in a postscript. For example:

P.S. The sample will be sent tomorrow.

13) Carbon Copy

Sometimes, copies of letters are given to relevant people who need to know the information contained in the letter, the name of these persons should be typed after "C.C:" or "X.C:". For example:

C.C. Mr. Buckley

2. Layout of the Business Letter

There are three main formats of a business letter in use at present: the full block style, the indented style, and the modified block style.

1) The Full Block Style

The block style is an American style, which has now come to be much more widely used than before. Its remarkable feature is that all typing lines begin at the left hand margin.

Kung Kee Wing Hing Trading Company
No. 16-20, Ko Shing Street
HongKong
Tel: (00852)25484259 Fax: (00852) 25487186

November 8, 2007

Your Ref. K.K. 678
Our Ref. K.O.1108
Mr. Koji Otani
Manager of Trading Department
Fukuda Ryu Company Limited
5-11, 1-Chome, Nishitemma, Kitaku
Osaka, Japan

Dear Mr. Koji Otani,
Subject: **20MT Canola oil**

开首段

阐述段

结尾段

Sincerely Yours,
For Ho Kun Kuan

2) The Indented Style

The indented style is a traditional British practice with the heading usually in the middle and the date line on the right-hand side. The complimentary close may be in the center or commence at the center point. The indented style takes 4 or 5 letters in the first line of each paragraph in the body of the business letter. It looks attractive and makes for easy reading, but it is not convenient to type.

Allen Incorporation
1470 St. Louis Street
Los Angeles,CA90015
U.S.A

Ref.No.

March 15,200…

China National Import &.Export Corp.
Shanghai Branch
Shanghai
China

Gentlemen:

Order No.789 for Tools

____
____________________开首段____________________
____

____
____________________阐述段____________________
____

____
____________________结尾段____________________
____

Yours sincerely,
Allen
Allen Inc

3) The Modified Block Style

The modified block style is a combination of the indented style and the block style. It is an eclectic style and is most widely used in international trade.

Xi'an Medicines & Health Products
Import & Export Corp.
No. 176, Qujiang Plaza, Square Road
Xi'an, China
Tel: (29)52227272 Fax: (29) 52227273

December 20, 2007

Your Ref. XMHOD0258/20
Our Ref. DtcOD0258/09

Sales Department
PSA Chemicals & Pharmaceuticals
109, Gaya Building, Yusuf Meherali Road
Bombay 400003, India
Dear Sir,
Order No. XMH20071206

____
__________开首段__________
____

____
__________阐述段__________
____

____
__________结尾段__________
____

Yours Faithfully,
McDonald
McDonald
General Manager

Section Two Principles of Business Letter Writing 商业信函写作原则

Only the letter which conveys the message is faultless can it be an effective business letter. So the following essential principles must be paid attention to if you want to write an appropriate letter. Generally speaking, we need to apply some specific writing principle while writing a business letter.

1. Consideration

The letters you send out must create a good impression. Try to put yourself in his or her place to give consideration to his or her varied wishes, demand, interest and difficulties. Emphasize the "You" attitude rater than the "I" or "We" attitude. Compare the following sentences:

You are authorized to draw at 90 days on the bank in Beijing for the amount of your invoice after shipment is effected.

We authorize you to draw at 90 days on the bank in Beijing for the amount of your invoice after shipment is effected.

2. Courtesy

It should hardly be necessary to stress the importance of courtesy in your correspondence. One of the most important things is promptness. Punctuality will please your customer who dislikes waiting for days before he gets a reply to his letter. In the business writing, you should

(1) Using "Please, Will you…, Will you please…" rather than "You should, You must, You have to".

(2) Using subjunctive mood.

We should be obliged if you let us have your opinion on their financial standing.

We would appreciate your providing us with any information you might have.

Should your goods prove to be satisfactory upon arrival, we are confident that further larger orders will be placed.

(3) Using positive feeling words "We are afraid, We would say, We may(might) say, We(would) think, It seems(would seem) to us, We(would) suggest, As you are (may be) aware, As we need hardly point out" instead of the negative feeling words "don't, be unable to, etc.".

3. Completeness

A business letter is successful and functions well only when it contains all the necessary information. An outline helps for letter to be full and complete. See to it that all the matters are discussed, and all questions are answered. Incompleteness is not only impolite but also leads to the recipient's unfavorable impression toward your firm.

4. Clarity

When the business letter is written, it must be clear, the language is eager to understand, and the subject must be prominence. If the customer must reread the message to grasp, the meaning of the passage is not clear, if we write clarity, the customer understands what we mean. Quick response, therefore, is the result. Compare the following sentences:

This chair will eliminate friend employees.(not clear)

This chair will reduce fatigue.(clear)

5. Conciseness

Conciseness is often considered to be the most important writing principle. It enable to save both the writer's and recipient's time. To achieve conciseness of your letter-writing, try to keep your sentences short, and avoid wordy languages and redundancy, or repetition, and eliminate excessive details. It is a good rule to confine each paragraph to only one point or topic. Compare the following sentences:

Please be advised that we have received your invoice No.248.(wordy)

We have received your invoice No.248.

6. Concreteness

What the letter comes to should be specific, definite rather than vague, abstract and general. For example, some qualities or characters of goods should be shown with exact figures and avoid words like short, long and good. Give specific time with date, month, year and even offer hour, minute, if necessary, but avoid expressions such as yesterday, next month, and immediately.

We wish to confirm our quotations yesterday.(vague)

Please make immediate shipment of our order to Bombay.(general)

7. Correctness

For business letter involve the rights, the duties and the interest of both sides, often as the base of all kinds of document. Therefore, we should not to overstate which would throw you in an awkward position.

Section Three Business Fax and E-mail Writing 商务传真与电子邮件写作

1. The Format of Faxes

When you send a fax, be sure to include a fax cover sheet like this:

FAX COVER SHEET

Date: October 18, 2002

PLEASE DELIVER THE FOLLOWING PAGE(S) TO:

NAME: Jack Tony

COMPANY/DEPARTMENT:Marketing Dept.

THIS FAX IS BEING SENT BY:

NAME/DEPARTMENT: Tom Smith, Design Dept.

NUMBER OF PAGES: 3 INCLUDING COVER SHEET

TIME SENT: 10:30 AM x PM -----.

IF YOU DO NOT RECEIVE ALL PAGES CLEARLY, PLEASE CALL(915)355-8960

2. The Guidelines of Faxes

When you send a fax, observe the following guidelines.

(1) Be careful about sending anything longer than three to four pages. You can tie up the recipient's phone line. Call before you fax to see whether the recipient will allow you to fax a longer document or would prefer that you send it another way.

(2) Make sure your fax is clear, but always include your phone and fax numbers in case the recipient needs to verify your message or has questions about it.

(3) Avoid writing any comments in the margins or at the very top or bottom of a fax. Your notes might be cut off or blurred in transmission.

(4) It may be permissible to send a fax to a company. After business hours, do not risk sending one after hours to a customer's home unless they've agreed or requested it.

3. The Layout of E-mails

1) heading
   -Date: automatic insertion
   -From: the sender's address
   -To: the recipient's address, an obligatory element
   -Subject: a description of what the message is about, an optional element
   -Priority: a signal of prime importance with the exclamation mark (!), an optional element
   -Cc (Carbon Copy): other recipients' email address, known to all recipients
   -Bcc(Blind carbon copy): other recipients' email address, unknown to other recipients
   -Attachment: reminding the recipients to check the message, a symbol like paper-clip
2) Salutation
   -Informal tone
3) The body
   -Reader friendly
   -No more than three paragraphs

4. Tips for Writing E-mail

(1) Avoid using all capital letters. Capital letters only for emphasis or for titles.
(2) Avoid using all lower-case letters.
(3) Check your E-mail regularly.
(4) Care about correctness.
(5) Never send spam.
(6) Announce attachments.
(7) Don't forward without permission.

Section Four Cases in Detail
具体案例分析

(一) 经典案例解析

CNIEC SHAANXI CORP. 28 Xiguan Street Xi'an, China 710082 Tel: 029 8862 3911 Fax: 029 8861 3616	Letterhead
Your Ref. 0709182A	Reference Number
Our Ref. 0709203C	Reference Number
29 August, 2007	Dateline
Minermet S.A. Avenue Mon-Repos 14 1005 Lausanne Switzerland	Inside Address
Attn: Miss Yuki Lee	Attention line

续表

Dear Sirs,	Salutation
Re. Shipment of 100 MT zinc Ingots under your S/C No. 2708	Subject Line
Dear Michael Scott, About items 1-7, if the female must be vertical, we could produce pitch 3.5/3.81/5.0/5.08m, that is to say, we couldn't produce item 6.7 because the mould is not finished at present. Mr. Michael Scott, we think, you only cancel item 6 and item 7. About female must be vertical, enclosing picture, please check it. if OK, please tell me. We are waiting for your reply, then we will send our price to you tonight. Waiting for your reply.	Body of the Letter
Yours faithfully,	The Complimentary Close
Jevin Li Jevin Li Sales director	Signature
Encl.	Enclosure
P.S.	Postscript
cc:	Carbon Copy

Notes

1. letterhead: 信头。信头部分英文地址的写法与中文完全不同，地址的名称按从小到大的顺序：第一行写门牌号码和街名；第二行写县、市、省、州、邮编、国名。写英文地址时，一般在每一行的末尾都不用标点符号，但在每一行的当中，标点符号不能省略。信头的写法可以使用齐头式和缩行式。

2. Reference Number: 参考编号。在商务信函中，采用参考编号不但便于日后查询信件或存档分类，还能够保证信件及时送达收信人。信函的参考编号一般可以由档案编号、部门代码或者有关人员姓名的首字母构成。如果收信人在写信时提供了参考编号，回信人在复函时就应该提及该参考编号。大多数进出口企业信笺纸的信头已经包括了参考编号部分(Our Ref. ——我方编号，即发信人编号；Your Ref. ——贵方编号，即收信人编号)，写信时应在相应的位置填上编号，否则，就要在信头的下方添加参考编号。在实际业务操作中，也可以在回信的第一段或者事由行提及参考编号。

3. Dateline: 日期。日期可以用数词；月份要用英语名称，不能使用缩略语；年份一概使用全称，不能简写，例如：不能以 07 代替 2007；日期应按月、日、年(美国英语)或日、月、年(英国英语)的顺序全文写出。

4. Attention line: 经办人姓名。有些商业信函需要发给公司或部门，不直接发给个人，在这种情况下，为了使收信公司迅速将信函转给经办人或经办部门办理，可以在封内地址和称呼中间加上经办人姓名。另外，在指明的收信人不在时，也允许公司的其他人查看信的内容。经办人姓名通常写在封内地址的下两行。

5. Subject Line: 事由。事由行的作用在于使收信人准确快速了解信函的基本内容和目的。

(二) 一般案例表述

Model Fax 1

FAX MESSAGE

TO: Shanxi Textile Imp. & Exp. Corp Trendsetters Inc.

ATTN: Mr. David, Manager160a Oak Avenue, New York, USA
FAX NO.: 0086-29-334876 Tel: 78928666 Fax: 78928668
FROM: Trendsetters Inc.
DATE: Sep.23, 2003
FAX NO.: 78928668 Page 1 of 3
PAGE: 1/3

Dear Mr. Chen,

This is an urgent request for a consignment to replace the damaged delivery that we received, and of which you have already been informed. Please airfreight the following items: Cat. No: Quantity: RN30Ag20L265070100. The damaged consignment will be returned to you on receipt of the replacement.

Yours sincerely,
Mr. Smith
Chief Buyer

Model Email 2

From: BethJ39903@aat.co.jp< BethJ39903@aat.co.jp >
To: Jackson < Jackson @usa.net>
Date: Thursday, January 28,1999 4:53 PM
Subject: Invoice received, goods missing

Dear Jackson,

Thank you for your original invoice for 15 Bella Handbags under our Order No.123. But we haven't yet received the goods. Would you please let us know whether it has been shipped or not?
Best regards,
Beth. J

资料链接 Material—link

1. Acronyms(often used in email)

Acronyms	Meaning	Acronyms	Meaning
HRU	How are you!	TTYL	talk to you later
UR	you are	WRT	with respect to
VR	we are	MGR	manager
B/cuz	because	IOW	in other words
HV	have	INFO	information
HVB	have been	IMM, IMMD	immediate
PLS	please	TKS, THKS	thanks
TDY	today	BTW	by the way

续表

Acronyms	Meaning	Acronyms	Meaning
A/O	at once	ASAP	as soon as possible
MKT	market	TIA	thanks in advance
BIZ	business	FYR	for your reference
F2F/FTF	face to face	VG	very good
A/S/L	age, sex, lodge	GTG	go to go
NBD	no big deal	FAQ	frequently asked questions

2. Top level domain name suffixes

Suffixes	Meaning	Suffixes	Meaning
.cn	China 中国大陆	.hk	Hong Kong 中国香港
.tw	Taiwan 中国台湾	.uk	United Kingdom 英国
.fr	France 法国	.us	United States 美国
.de	Germany 德国	.br	Brazil 巴西
.it	Italy 意大利	.tr	Turkey 土耳其
.nl	Netherlands 荷兰	.es	Spain 西班牙
.jp	Japan 日本	.kp	Republic of Korea 韩国
.sg	Singapore 新加坡	.my	Malaysia 马来西亚
.eg	Egypt 埃及	.za	South Africa 南非
.ar	Argentina 阿根廷	.vn	Vietnam 越南

3. Writing Guide

1) 给客户写信时的注意事项

(1) 要简明和言之有物。(Be concise and to the point.)

(2) 信件内容应避免混乱、冗长或带有攻击性，尽量以客气、友好和不拘泥的形式书写。(Don't write confused, overlong or pointed letters and try to be polite, friendly and informal.)

(3) 要传达信息而不要哗众取宠。(Try to communicate instead of writing to impress.)

(4) 先说重要信息。(Place primary information upfront in organizing sentences, paragraphs and the whole passage.)

(5) 信件内容要清晰易读。(Keep your writing clear and completely readable.)

(6) 使用浅显易明的文字。(Use plain language.)

(7) 注意文化差异。(Consider cultural differences.)

2) 英文信封的内容

(1) 发信人的名称、地址(Return Address)。

(2) 收信人的名称、地址(Mailing Address)。

(3) 邮递指示(Mailing Direction)。

(4) 其他。

3) 英文信封通常采用的两种书写形式

(1) Block Style 齐头式。

(2) Indented Style 缩进式。

4) 电子邮件地址的组成

一个完整的 Internet 邮件地址由两个部分组成，格式如下：

1oginname@full host name .domain name

即：登录名@主机名.域名

中间用一个表示“在”(at)的符号@分开，符号的左边是对方的登录名，右边是完整的主机名，它由主机名与域名组成。其中，域名由几部分组成，每一部分称为一个子域(Subdomain)，各子域之间用圆点“. ”隔开，每个子域都会告诉用户一些有关这台邮件服务器的信息。

5) 顶级域名

目前互联网上的域名体系中共有 3 类顶级域名：类别顶级域名、地理顶级域名、个性化域名(又称为新顶级域名)。类别顶级域名共有 7 个，也就是现在通常说的国际域名：.com(用于商业公司)；.net(用于网络服务)；.org(用于组织协会等)；.gov(用于政府部门)；.edu(用于教育机构)；.mil(用于军事领域)；.int(用于国际组织)。地理顶级域名共有 243 个国家和地区的代码，例如.cn 代表中国，.uk 代表英国，这样以.cn 为后缀的域名就相应地叫做“国内域名”。国际互联网名称和编号分配公司(ICANN)2008 年 6 月 26 日在巴黎年会上全票通过个性化域名方案，自 2009 年开始有了以自己公司名字结尾的域名，如.ibm、.hp、.qq、.baidu 等，一个形象的比喻是这些域名的所有者在某种意义上就是一个域名注册局。所以从某种意义上来说，以后将会有无穷多的“国际域名”。

Section Five Selected Sentences
精选句型表达

1．We confirm telegrams/fax messages recently exchanged between us and are pleased to say that…

我方确认近来双方往来电报/传真。并欣告……

2．We confirm cables exchanged as per copies (cable confirmation) herewith attached.

我方确认往来电报，参见所附文本。

3．Although no communication has been exchanged between us for a long time, we trust that you are doing well in business.

虽然久未通信，谅你方生意兴隆。

4．Although we have not heard from you for quite some time, we hope your business is progressing satisfactorily.

虽然好久没接到你方来信，谅业务进展顺利。

5．We have pleasure in sending you our catalog, which gives full information about our various products.

欣寄我方目录，提供我方各类产品的详细情况。

6．We are pleased to send you by parcel post a package containing…

很高兴寄你一邮包内装……

7. We have the pleasure in acknowledging the receipt of your letter dated…
欣获你方……月……日来信。

8. We acknowledge with thanks the receipt of your letter of…
谢谢你方……月……日来信。

9. We have duly received your letter of…
刚刚收悉你方……月……日来信。

10. We thank you for your letter of …contents of which have been noted.
谢谢你方……月……日来信，内容已悉。

11. Referring to your letter of…, we are pleased to…
关于你方……月……日来信，我们很高兴……

12. Reverting to your letter of, we wish to say that…
再洽你方……月……日来信，令通知……

13. In reply to your letter of …, we…
兹复你方……月……日来函，我方……

14. We wish to refer to your letter of…concerning…
现复你方……月……日关于……的来信。

15. In compliance with the request in your letter of …, we…
按你方……月……日来函要求，我方……

16. We owe your address to…
我方从……获得你方地址。

17. We should be glad if you would let us know whether…
如果贵方告知是否……，我们将很高兴。

18. May we have details of…？
我们可以得到……的详情吗?

19. We are sending you under separate cover…
兹另封寄上……

20. We attach for your information the copy of a letter received today from…
附上今日收到的从…来信的复印件，供你方参考。

21. We have been informed by…
……已通知我方。

22. Your letter of the…crossed ours of the same date.
贵方……月……日函刚好错过我方同日信函。

23. We are surprised to learn from your letter of…that…
从你方……月……日函惊讶地获悉……

24. Since receipt of your letter of …, we have been trying to find out more about…
收到贵方……月……日信函后，我们一直设法得到更多关于……

25. We would point out that…
我方指出……

26. For your information, we would add that…
我方要补充说明……供你参考。

27. They mainly trade with Japanese firms.

他们主要和日本商行进行贸易。

28. For the past five years, we have done a lot of trade with your company.

在过去的 5 年中，我们与贵国进行了大量的贸易。

29. Our trade is conducted on the basis of equality.

我们是在平等的基础上进行贸易的。

30. There has been a slowdown in the wool trade with you.

和你们的羊毛贸易已有所减少。

31. Our foreign trade is continuously expanding.

我们的对外贸易不断发展。

32. Trade in leather has gone up (down) 3%.

皮革贸易上升(下降)了 3%。

33. Trade in general is improving.

贸易情况正在好转。

34. Our company mainly trades in arts and crafts.

我们公司主要经营手工艺品。

35. They are well-known in trade circles.

他们在贸易界很有名望。

36. We trade with people in all countries on the basis of equality and mutual benefit.

我们在平等互利的基础上和各国人民进行贸易。

37. To respect the local custom of the buying country is one important aspect of China's foreign policy.

尊重买方国家的风俗习惯是我国贸易政策的一个重要方面。

38. Attached is the design document, please review it.

设计文档在附件里，请评阅。

39. For other known related to individual features, please see attached release notes.

其他个人特征方面的信息请见附件。

40. Attached please find today's meeting notes.

今天的会议记录在附件里。

Abstract

通过本章学习，①了解商务信函的基本结构；②掌握商务信函的写作原则；③通过熟悉标准模板掌握传真和电子邮件写作的基本方法；④熟练掌握商务信函经典句型的表达。

Useful Words & Expressions

1. Confidential(机密)
2. Top Confidential(绝密)
3. Private(私人亲启)
4. Personal(亲启)

5．Urgent(急件)
6．Top Urgent(特急件)
7．Shipping Documents/Business Papers(装船单据)
8．Printed Matter(印刷品)
9．Sample of No Commercial Value(无商业价值的样品)
10．Kindness/Courtesy of Mr…(烦请……先生转交)
11．With Compliments of…(……敬赠)
12．Photographs: Please do not bend.(照片：请勿折叠)

Exercises

1. Multiple choice.

(1) We ____ some brochures ____ to illustrate the products we manufactured.

A．enclose, to you　B．enclose you,\　C．enclose, \　D．enclose, you

(2) If you will send us a catalog by air, we shall ____ very much.

A．appreciate　B．appreciating　C．appreciation　D．appreciate it

(3) As it only ____ a small quantity, we hope you will have no difficulty in settling this matter.

A．involves　B．involved　C．has involved　D．may have involved

(4) You can find ____ for black tea here.

A．a ready market　B．most popular

C．great popularity　D．selling fast

(5) We trust you will do your best to have this matter ____ right away.

A．settle　B．to settle　C．settling　D．settled

(6) By joint efforts we can ____ both friendship and business.

A．increase　B．promote　C．expand　D．extend

(7) We ____ you for the special offer you send us.

A．thank　B．appreciate　C．be grateful　D．be indebted

(8) As it involves only a small ____, we hope you will have no difficulty on promotion.

A．quality　B．figure　C．quantity　D．number

(9) We cannot entertain your suggestion ____ it does not seem workable.

A．because　B．for　C．so　D．therefore

(10) We enclosed our Purchase Confirmation No. 4848 ____ duplicate.

A．in　B．for　C．with　D．through

2. Fill in the blanks.

(1) Our foreign trade policy is based ________ equality and mutual benefit.

(2) To trade ________ the people of all countries on the basis of equality and mutual benefit

is our established policy.

(3) ________ you know, this is a popular brand which can see easily in our market.

(4) Please take the necessary steps ________ delay.

(5) We hope this unfortunate incident will not affect the friendly relations ________ us.

(6) Please cable us as soon as ________, giving us all necessary information.

(7) As to chemical products we are well connected ________ the major producers in America.

(8) We refer ________ you letter of May 2.

(9) They are not interested ________ small quantities.

(10) Will you send us ________ return mail pamphlets and price list ________ your exports?

3. Rewrite the following sentences.

(1) As to the steamers sailing from Hong Kong to San Francisco, we have bimonthly direct services.

(2) We shall be able to supply 10 cases of the item only.

(3) We sent you 5 samples yesterday of the goods which you requested in your letter of May 20 by air.

(4) We wish to acknowledge receipt of your letter of 5 June.

(5) Enclosed herewith please find two copies of the file.

4. Correction.

Directions: Read the following e-mail. Do you think it is suitable for the business? Try to rewrite it.

Dear Sirs,

Your message has been received. Thank you.

It is difficult to understand your inquiry of 56mm 8ohm waterproof speaker which can handle 102dB, because through our vast experience, it is almost impossible in technology. Can you supply us with your sample? If so, it would be big help to this project.

Hope we could work together.

Yours faithfully,

5. Read the following letter carefully and identify the numbered labels in the letter.

March 23, 2004

Mr. Jame

Director of Personnel (1)

Windsor Mils Inc.

212 Magnolia Avenue (2)

Spartanburg, South Carolina 29301

The United States of America

Attention Mr .Li (3)

Dear Mr. Zhang,

Re / Subject: Claim No. MA-457972 (4)

We have decided to accept the 8% discount you offered and terms of payment, viz. Documents against Payment, but would like these terms to be reviewed in the near future.

Would you please send the shipping documents and your sight draft to Northminster Bank (City Branch) Deal Street, Birmingham B3 ISQ?

If you do not have any of the listed items in stock, please do not send substitutes in their place.

We would appreciate delivery within the next six weeks, and look forward to your acknowledgement.

Cordially, (5)

Systems A/S Corporation (6)

Joe Grossman (7)

Sales Manager

XYW : SH (8)

Encl: Order form No. AB 3015 (9)

CC to Mr. Zhang (10)

6. Plan the layout according to the following particulars.

Sender: China National Import & Export Corporation
Shanghai Branch Shanghai China

Receiver: Alfred & Co.
Sherman Oak, California
91403
U.S.A.

Date: Twenty second of March 2001

Our Reference No. : 351/10578

Remarks: This letter is to be signed by a staff member on behalf of the firm.

7. Address an envelope based on the following addresses.

Sender: Kenneth Harvey & Co., 361 1st Cross Street New York, N.Y., U.S.A.

Receiver: John Simon & Co., Fern hall Driver, Red bridge London E.C.1, England.

Case Practice

以本章的导入案例为背景，请以公司销售经理李小燕的名义写一封祝贺信，并附上产品目录及插图，为以后建立业务关系打下基础。注意信函的格式和语言表达。

Chapter 2 Establishing Business Relations and Status Enquiries

建立商务关系和资信调查

案例导入 Case-lead-in

某日，阳光公司自澳大利亚驻华大使馆商务参赞处获悉，澳大利亚悉尼市 Flushing 大街 56 号的 Nelson & Peterson 有限公司(邮政编码 94672)拟购买山地车，并想在中国内地寻求与其建立长期合作关系的客户。

Section One Establishing Business Relations 建立商务关系

1. Importance of Establishing Business Relations

In international trade, establishing business relations with prospective trade partners is the first and foremost step, which is a foundation stone for a company's development. No customer, no market. No market, no business. A foreign trade company needs extensive business connections to maintain or expand its business activities. Therefore, establishing business relations is one of the important undertakings in the field of foreign trade, which aims at transforming prospective trade partners into real ones. The principal purpose of business correspondences is to establish business relations and maintain goodwill. Both the importer and the exporter will benefit from a favorable business relation. To companies engaged in foreign trade, business connections are valuable. Therefore, traders must not only do everything possible to consolidate their established relations with companies having precious business but also develop and revitalize their trade by searching for new connections from time to time.

2. Channels for Obtaining Information about Prospective Trade Partners

If a company wishes to open up a market to sell something to or buy something from companies in foreign countries, the first step is to find out whom he is going to deal with and some information related to him, especially contact information. How to find potential trade partners is a great challenge for a new foreign trade company. Usually, such information is obtainable through the following channels.

1) Chamber of commerce both at home and abroad 商会

2) Chinese Commercial Counsellor's Office in foreign countries 商务参赞处

3) Trade directory 工商行名录

4) Attendance at the trade fairs, exhibitions and expositions at home and abroad 交易会、展览会或博览会

5) Advertisements in the media, such as newspaper, magazine, radio, TV and so on 媒体广告

6) The Internet 互联网

7) Market survey 市场调研

8) Mutual visits by trade delegations and representatives 贸易代表团

9) Bank 银行

10) Yellow page 黄页

11) Self-introduction or enquiries received from the merchants abroad 自我介绍或外商的询盘

12) Introduction or recommendation from business connections 贸易伙伴的介绍

With the development of the Internet, most traders take advantage of search engines, among which the most popular is Google, and the second is B2B(Business to Business)electronic business trade platform, such as alibaba(阿里巴巴), Global Sources(环球资源), Made-in-China(中国制造网), Hi-supplier(中国海商网), HKTDC(香港贸发网), hc360(慧聪网), dhgate(敦煌网). Among these B2B electronic business trade platforms, alibaba takes up an absolute advantage.

In addition, you should make best of Google, exploring the local websites in different countries. Some common Google websites are listed here.

US：www.google.com

UK：www.google.co.uk

Germany：www.google.de

France：www.google.fr

Japan：www.google.co.jp

Italy：www.google.it

Holland：www.google.nl

Switzerland：www.google.ch

Denmark：www.google.dk

Finland：www.google.fi

Canada：www.google.ca

Australia：www.google.com.au

You can explore local search engines to seek for more opportunities as well. Some useful websites are offered here.

www.sensis.com.au 澳大利亚本土最大的搜索引擎，相当于百度在中国的实力

www.kellysearch.com 美国的搜索引擎

www.virgilio.it 意大利的搜索引擎

www.wlw.de 德国的搜索引擎

www.ypag.ru 俄罗斯的黄页

www.yellowpages.biz.pk 巴基斯坦的黄页

Generally speaking, if you have found out the potential partner's e-mail address, then it's very convenient for you to communicate with him. In effect, sending e-mails to potential trade partner has become a common practice in international trade. That's to say, it's especially important to find out the right e-mail address of the potential trade partner. If you find out the right person and his right e-mail address, you just open a door for further business connections. One effective method is to put some public e-mail domain names after the key words you are searching, such as *promotional gifts@hotmail.com*. Of course, different countries and regions have different public e-mail domain names. Common public e-mail domain names are as follows.

U.S.: @comcast.net

Japan：@yahoo.co.jp

Hong Kong：@netvigater.com

Germany：@t-online.de

France：@excite.com

Australia：@westnet.com.au

Sweden：@caron.se

In addition, you can use the "site" function to make your search more precise, such as *site: promotional gifts@comcast.net*, but the shortcoming is that it is very likely to leave out some important trade partners.

Although the Internet is widely used now, it's still a quite difficult job to seek prospective partners on the Internet, which involves a great amount of time and energy. Participating in fairs is one of the most important marketing modes for companies and it is also the first choice to develop new markets. A fair is a neutral place where the seller or buyer can negotiate with each other face-to-face on the basis of equality. Besides, it can make the buyers recognize the exhibits thoroughly. The most famous one in China is *China Export Commodities Fair* (also called *Guangzhou Fair* or *Canton Fair*, 广交会). Fairs held by *Hong Kong Trade Development Council* (HKTDC, 香港贸易发展委员会，简称香港贸发局) also enjoy great popularity with their top performance. If your company can afford it, you can also attend varieties of fairs abroad.

3. Contents of Letters about Establishing Business Relations

After obtaining the desired names and addresses of the companies from any of above channels, writing letters to prospective customers for the establishment of business relationship is a routine in international trade. This type of letter is an outgoing letter and may be called a "First

Enquiry". A successful business letter is a key to establishing business relations with potential customers and opening up an oversea market. To attract the receiver's attention, your letter should arouse his interest and encourage him to take action. Generally speaking, this type of letter should be simple, clear and concise, including the following contents.

(1) Tell the receiver how you get his name and information.

(2) Make a self-introduction of your own company.

(3) Express your expectation of establishing business relations and an early reply.

(4) If possible, offer the receiver the reference as to your company's credit standing.

The core of business letter is "short, short, short again; delete all extra words; make everything clear". To businessmen, time is money. To make your letter short and clear is to save your customer's time as well as yours. Your letter should be polite, cordial, warm and kind. Such words as "please, help, kindly, could, thank you, appreciate" are often applied.

Any letter of this kind received must be answered in full without the least delay and with courtesy so as to create goodwill and leave a good impression on the reader. Even though you refuse the other party's request, you should explain the reasons for refusal with courtesy and without delay, leaving room for future potential trade. It's unwise to put it aside.

Section Two Status Enquiries
资 信 调 查

1. Importance of Status Enquiries

Status enquiries are an examination of an importer's credit history, which is a prerequisite and important factor in international trade. It is of great importance to obtain any information possible concerning the partner one is about to enter into relations with. No matter whether you are an importer or an exporter, it is necessary for you to make a careful investigation of the partner's credit status, which can avoid some potential ventures in business. With the help of a status enquiry, a foreign trader can know the customer's conduct, capacity and capital so as to be able to decide whether or not to risk doing business with him.

2. Channels for Obtaining Information about Status Enquiries

There are various channels to obtain information about status enquires. The main ones are as follows.

1) Banks 银行

2) Chinese Commerce Agencies in Foreign Countries 中国驻外商务机构

3) Foreign Countries Commerce Agencies in China 外国的驻华商务机构

4) Enquiry Companies at Home and Abroad 国内外咨询机构

5) Chamber of Commerce 商会

6) Other or Similar Industries Enterprises 其他同行业或是相近行业的企业

Among all channels mentioned above, the most widely-used one is applying to the bank. Therefore, status enquiries are often referred to as "bankers" references. The information obtained from a bank is generally most reliable. However, a bank will not give information direct to an unknown trader unless the enquiry is from one of its fellow banks. Therefore, when taking up a bank reference, the trader must do so through his own bank.

Apart from those channels, you can obtain some information through other ways, such as the customs data, to see whether the partner has done some business with others before. You can search some information about your potential trade partner on the Internet as well. As an exporter, you'd better make status enquiries through different channels to ensure you are dealing with trustworthy importers.

3. Contents of Status Enquiries

For the information about status enquiries, the more detailed, the better. Generally speaking, the main contents are as follows.

(1) The financial standing(assets and liabilities).

(2) The credit.

(3) The reputation.

(4) The management scope.

(5) The management methods.

(6) The management capacities.

4. Contents of Letters about Status Enquiries

Letters enquiring status are more or less stereotyped. Some large companies make such enquiries on specially printed forms containing the questions they would like to have answered.

Your letter of status enquiries should inform your receiver of the following particulars.

(1) The name of your customer and his company address.

(2) What you need to know about your customer.

(3) Your assurance of keeping the reply as confidential.

Status enquiries are generally headed "confidential" or "private and confidential". These words are also written on the envelope.

After obtaining the information, the enquirer will make an objective analysis about the prospective customer according to the "three C" principles: capital, capacity and conduct. Capital refers to the assets, profits, liabilities, and the capital turnover. Capacity refers to the management capacity, management skill and comprehensive index of the future client. Conduct refers to its credit and reputation. The conclusion can finally be reached according to the "three C" principles.

Traders asking for information must bear in mind that they are asking a favor and therefore should write in polite and appreciative terms. When the information is received, no matter it's favorable or unfavorable, a suitable letter of acknowledgment and thanks must be sent. This is no more than common courtesy.

Section Three Cases in Detail
具体案例分析

(一) 经典案例解析

Dear Sirs,

We owe your name and address to the Commercial Counsellor's Office of the Swedish Embassy in Beijing who have informed us that you are in the market for Textiles.

We avail ourselves of this opportunity to approach you for the establishment of trade relations with you.

We are a state-operated corporation, handling both the import and export of Textiles. In order to acquaint you with our business lines, we enclose a copy of our Export List covering the main items suppliable at present.

Should any of the items be of interest to you, please let me know. We shall be glad to give you our lowest quotations upon receipt of your detailed requirements.

In our trade with merchants of various countries, we always adhere to the principle of equality and mutual benefit. It is our hope to promote, by joint efforts, both trade and friendship to our mutual advantage.

We look forward to receiving your enquiries soon.

Yours faithfully,

Jacqueline

Notes

1. owe…to… 得知……

例句：We owe your name and address to the Commercial Counsellor's Office of the Swedish Embassy

2. Commercial Counsellor's Office 商务参赞处

3. be in the market for… 想要购买……

例句：We are in the market for Groundnuts.

be in the market 要买(或卖)

例句：Please advise us when you are in the market.

4. avail oneself of … 利用……

例句：We avail ourselves of this opportunity to express our thanks to you for your close cooperation.

5. approach *v.* 与……接洽

例句：We have been approached by several buyers for the supply of walnuts.

6. state-operated corporation 国营公司

7. handle *v.* 经营

例句：This shop handles paper and stationery.

8. acquaint sb. with sth. 使某人了解某事

例句：You will have to acquaint us with the details.

9. line *n.* 行业；(一类)货色

例句: We have been for many years in the chemical line.

This is a good line of hardware.

10. enclose *v.* 随函附上

例句: We enclose a copy of our pricelist.

Please refer to the pricelist enclosed with (or : in) our letter of August 5.

Enclosed please find a copy of our pricelist.

(Or: Please find enclosed a copy of our pricelist.)

We believe you will find the enclosed interesting.

enclosure *n.* 附件 (信内有附件时，常用 Encl. 或 Enc. 注明于信末左下角，如例文。)

例句: We thank you for your letter of April 15 with enclosures.

11. covering *a.* 包括……的；涉及……的；有关……的

例句: Please let us have your pricelist covering your typewriters.

12. sth. be of interest to sb. 使感兴趣；有兴趣

例句: This article is of special interest to us.

注意区分: sb. be interested in sth.

13. upon (or : on) receipt of… 收到……后，(即……)

例句: On (or : Upon) receipt of your instructions we will send the goods.

14. requirement *n.* 需要；需要之物

例句: We can meet your requirements for (or: of) Walnutmeat.

15. trade *n.* 贸易；行业

例句: They have been in the wool trade for quite a number of years.

trade *v.* 从事贸易；做生意；经营

例句: They trade in cotton piece goods with many countries.

16. adhere to = stick to 忠于；坚持

例句: We always adhere to our commitments.

17. principle of equality and mutual benefit 平等和互利的原则

18. both trade and friendship to our mutual advantage 对双方都有利的贸易和友谊

例句: It is our hope to promote, by joint efforts, both trade and friendship to our mutual advantage.

(二) 一般案例表述

1. Self-introduction

Dear Sirs,

This is Water from SHV Company. I've been working in DVD field for more than five years. Hope that I can serve you with my professional experience from now on. Please feel free to study our offer as below.

First of all, I would like to introduce you some information about our factory. SHV Company is a professional manufacturer in producing Portable DVD Player, covering 7', 8.5', 9', 10.2'. And SHV got the supports as below.

Staff Number: over 300.

Production lines: four lines.

Monthly capacity: 60 000pcs.

Quality control: FCC, CE, EMC, CCC, RoHS.

Factory management: ISO9001 International Quality Management System and ISO14000 International Environment Management System.

Markets: ××× from Spain, ×××, ××× from Italy, ××× from Germany, ××× from Ukraine, ××× from Bulgaria, ××× from Russia, ××× from Israel, ××× from Iran, ×××, ××× from India, ××× from Middle East, ××× from Paraguay, ××× from Panama, etc.

Now I would like to offer you the fast sale item with best price for your reference first.

Model: Item A701, 7' swivel screen with TV tuner, USB & Card Render.

Offer: FOB Shenzhen US$50.

MOQ: 1 000pcs.

Samples and more information are available for your study anytime. We appreciate your kind reply soon.

We are looking forward to our cooperation in near future.

Best regards,

Water

Notes

(1) 第一次主动联系客户，介绍自己在行业内的经验和业绩，让客户产生信心。

(2) 介绍公司的产品和实力，以增加客户信心。

(3) 根据客户所在国家目前销售产品的情况，向客户推荐适当的产品。

(4) 报价时要包含产品的重要信息，例如产品的主要功能、报价条款、价格、订单起订量等。

(5) 最后，提出合作的愿望。

2. Contact Customers after the Fair

Dear Sirs,

Thank you for your kind visit at our booth 3.2F18 during Canton Fair. This is Water from SHV Company. I hope you could feel free to study our offer about Portable DVD Player.

SHV Company is a professional manufacturer in producing Portable DVD Player. The products are spreading countries and regions including Asia, Europe and America, products covering 7', 8.5', 9', 10.2'. We've been investing US$38 million to set up a high-tech industry zone named SHV Technology Co., Ltd in Zhejiang Province, which covers 82 000 square meters and 200 000 square meters of building. With our strong R&D and workmanship, believe we can become your good partner and friend.

According to the memo during Canton Fair, we would like to list the following offers for your record.

Model: Item A903, 9' swivel screen with TV tuner, USB & Card Reader.

Offer: FOB Shenzhen US$50.

MOQ: 1 000pcs.

Samples and more information are available as requested. We appreciate your kind ideas about our cooperation.

We are looking forward to our initial cooperation soon.

Best regards,

Water

Notes

(1) 参加展会是很多公司选择推广产品的一种很重要的方式。在展会之前，通常都要向所有的老客户和潜在的客户发邀请函。这也是向客户展示实力的一次机会。通常邀请函都会做成图片的形式，方便发送给用户参考。内容包括：参展公司名称、参展日期、展位号、主展产品等重要信息。

(2) 展会之后，联系客户时提及展位号，使客户更容易回忆起自己。

(3) 开门见山地说明自己销售的产品，容易抓住日理万机的客户的注意力。

(4) 简短的公司和产品介绍可以让客户在短时间内熟知自己的实力和优势，以拉近合作的距离。

(5) 根据展会上的笔记总结正式向客户报价。

(6) 最后，提出合作的期望。

3. Contact Customers by B2B Web Information

Dear Sirs,

I got your business information online. We would like to cooperate with you on CARDS，and become your good partner in near future.

With more than 12 years experience in manufacturing all kinds of PVC cards, paper cards, metal cards and smart cards in China, we've grown up into a main supplier in Italy, Germany, Sweden, France, Denmark and New Zealand etc. The daily output can reach millions of cards. Including PVC blank and printed cards, paper cards, scratch cards, magnetic cards, IC cards, game cards, gift cards, member cards, pokers, playing cards, metallic cards, phone cards, irregular-shaped cards, ATM cards, IC cards, ID cards, RFID tags etc. We welcome your ODM projects. All sizes and thickness can be done here.

We welcome your enquiries. Please visit our official website at http://www.ucard.biz. It will be appreciated that if someone from your company could contact me freely. My email is: water@ucard.biz.

Please let us become partners and start the initial cooperation soon.

Looking forward to hearing from you.

Beat regards,

Water

Notes

(1) 利用搜索引擎获取客户信息。首先，说明信息来源和目的。要直截了当，为客户节省时间，使客户一看便知道自己是做什么产品的，如果客户感兴趣便会继续看，或者作为考虑的合作对象，而不是视为垃圾邮件。

(2) 公司产品种类和市场情况的简短介绍，表示可以满足客户的需求。

(3) 第一次联系的人也许不是直接的对口人，提出如果有人联系自己，邮件也是一种很好的联系方式。

(4) 最后，提出合作的愿望。

4. Contact Previous Customers

Dear Marcus,

How are you doing? This is Water from ABC Company, Ms. Grace's colleague. She already left the company some time ago. It's been a long time no contact with you and your company. We are glad to contact you again about external battery pack for Mobile Phone and Notebook.

I would like to update you some latest models and new offers for your reference. We hope we can enlarge our business scale. Please find the details as attached.

Looking forward to hearing from you soon.

Best regards,

Water

Notes

(1) 对已联系或者已合作的客户，函电撰写主要体现服务，不让客户感觉到突兀。

(2) 对暂时无合作，曾经联系密切，有邮件阅读回执的客户要保持联系，在某个特定的时间提醒客户产品的报价，以及产品的市场销售情况等。假如知道对方公司和自己公司生产的产品相符，要多参考客户公司的网页，根据网页上的信息，不断向客户展开猛烈的"攻击"。另外，适当的电话联系也是必需的，或者以传真的方式，或者直接给客户发邮件。尝试不同的方式反复联系，提高成功的可能性。

资料链接 Material—link

1. Standard Model

Model 1:Self-introduction

Dear Sirs,

Through the courtesy of the Chamber of Commerce in Tokyo, we have learned that you have been supplying the best quality foods all over the world, and we are sure there is a large demand for various exotic foods in our country. We are writing to you in the hope of establishing business relations with you.

We are the largest food trading company in Japan with offices or representatives in all major cities and towns in the country. We have been importing a large variety of foods from Europe and the U.S.A. and consider that we have considerable experience in this field.

A bright prospect for your products in our market is foreseeable. We look forward to hearing from you and assure you of our close cooperation at all times.

Yours faithfully,

Model 2: Asking to Establish Business Relations

Dear Sirs,

Your name and address have been recommended to us by the Commercial Counselor's Office of our Embassy in your country as well-established importer of light industrial goods in your country. We now avail ourselves of this opportunity to write to you and see if we can establish business relations by a start of some practical transactions.

Our corporation is established for the purpose of carrying on import and export business as well as other activities in connection with foreign trade. We are active in commercial intercourse with the trade and financial circles of various countries and districts. We are striving to expand economic cooperation and exchange of technology with foreign countries, and to utilize common and reasonable international practices in a flexible way.

To acquaint you with light industrial goods we handle, we are sending you, by separate airmail, a commodity list and several sample books for your reference. We welcome your inquiries.

Yours faithfully,

Model 3: Asking for Catalogues

Dear Sirs,

We owe your name and address to Bank of China, Lagos Branch, through whom we have learnt you are exporters of Chinese Textiles and Cotton Piece Goods. For your information, textiles are our main imports, but now we are especially interested in importing Printed Shirting from your country.

If you can assure us of workable prices, excellent quality and prompt delivery, we shall be able to deal in these goods on a substantial scale.

We would therefore highly appreciate it if you would send us catalogues, sample books and all necessary information regarding Printed Shirting by airmail, so as to acquaint us with the material and workmanship of your supplies.

We are looking forward to your early reply.

Yours faithfully,

Model 4: Credit Enquiry

Gentle*men*,

We have received a sudden bid from Freemen Brothers Company, London, with which you are now doing business and the firm gave us your name as a reference.

We shall appreciate it if you will let us have the following information.

1. *How long have you been in business relations with the firm?*
2. *What credit limit have you placed on their account?*
3. *How promptly are terms met?*
4. *What amount is currently outstanding?*

Any information you may give us will be treated as strictly confidential and expenses accruing from this inquiry will be gladly paid by us upon receipt of your bill.

Very truly yours,

Model 5: Favorable Reply to Credit Enquiry

Private & Confidential

Dear Sirs,

We have now received from the National Bank of Nigeria the information you asked for in your letter of April 4. The Auto Engineering Co., Ltd. you mentioned is a private company runs as a family concern by three brothers and was founded fifteen years ago. It enjoys a good reputation. As far as our information goes, it is punctually meeting its commitments and a credit in the sum you mentioned would seem to be safe.

This information is confidential and is given without any responsibility on our part.

Yours faithfully,

Model 6: Unfavorable Reply to Credit Enquiry

Dear Sir,

We are sorry to say that our experiences with the company which you inquired about in your letter of June 17 have been unsatisfactory.

It is true that we were in business relations with the firm of the last two years and on several occasions we have had lots of trouble in effecting settlements.

The company still owes $1 400 for purchase made over seven months ago. The account is now in the hand of our attorneys for collection.

May we ask that you treat this information as strictly confidential without responsibility on our part?

Very truly yours,

2. *Writing Guide*

(1) 建立商务关系的信函应包含哪些内容?

When you want to establish business relations with your potential customers, you should tell the receiver:

① *How his name is known.*

② *What you handle.*

③ *What you want to do, that is, what you want to sell or what you want to buy.*

④ *You are looking forward to his early reply.*

(2) 如何获得潜在客户的资信情况?

In order to obtain the credit standing of your potential customer, you should take following steps.

① *Find a proper channel or trustworthy organization for the credit enquiry.*

② *Name clearly your requirement in the credit enquiry.*

③ *It's better to make credit enquiries through different channels to ensure you are dealing with trustworthy importers.*

Section Four　Selected Sentences
精选句型表达

1. Resources of Information 信息来源：我们从……处得知……/通过……我们了解到……

(1) We owe your name and address to the Journal of Commerce.

我们从《商业日报》得知贵公司的名称和地址。

(2) We obtained your name and address from …

我公司从……得知贵公司的名称和地址。

(3) We learned your company from the Internet that you are one of the leading manufactures in this line.

我们从网上了解到贵公司是这一行业的主要生产商之一。

(4) Through the courtesy of …, we have your name as a firm who is interested in doing business with us.

经由……引荐，我们得悉贵公司有兴趣与我方进行贸易。

(5) On the recommendation of …, we have learned with pleasure the name and address of

your firm.

承蒙……推荐，我方得知贵公司的名称和地址。

(6) You were recommended to our company by…

贵公司由……推荐给我公司。

(7) We are indebted for your name and address to …

我们得知贵公司的名称和地址，要感谢……

(8) Your company's name has been given to us by …

我们从……了解到贵公司。

(9) Having had/obtained the name and address of your company through ABC Trading Company, we know that you deal in textiles.

通过 ABC 贸易公司的介绍，我们得知贵公司的名称和地址，并熟悉你方经营纺织品。

2. Purpose of Writing 写信的目的：建立业务关系

(1) We are writing to you and hope to enter into business relations with you.

我方写信给贵方，望建立业务关系。

(2) We are writing to you and willing to open up business relations with you.

我方写信给贵方，以期与贵公司建立业务关系。

(3) We would like to take this opportunity to establish business relations with you.

我方愿借此机会与贵公司建立业务关系。

(4) The purpose of this letter is to explore the possibilities of developing trade with you.

本信目的是探索与你们发展贸易的可能性。

(5) We are willing to enter into business relationship with your company on the basis of equality and mutual benefit.

我们愿在平等互利的基础上与贵公司建立业务关系。

(6) We are willing to enter into business relations with your firm on the basis of equality, mutual benefit and exchanging what one has for what one needs.

我们愿在平等互利、互通有无的基础上与你公司建立业务关系。

(7) We wish to establish friendly business relations with you to enjoy a share of mutually profitable business.

我们愿与你们建立友好业务关系，分享互利的交易。

(8) We learn from … that your firm specializes in …, and would like to establish business relationship with you.

从……获悉你公司专门经营……，现愿与你公司建立业务关系。

(9) We have the pleasure to introduce ourselves to you with the hope that we may have an opportunity of cooperating with you in your business extension.

我们有幸自荐，盼望能有机会与你们合作，扩展业务。

(10) We take the liberty of writing to you with a view to building up business relations with your firm.

我们冒昧通信，以期待与贵公司建立业务关系。

(11) The high reputation, which you are enjoying as camera importer, has rendered us desirous of entering into business relations with you.

你公司是信誉卓著的照相机进口商，我公司极愿与你公司建立业务关系。

(12) As you are one of the leading importers in …, we have pleasure in contacting you in the hope of establishing business relations and rendering you assistance in a wide range of your requirements.

鉴于你们是……的主要进口商之一，特此联系，盼能建立业务关系，以有助于满足你们各项需求。

(13) We understand that you are interested in both the import and export of …, and it is on this subject that we wish to introduce ourselves in the hope of establishing mutually beneficial business relations between our two corporations.

了解到你们对……(商品)的进口和出口都感兴趣，故愿自荐，希望在我们两公司间建立互利的业务关系。

(14) Having had your name and address from the Commercial Counselor's Office of the Embassy of the People's Republic of China in…, we now avail ourselves of this opportunity to write to you and see if we can establish business relations by a start of some practical transactions.

从中华人民共和国驻……大使馆商务参赞处获悉贵公司名称和地址，现借此机会与贵方通信，意在以达成一些实际交易为开端，建立业务关系。

3. Self-introduction 自我介绍：公司经营管理范围等

(1) Our company handles/deals in/ deals with/ trades in/ specializes in/ is in the line of…

我公司经营……

(2) We take this opportunity to introduce ourselves as large importer of …in our country.

乘此机会，兹介绍，我公司为国内……大进口商。

(3) We have been trading in the goods for years. We are a big supplier/exporter/importer for our local market.

我方多年来一直从事此产品贸易，是本地区最大的供应商/出口商/进口商。

(4) As you may be well aware, we are a state-operated corporation handling such items as … in both import and export business.

也许你们已有所知，我们是国营公司，经营……(商品)的进出口业务。

(5) We write to introduce ourselves as large dealer in … with good connections in the country.

现函告，我公司为……大经销商，在国内拥有大批客户。

(6) Having many years' experience in this particular line of business, we write to introduce ourselves as exporter of …

现函告，我方为……出口商，在此行业已有多年的经验。

(7) Being closely connected with reliable wholesalers here, we shall be able to do considerable import business with you.

我公司与此地可靠的批发商有密切联系，能与你公司建立可观的进口业务。

(8) We manufacture plastic items for several years, with the strength of storage box, promotional items, travelling bottles, etc.

我们生产塑料产品多年，在储物盒、促销品、旅行水壶等方面有优势。

4. Ask for Information 要求寄送有关资料

(1) It would be very helpful if you could send us statistics on your sales.

如果你们能将你们的销售统计资料寄给我们，那就太有帮助了。

(2) We would like to ask you to kindly send us the related information.

我们希望你们能将相关资料寄给我们。

(3) We shall appreciate your catalogue and quotations.

若能收到贵方的商品目录和报价，将不胜感激。

(4) We have little information about your goods. We will really appreciate it if you can send me your catalogues and price list for our reference.

因我方对你方产品知道的不多，很希望你方能寄商品目录及价目单，以供我方参考。

5. Offer Status Enquiries 提供信用咨询

(1) For our credit standing, please refer to the following bank.

关于我方资信情况，请向以下银行查询。

(2) As to our standing, we are permitted to mention the Bank of … as a reference.

关于我方资信情况，请向……银行查询，以供参考。

(3) As to our credit and financial standing, we would refer you the Bank of China and the Chamber of Commerce in Guangzhou.

至于我们的信用和财务状况，请向中国银行和广州商会了解。

(4) Our banks are the Bank of …,they can provide you information about our business and finances.

我方开户行是……银行，他们可以向贵方提供我方的商业和财政状况。

6. The Ending of Establishing Business Relations 建立商务关系的结束语

(1) We look forward to establishing a friendly relationship with you soon.

期盼早日与贵公司建立贸易关系。

(2) Your early reply will be highly appreciated.

如能早日回复，我方将不胜感激。

(3) Awaiting your favorable reply.

期盼佳音。

(4) We are looking forward to your early reply with much interest.

期盼贵方早日回复。

(5) We are glad to send you this introductory letter, hoping that it will be the prelude to mutually beneficial relations between us.

我们欣然寄发这封自荐信，希望是互利关系的前奏。

(6) We wish to enter into direct negotiation with you with a view to introducing your special lines in our market.

盼直接洽谈，以便将你公司特种经营商品引进我地市场。

7. Ask for Credit Information 资信调查

(1) As we are on the point of transacting some important business with them, we should like to know exactly how their credit standing is.

因为本公司正要与该公司进行重要交易，所以希望事先正确地了解该公司的信用状况。

(2) We shall appreciate it if you will let us know their financial position.

如贵方能告知该公司的财务状况，我方将不胜感激。

(3) I shall feel under great obligation if you will advise me confidentially respecting the reputation they enjoy among your neighbours and correspondents.

恳请惠予告知该公司的近邻与顾客对该公司的评价，本人将深感谢意。

(4) We shall be glad to consider open account terms if you will kindly supply the usual trade reference.

若你方能提供通常贸易资信的情况，我们将乐意考虑用记账方式付款。

(5) When opening new accounts, it is our practice to ask customers for trade references.

开立新账户时，向客户要求商业信用是我方的惯例。

(6) As requested in your letter of …, we are pleased to give below the names of two dealers to whom you may refer.

应你方……日来函要求，我们愉快地提供下面两位商人的姓名，供贵方查询。

(7) We should be very grateful to you for an answer, and enclose a postal reply coupon.

如蒙答复，不胜感激，现随函附寄回邮代金券一张。

(8) Will you please be kind enough to obtain for us all information possible respecting the standing of Messrs. Toyoda & Co., of Yokohama?

恳请贵方尽量收集有关横滨市丰田公司的信用状况方面的材料。

(9) ABC Corp. has given us your name as a reference, and we should be very much obliged if you would advise us whether they are of good repute and should be allowed credit up to that amount.

ABC 公司推荐贵方做他们的资信证明人，如果贵方愿意告知我方该公司是否声誉良好以及那个赊账额是否可行，我方将不胜感激。

(10) We should appreciate it if you would provide us with reliable information respecting Messrs. J. C. Maxwell Company. We wish to know if their financial standing is considered strong.

如果贵方能为我方索取有关 J.C.麦斯威尔公司的可靠信息，我方将不胜感激。我方希望了解该公司的财务运作是否很强。

(11) Messrs. J.M. Shneider & Co. has recently written to us that they are the leading importer in Germany and wish to establish business relations with us in the line of machine tools. As we know nothing about the firm we should be obliged to you if you would get for us some information about this company.

施耐德公司最近写信告诉我方，他们是德国的大进口商，希望在机床业务方面与我方建立业务关系，因为我们对该公司情况不了解，你方如能为我方获取有关该公司的资料，我方将不胜感激。

(12) We should appreciate it if you could obtain for us all information about the financial and credit standing of Messrs. James Neil & Co. in London. The reference they have given us is Hong Kong Standard Chartered Bank.

如果贵方为我方获取伦敦 James Neil 公司财务和信用情况，我方不胜感激。他们提供的资信证明人是香港渣打银行。

(13) Will you please be so kind as to furnish us with details, as exact as possible, as to the credit which may be safely allowed to the firm whose name is given on the attached slip?

关于附寄的纸条上所写的那家公司，可以提供他们的安全的赊账额是多少吗？惠请提供尽可能准确的详细信息。

(14) You would greatly oblige me by obtaining for me information as to the present financial position of the firm named on the attached slip.

如有幸由贵处得知附件中所提及的公司目前的财政情况，本公司将不胜感激。

(15) It would give us great pleasure to be able to render you a similar service， should opportunity occur.

以后如有机会，我们将乐于为贵公司提供同样的服务，作为对这次协助的报答。

(16) Messrs. Smith & Co., of your city, desire to open an account with us, and have given us your name as a reference.

贵商史密斯公司希望与本公司开展交易，指定贵处为信用出证人。

(17) Messrs, Yawata & Co., of Yokohama, is desirous of entering into business relations with us and has given us your esteemed address as reference.

本公司接到横滨市八幡公司来函，表示愿意与本公司建立贸易关系，并指定贵方为该公司信用证明人。

(18) Any information you may give me will, of course, be treated as strictly confidential.

诚然，贵方所提供的任何信息一定会严格保密。

(19) You may rest assured that anything thus communicated will go no further.

请你放心，信中内容我们绝不会泄漏出去。

8. General Reply 一般信用回复

(1) Calcutta bankers advise that the company was originally established in 1947 by Mr. Charles E. Smith, to conduct a business in chemicals, cement, paper, milk-products, etc., as importer and indenter.

根据加尔各答的银行通知，该公司是由 C. E. 史密斯先生在 1947 年创立的，其主要业务为药品、水泥、纸张及乳制品等货物的进口与购买。

(2) We are informed, “The company is a newly-formed corporation, having been chartered in September of 2005 with an authorized capital of $50 000 with only $5 000 recorded as having been paid in”.

据我们所得到的情报：“该公司为新创立的公司，2005 年 9 月创立时，其登记资本额为 50 000 美元，但股东实际上缴纳金额总计仅为 5 000 美元而已。”

(3) Any statement on the part of this bank or any of its officers as to the standing of any person, firm or corporation, is given as a mere matter of opinion for which no responsibility, in any way, is to attach to this bank or any of its officers.

任何有关个人、公司以及其他任何组织的信用状况，本银行或本行职员所提供的情报，无论内容如何，仅供参考。对此本银行或本行职员，不负任何责任。

(4) It is, of course, understood that this is no more than a personal opinion, for which we accept no responsibility, and we trust that it will be treated with the strictest discretion.

诚然，你方应该了解，这只是个人意见，我方对此不负任何责任，务必请谨慎处理此信息。

(5) This is a strictly confidential response to a request made by the firm.

这是对该公司的要求严格保密的回函。

(6) The foregoing information is given in confidence and for your private use only.

以上情况，乃属机密，仅供你方参考。

(7) We shall be pleased to render you any further services, and we ask you to consider this information as given in strict confidence.

今后如有吩咐，我们将乐于为您效劳，但对本报告，务必严守秘密。

(8) This is without obligation on my part, though I am fully convinced that you will find my information borne out by the fact.

本人所说均为依据事实的直言，可证明确有其事，但对文责方面，本人实在无法负责。

9. Favorable Reply 信用良好的回复

(1) The financial status is sound.

财务状况健全。

(2) The firm enjoys the fullest respect and unquestionable confidence in the business world.

该公司在实业界颇受尊敬、信誉很高。

(3) We have much pleasure in stating that they are a small but highly respectable firm, and very old and valued customers of ours.

我们很乐于说明：该公司虽小但信用颇好，对本公司来说，是交易甚久且最重要的一位客户。

(4) The company you mentioned is an old-established one who has long enjoyed the highest reputation.

您所提及的公司是长久享有最高声誉的老字号。

(5) The firm you enquired about is one of the most reliable importers in our district and has for many years enjoyed good reputation among the traders.

贵方所调查的公司是我方地区最可靠的进口商之一，多年以来在同行中享有良好的声誉。

(6) Established in 1979 as importer and exporter, they have now a sound business standing with an excellent business turnover.

该公司创建于 1979 年，从事进出口贸易，如今已拥有很好的商业信誉和营业额。

(7) As far as we know, they are sound enough, but we have no certain knowledge of their true financial position.

就我们所知，该公司经营稳健，但对于他们具体的财务状况我们并不清楚。

(8) The corporation trades principally in electric and electronic commodities with America and Japan. We have a high regard for their business ability and financial standing. Their reputation here is decidedly good. We hope that you will treat it as confidential.

该公司主要与美国和日本开展电器和电子商品交易。我方对他们的经营能力和财务资信有很高的评价。该公司的名声在此地非常好。我方希望贵方把这作为机密处理。

(9) We inform you that we can give nothing but favorable information about the firm in question.

我们只能向您报告，该公司在各方面均博得好评。

(10) They command considerable funds and an unlimited credit, and the executives are thorough business men.

该公司的资金雄厚，其信用可以说“无限”，而其高级职员可称之为精明强干。

(11) We learned that though they had not been long established, stood pretty well, but were not supposed to be rich.

该公司自创办至今虽然时间很短，但在实业界已有相当信用，然而仍不能算是富有的公司。

(12) Replying to your letter of yesterday, we are happy to inform you that the house referred to enjoys an unlimited credit.

昨天接到贵函，我们很乐意向您报告有关查询事项。该公司博得客户极大信赖，特此复函。

(13) Our opinion is that we can safely trust them for the amount of business you mentioned.

我们的意见是，对于你方提到的交易额，我们可以完全信任他们。

10. Unfavorable Reply 信用不佳的回复

(1) This company is being pressed by creditors and its position is precarious.

这家公司正受迫于债权人，状况不稳定。

(2) We are sorry to say that our experiences with the company which you inquired about in your letter of June 9 has been unsatisfactory.

我们遗憾地说，我们与贵公司 6 月 9 日来信询及的公司的业务往来一直不太令人满意。

(3) Of late, payments have been quite irregularly made, and more than one occasion we have had to press for them.

该公司最近在付款方面几乎没有准则，我们曾一再催告，然而毫无结果。

(4) As this is the case, we deem it rather advisable for you to refrain from having relations with that company.

既然情况如此，本公司认为贵方避免和那家公司往来是相当明智的。

(5) They are inexperienced in business and extreme caution is advised in granting credit.

他们缺乏经营经验，让他们赊账时需谨慎。

11. Decline to Offer Credit Information 拒绝提供资信证明

(1) Replying to yours of 10th inst., we inform you that we have no personal knowledge as to the standing of Messrs. Yada & Co., of our city.

本月 10 日您来函询问本市矢田公司的信用状况，对此我们也不太明了。

(2) We have no information in our files concerning the firm in question.

我方档案中没有关于您所询问公司的资料。

(3) We are sorry we are not able to give precise information you ask.

我们无法向贵公司提供您所需要的确切情报，对此，我们深感遗憾。

(4) We do not know enough about this firm to give satisfactory answers to your enquiry.

对于这家公司我方不甚了解，所以无法给予令贵方满意的答复。

(5) We regret our inability to tell you anything positive concerning the firm mentioned in your letter of the 30th ult.

对于上月 30 日贵函所要查询的公司，我们实在无法报告确切情况，甚为遗憾。

(6) We are sorry that we are not able to give precise information you asked.

遗憾，我们未能为贵方提供所要求的确切消息。

Abstract

通过本章学习，①了解获取外商信息的途径；②了解资信调查的主要内容及其方式；③熟练掌握建立商务关系信函和资信调查信函的书写技巧和注意事项；④通过熟悉标准模板掌握书写建立商务关系信函和资信调查信函的基本方法；⑤掌握有关书写建立商务关系信函和资信调查信函的经典句型及表达方式。

Useful Words & Expressions

1. recommendation 推荐；介绍
2. on the recommendation of … 由……推荐/介绍
3. through the courtesy of … 承蒙……介绍或引荐
4. to write to/write a letter to/address a letter to 致函
5. to come to know/understand/one's knowledge 获知；得知
6. avail oneself of this opportunity 利用这次机会
7. take the liberty of doing sth. 冒昧地去做某事
8. owe one's name and address to …由……得知某人的姓名和地址
9. to be indebted to 感谢
10. goodwill 信誉；商誉；友好；亲善
11. prospective 潜在的；预期的；有希望的
12. to establish/enter into/set up business relations 建立业务关系
13. to establish direct business relations with sb. 与某人建立直接的业务关系
14. to continue business relations 继续业务关系
15. to maintain business relations 保持业务关系
16. to improve business relations 改善业务关系

17. to promote business relations 促进业务关系
18. to speed up business relations 加快业务关系的发展
19. to enlarge (widen) business relations 扩大业务关系
20. to restore (resume) business relations 恢复业务关系
21. to interrupt business relations 中断业务关系
22. to consolidate business relations 巩固业务关系
23. enclose 附寄
24. enclose herewith 随函附寄
25. enclosure 附件(常缩写为 Encl. 或 Enc.)
26. catalogue 目录
27. quotation 报价
28. for your reference/guidance /consideration 供您参考
29. for your information 现告知
30. specific inquiry 具体询价
31. enquiry note/sheet 询价单
32. make offers 报价
33. make sb. a quotation for sth. 向某人就某商品报价
34. latest price list 最新价格表
35. promptly 立即
36. representative 代表
37. chamber of commerce 商会
38. Commercial Counselor's Office 商务参赞处
39. take advantage of 利用
40. acquaint oneself with 使了解
41. specialize in/be specialized in 专营
42. deal with/deal in/handle/ trade in/be in the line of 经营
43. on the bases of equality and mutual benefit 在平等互利的基础上
44. pamphlet 小册子
45. a range of 一套
46. import and export corporation 进出口公司
47. extend export business 扩大出口业务
48. be of the latest style 最新式样
49. financial position 财务状况
50. trade reputation 贸易声誉
51. enjoy a high reputation 享有好的声誉
52. enjoy popularity 享有盛名；受欢迎
53. captioned goods/mentioned goods/subject articles 标题商品
54. on display 展出
55. meet with great favor 受欢迎

56. be in a position to 能够
57. fresh orders 新订单
58. credit standing 信用地位
59. capital turnover 资金周转
60. assets & liabilities 资产与负债
61. state-operated 国营的
62. currency, Chinese currency, British currency 货币，中国货币，英国货币
63. a long-term investment 长期投资
64. a profitable investment 有利可得的投资
65. a safe and sure investment 安全可靠的投资
66. a heavy investment 巨额投资
67. investment intent 投资意向
68. investment partner 投资伙伴
69. direct investment 直接投资
70. investment environment 投资环境
71. investor 投资者
72. joint venture enterprise 合资企业
73. cooperative enterprise 合作企业
74. exclusively foreign-owned enterprise 外商独资企业
75. state-owned enterprise 国营企业
76. state-designated second grade enterprise 国家指定二级企业
77. collective-owned enterprise 集体企业
78. individual-owned enterprise 私营企业
79. merchandising enterprise 商业企业
80. township/rural enterprise 乡镇企业
81. classified catalogue 分类目录
82. descriptive catalogue 带有说明的目录
83. illustrated catalogue 有插图的目录
84. catalogue of industrial products 工业产品目录
85. financial position/standing 财务状况
86. cash position 现金头寸
87. easy position 头寸宽裕
88. to cover position 轧平头寸
89. sales confirmation 销售确认书
90. sales contract 销售合同
91. in your district 在你地区；在你处
92. as requested/at your request/as you requested 按照要求
93. under separate cover/by separate mail/by another mail separately 另外邮寄
94. be in the market for sth. 想要购买

95. take this opportunity to do sth. 借此机会做某事
96. at an early date 尽早
97. referring to your letter of …有关/关于贵方……来函
98. in compliance with 按照
99. in the line of … 在……业务范围之内
100. reference 证明人
101. account 账户
102. it goes without saying 不言而喻
103. private & confidential 机密并亲启
104. initial contact 首次联系
105. the Standard Chartered Bank 渣打银行
106. on/upon receipt of … 一收到……就……
107. favorable reply 合意的答复
108. exclusive agent 独家代理
109. expire (合同、文件等)到期；失效；终止
110. in question 正被谈论的；该
111. in reply to 答复
112. in view of 考虑到；鉴于
113. ult. 上月的(ultimo 的缩写)

Exercises

1. What are the channels through which general information about a company to be dealt with can be obtained?

2. How to establish business relations through correspondence?

3. What is a status enquiry? Why is it important to obtain all the information possible respecting the firm one is about to enter into relations with?

4. What are the channels through which you can make a status enquiry?

5. Choose the best answer to complete each of the following sentences.

(1) We would like to take this ____ to establish business relations with you.

A. step B. opportunity C. advantage D. opening

(2) Our company has wide experience ____ the textiles line.

A. on B. in C. about D. of

(3) We would ____ very much if you send us some samples immediately.

A. thank you B. appreciate it C. appreciate D. appreciate you

(4) They have ____ us that you are ____ the market ____ chemicals.

A. inform, in, on B. informed, in, for C. advise, in, on D. advised, in, of

(5) We have received your enquiry of October 15 ____ we learn that you are interested in our black tea.

A. in which B. from which C. which D. at which

(6) We shall appreciate ____ us your most competitive prices.

A. your quoting B. you quoting C. you to quote D. quote

(7) To give you a general idea of various goods now available for export, we ____ a brochure and a sample.

A. enclose you B. enclose C. enclose to you D. enclose for you

(8) You may refer to our bank, Bank of China, for our financial____.

A. understanding B. outstanding C. upstanding D. standing

(9) You are recommended to us ____ a large buyer of Textiles by one of our clients.

A. as B. of C. for D. with

(10) Our new pricelist will ____ from the beginning of next month.

A. affect B. take effect C. come into D. make out

6. Put the following sentences into English.

(1) 我们愿意在平等互利，互通有无的基础上与贵公司建立业务联系。

(2) 承蒙中国外贸组织的介绍，我们得知贵公司有意在本地市场做生意。

(3) 我们是经营轻工产品的国营公司。

(4) 瑞典一进口商要求我们按承兑交单方式运去一批试销商品。

(5) 贵国驻华大使馆商务参赞处告知，你拟从我国进口车床(lathe)，故特致函你公司，希望能在该项产品方面建立业务关系。

(6) 我们是世界上最大的丝绸进口商之一。我们过去一直是从日本进口的，现在我们想到中国市场订购。

(7) 在收到你方具体询价时，我将立即寄上报价单及样品。

(8) 为了使你们对我们可供出口的各类纺织品有一个总的概念，随函寄上样本和价格单各一份，供你们查阅。

(9) 我们想请你们代为查询一下伦敦一家商行的财务和信用情况，他们是 James Neils & Co.。他们的银行是香港汇丰银行。谢谢。

(10) 敬启者：

我们是这个城市最大的轻工产品进口商之一。很想和你们建立业务关系。

目前我们对你们的电器产品感兴趣，详情请看附寄的第 1345 号询价单。如能尽早收到你们的报价将不胜感谢。

谨上

Case Practice

以本章的导入案例为背景，以阳光公司业务员赵紫娟的身份为公司起草一份建交信函，详细介绍自己公司的信息和产品信息，表达与之建立业务关系的愿望。

Chapter 3 Enquiry and Offer

询盘与报盘

案例导入 Case-lead-in

华信贸易有限公司(Huaxin Trading Co., Ltd.)成立于1980年，是经国家批准的具有进出口经营权的综合性贸易公司。其经营范围包括机电设备、金属材料、建筑材料、化工原料、轻工产品等。公司与多家供货厂商有固定的业务往来，货源基础雄厚。同时，面对多变的国际市场，公司也十分重视新产品的开发。例如，日用品部与其挂钩工厂联手开发了一项新产品——HX系列瓷器。该系列选用上等瓷土烧制，以精美礼盒包装，加之手工绘制图案，美观大方，质量上乘，极具竞争力。一日公司收到客户James Brown & Sons 公司的还盘如下。

March 25, 2008

Dear Mr. Huang,

Thank you for your e-mail of March 16, 2008 and your samples.

For your information, our customers are quite satisfied with the lab report of your samples, but they are still holding back.

After careful examining and comparison with similar products of other markets, we find your quotation is really much higher. Unless the prices could match with the market level, it is difficult to persuade customers to purchase from you.

So, we would counter offer as follows:

Art No. HX1115 USD23.00 per set CIFC5 Toronto
Art No. HX2012 USD19.20 per set CIFC5 Toronto
Art No. HX4405 USD22.90 per set CIFC5 Toronto

Actually, competitive prices for a trial order can often lead to a high market share with enormous profits in future. We hope you will take this factor into account and wait for your early reply.

Yours truly,
James Brown & Sons
Paul Lockwood
Purchasing Division

Section One Enquiry
询 盘

1. Definition of Enquiry

Enquiry is the first real step in international trade negotiations, which brings a would-be buyer and a potential seller together. An enquiry is a request for a reply informing an importer of prices, catalogue, samples and/or a quotation sheet, delivery date and usual payment terms before placing an order with a prospective exporter. In international trade, an enquiry is usually made by the buyer, which should be concise, specific and polite. Sometimes, it can also be made by the seller, which is an invitation to bid. Enquiries may be either dispatched by mail, cable telex, fax, or handed to the suppliers through personal contact, and even by telephone or face-to-face talk.

2. Classification of Enquiry

1) General Enquiry

If the importers want to have a general idea of the goods which the exporter is in a position to supply, they may make a request for a price list, a catalogue, samples and other terms. This is a general enquiry.

Generally, it is also a first enquiry without first writing a letter to establish business relations.

2) Specific Enquiry

If the importers intend to purchase goods of a certain specification, they may ask the exporter to make an offer or a quotation for specific goods. That is a specific enquiry, which has a stronger intention to make an order than general enquiries. A specific enquiry may request detailed information about the specific goods, such as price, quality, specifications, terms of payment, delivery date, samples and so on.

3. Contents of an Enquiry Letter

Nowadays, many companies use a printed enquiry form instead of letters. An enquiry usually includes the following contents.

(1) State how you get to know about the firm, if this is an initial letter. Or to express your thanks/reference, if this is a reply.

(2) Express your interests in the products produced by the suppliers.

(3) Making an enquiry depending on your needs in detail or simply, including quotation, catalogue, price list, samples or offer etc. , and even payment terms.

(4) Express your hope for an early favourable reply.

Enquiries should be addressed to the company because it is a transaction between two companies not two individuals, and in this way, your letter will receive quick attention as well. It is essential in making enquiries to consider carefully to which region or regions the enquiries are to be approached in one and the same region. Failure to take into consideration the relevant situation would lead to an adverse effect on future transaction.

The reply to enquiries should be prompt, courteous and helpful. In case the goods enquired for are currently out of stock, the supplier should inform the enquirer when they will be available and, by taking this opportunity, introduce some other products as substitutes so as to create a good impression, which hopefully will result in more business. For some general enquiries, it's all right to make a reply by sending printed catalogues and price list.

Section Two Offer and Counter-offer 报盘和还盘

1. Definition of Offer and Counter-offer

Offer and counter-offer are two directions of a transaction. An offer is the expression of the wish of the seller to sell particular goods under stated terms, including quantity, prices, shipment, terms of payment, etc. It usually follows an enquiry that is either written or oral. Sometimes, an offer is not in response to a buyer's enquiry, but made voluntarily by the seller, which is named a bid. That's to say, the seller will bid to the buyer without the latter's enquiry. An offer is usually made either by way of advertisements, circulars and letter or in rely to enquiries.

A counter-offer is virtually a partial rejection of the original offer and also a counter proposal initiated by the buyer or the offeree.

2. Classifications of Offer

An offer can be divided into a firm offer and a non-firm offer.

1) Firm offer

An offer, usually in written form, which states it may not be withdrawn, revoked or amended for a specific period of time, is called a firm offer. A firm offer must be subject to the following conditions.

(1) The writer encloses complete, affirmative, specific terms of business. The major conditions of the contract are required as to delivery date, time of shipment and terms of payment as well as names of goods, quality, specifications, prices, quantity, packing and insurance.

(2) The validity period is indispensable to a firm offer. Specifically, the beginning and the ending date and place of the validity must be given.

2) Non-firm offer

An offer, which is not binding upon the sellers and the details of the offer may change in certain situations, is called a non-firm offer. It has no regulations concerning specific time limit and usually states some terms to express reservation, such as "subject to our final confirmation", "subject to goods being unsold" and "only for reference".

A quotation or a proforma invoice can also play the role of both a firm offer and a non-firm offer according to their contents. However, a catalogue or a price-list can only be used as information for the receiver's reference. The greatest difference between a firm offer and a non-firm offer is that the former involves the offeror in contractual obligations, while the latter does not.

3. Contents of Letters on Making an Offer and a Counter-offer

An offer usually includes the following points.

(1) An expression of thanks for enquiry.

(2) Details of prices, discounts and terms of payment.

(3) A statement or clear indication of what the prices cover (eg. freight and insurance, etc.).

(4) An undertaking as to date of delivery or time of shipment.

(5) The period for which the quotation is valid.

(6) An expression of hope that the quotation will be accepted.

When a buyer rejects a quotation or other offer, he should write and thank the sellers for his trouble and explain the reason for rejection. Not to do so would show a lack of courtesy. In making a counter-offer, one has to state the terms most explicitly and use words very carefully so as to avoid ambiguity or misunderstanding.

A letter of counter-offer should cover the following points.

(1) Thank the seller for his offer.

(2) Express regret at inability to accept.

(3) State your reasons directly why an adjustment is necessary.

(4) Make a counter-offer if, in the circumstances, it is appropriate.

(5) Hope to receive favorable reply or suggest other opportunities to do business together.

In international trade, by receiving a counter-offer, the seller may not accept some terms and conditions of the buyer's counter-offer, and may send a re-counter offer to his buyer. In this way, a business transaction is concluded after several rounds of such business negotiations. There could be many re-counter offers before a business transaction is concluded.

Section Three Cases in detail
具体案例分析

(一)经典案例解析

Offer and Counter-offer

Dear Sirs,

We thank you for your enquiry of August 22 and are pleased to send you our quotation for the goods you required as follows.

Commodity: "White Rabbit" Brand Woolen Mixed Blanket No.33.

Size: 74×84in

Weight:4lbs

Colour: yellow, brown, green assortment

Quantity:1 000pcs.

Price: US$40.00 per piece CIF Montreal

Shipment: October

You are cordially invited to take advantage of this attractive offer. We are anticipating a large order from the United States, and that will cause a sharp rise in price.

We look forward to receiving your order.

Yours faithfully,

(Reply)

Dear Sirs,

"White Rabbit" Brand Woolen Mixed Blanket

Thank you for your quotation of August 24 for 1 000 pieces of the captioned goods.

We immediately contacted our customers and they showed great interest because there is a growing demand for woolen blankets. The prices you quoted, however, are found too much on the high side. ABC Company, one of our customers, told us that they would possibly order 2 000 pieces of the goods, provided that you can reduce your price to US$38.00 per piece. ABC is one of the leading importers in our country, so there is a good chance of finalizing and order with them if the present price can be lowered to meet their requirement. We hope you will take advantage of this chance so that you will benefit from the expanding market.

We are most anxious that you will do your utmost to reduce the price and we await your reply with great interest.

Yours faithfully,

Notes

1. woolen mixed blanket 混纺毛毯
2. pcs. 是 pieces 的缩写；piece 的缩写为 pc.
3. We are anticipating a large order from the United States,…

我们预计美国方面将有一个大的订单到来，……

anticipate *v.t.* 盼望、期望，后接名词、动名词或 that 引导的从句。

We anticipate your acceptance. 盼望你方接受。

We anticipate receiving your early reply. 盼你方早日回复。

We anticipate that fresh supplies will arrive next month. 我们预计新货将于下月送到。

anticipate 与 expect 的区别：

这两个动词都表示预期某事将发生，但有所不同。在意思上，anticipate 所预期的一般都指可喜的事，expect 则不一定。

We anticipate (or:expect) our products will be a quick seller in your market.

The firm expects heavy losses this year. (一般不用 anticipate)

在结构上，除两个动词都可以用名词及 that 从句作为宾语外，anticipate 后面可接动名词，不可接不定式，expect 则可接不定式，不可接动名词。

We anticipate shipping the goods next week. =We expect to ship the goods next week.我们期望下周装货。

expect 还可接：名词或代词+不定式构成的复合宾语，anticipate 则不可。

正：We expect the shipment to arrive in a few days. 我们预期装运的货物将于日内到达。

误：We anticipate the shipment to arrive in a few days.

4. a sharp rise in price 价格急剧上涨

5. the captioned goods 标题项下的货物(这里指"White Rabbit"Brand Woolen Mixed Blanket)

类似的表达法还有：

the subject article (goods)

the goods (article) mentioned in the subject lined

6. growing demand 增长的需求

a large demand 大的需求

a great demand 很大的需求

latent demand 潜在的需求

overfull demand 过多需求

demand and supply 供与求；供求

7. on the high side (指价格)偏高

We regret to say that we cannot accept your offer, as your price is found (to be) on the high side. 谦告由于你方价格偏高，我们不能接受你方报盘。

类似的表达方式有：

Your price is a bit high. 你方价格有点高。

Your price is too high.你方价格太高。

Your price is rather stiff. 你方价格相当高。

Your price is excessive. 你方价格过高。

注意: out of line with the market (与市价不一致)，unreasonable (不合理)，unworkable (不可行)，impracticable (行不通)，infeasible (行不通)，unrealistic (不现实)等如果出自买方之口，往往指价格偏高，如果出自卖方之口，则往往指价格偏低(on the low side)。

8. provided *conj*. 假若；倘使；假如；以……为条件(与 that 连用)

We will send you an order for 5 000 metric tons, provided that you can ship in May. 如果你方能在 5 月份装船，我们将订购 5000 吨。

9. finalize an order with them 接受他们的订单

(二) 一般案例表述

1. Enquiry from Customer

Dear Julia,

I hope you are doing well.

My name is Marcelo. I represent R&S Corp., from Buenos Aires, Argentina. We met each other at the Las Vegas'CES, last January. At that time we talked about your products. Actually we are WalMart's Argentina traders, relating to DVD, DivX, DVD Recorder, Portable DVD and LCD TV. I remembered that during our meeting you informed me about some prices that were suitable for us. So, at this moment, I'd like to know your quotation of prices—FOB China—of the following articles, for WalMart's Argentina.

DVD 5.1 full size

DVD 5.1 1/2 size with display

DivX 5.1 full size

DivX 5.1 full size with USB

This request is for WalMart's order, which will be around 20000pcs of each article. Please, I'll appreciate you will send me your products , pictures and price. If those are different from the catalogue you gave me at the CES, or just let me know which catalogue's articles you are quoting. Please answer me as soon as possible. Thanks a lot.

Hope to hear from you soon.

Best regards,

Marcelo

Reply to the above

Dear Marcelo,

Thank you very much for your kind enquiry to us. Your detailed company and market information impressed us deeply. Glad to see that there is a chance for both R&S and Mizida in entering into some projects cooperation in near future.

Further to the enquiry, we would like to make you the offer as below. Photos are as attached.

DVD 5.1 full size, DVD-592, US$21, if with DivX, US$21.5

DVD 5.1 1/2 size with display, DVD-558B, US$20

DVD 5.1 full size with USB, DVD-602/561, US$23

The whole offer is upon FOB Shenzhen price.

And base on your potential quantity 20000pcs per item.

Wish they could meet your request.

We are ready to provide more information and samples as requested. We appreciate your comments and look forward to working together with you soon.

Best regards,

Julia

Notes

(1) 展会之后或者是从互联网推广联系得到的客户，在一段时间内没有订单，一方面可能是市场销售和客户的推广计划等方面的原因，在当时确实没有订单需求；另一方面说明客户当时已经有较为稳定的合作伙伴。但往往客户也会将同等的供应商列为参考对象，当有合适的产品或者新项目的时候，客户将会主动联系。所以需要不间断地跟进，比如价格更新、产品更新或者是信息交流。

(2) 分析客户的邮件。邮件中客户陈述说明相识于何处，客户的公司和产品介绍以及销售的场所，还有关于产品的规格等较为详细的要求。这类有实质性内容的邮件，说明合作可能性往往较大。

(3) 回复邮件要根据客户的市场特征、订单数量、价格要求等，推荐最合适的产品，报最有竞争力的价格。客户也喜欢和实力相当的公司合作，但需要产品质量过关以及有竞争力的价格。

(4) 报价的内容要清晰。比如价格条款、起订量和相关的单价、产品的主要规格或者功能说明等。这些内容一定要清晰，不能模糊，以免引起误解。并附上精美的图片，让客户可以更直观地选择。为了满足不同客户的需求，还可以采取不同的方式来报价：①对比式报价(同类、同行比较)；②图片式报价(产品图片加标注)；③分析式报价(介绍产品亮点优势)；④分割式报价(详细价格构成)；⑤买家母语报价(英语和买家母语对照)。切忌千篇一律。如果买家没有标注采购数量，就应该做到梯形报价。

(5) 报价时，还要善于抓住买家的心理。一般买家比较关注的点是：发货期快、价格有绝对的优势、有多年的生产或外贸经验、有参加买家当地的展会或业内知名展会、有自己的研发团队、有跟知名品牌或企业的合作、有证书，品质有保证、提供 OEM(Original Equipment Manufacturer)个性化定制服务。

(6) 报价黄金法则：①开价一定要高于实际想要成交的价格；②无论如何，让客户感觉自己赢得了谈判；③让对方感觉物有所值，甚至物超所值。

(7) 期望合作，表现诚意和热心。

2. Asking for Quotation

Dear Water,

Good day. Here is Echo from ETA (Germany), Shenzhen office. Thank for your products presentation.

We are interested in your products; please kindly fill in our quotation sheet here attached.

Any questions please contact me freely.

Br/Echo

Reply to the above

Dear Echo,

Thank you for your kind e-mail, showing interests in our products.

Could you let us know more details? Which item would you like most? We hope to talk by details. Please find the attached file for reference.

More information is available as requested. Looking forward to hearing from you soon.

Best regards,

Water

Notes

(1) 国外的客户通常都有固定的报价单，或者是公司调查表要求供应商填写。内容不尽相同，产品报价单主要是针对具体的产品型号，而公司调查表更侧重于对大的方面的了解，如公司实力、产品特点、质量控制等。这些都是客户对工厂深入了解的一种方法。所以在回复客户的邮件时，需要结合公司的实际情况加以描述。这也是向客户展示产品、展示公司实力的一个机会，必须认真对待。

(2) 回复客户的邮件，不能只是单纯的回复。因为作为厂家，主要目的是销售产品，主动向客户介绍产品是必要的。在不明确客户的需求时，要适当询问。在询问的同时，还要向客户提供更多的合作信息，体现出一种贴心的服务，而不是客套。

3. Reply to Customer's Low Price Request for Lager Order

Dear Ms. Olga Litvi,

Thanks for your enquiry. Surely we can manufacture the aerosol cans with your parameters.

The price I offered you is quite competitive as per MOQ. Could you please kindly tell me your potential quantity? We would like to update you the new offer immediately.

We understand that you are a big supplier of building materials in Russia. You may be interested in our spray adhesive, too. It is one of our most advantaged products. We produce all kinds of spray adhesives with superior quality and low price, some of which can be used in construction decoration. We have our own brand-SUPER, OEM brand is also welcomed. Please study our offer as attached.

Hope to receive your quick response.

Best regards,

Walter

Notes

(1) 分析客户类型，订单数量不同，产品的价格也会有所不同。首次报价一般只报最低订单量的价格。客户都会广泛询价，所以客户回复邮件也不会很全面，只是单方面觉得价格报高了，而没有太多详细的规格以及数量等内容。分析出客户的特点之后，以引导的方式回复更适合此类客户。除了回复客户提出的问题之外，适当地向对方提出一些问题，或者直接告知对方关于不同的订单数量和价格之间的关系等一些情况的基本操作。

(2) 了解客户需求。得到客户资料之后，以不同的了解方式去搜索客户公司资料并了解客户的实际需要。针对自己公司的实际供货能力，向客户推荐更多产品，也让客户有更多选择，这样可以增加合作项目。

资料链接 Material—link

1. Standard Model

Model 1: Showing Interest in Products

Dear Sirs,

We have read your advertisement in "Economic Reporter" and we are glad to know that you are one of the leading exporters of silk blouses in China. We are interested in the products and would like to be informed of details of your various types, including sizes, colors and prices.

We are large dealers in silk garments, having over 15 year's experience in this particular line of business. Silk blouses of good quality and moderate prices command a good sale in our market.

When replying, please state terms of payment and discounts you would allow on purchases of quantities of over 100 dozen of individual items.

We look forward to your early reply.

Sincerely yours,

Model 2: Making an Enquiry

Gentlemen,

Please be informed that one of our clients is in the marked for peanuts. It will be highly appreciated if you could quote us your rock-bottom prices for the same, with indication of date of shipment.

We would like to stress the point that the peanuts enquired for are handpicked Shandong peanuts, 2 001 crop and packed in new gunny bags of 100 kgs each. Meanwhile, the goods should be surveyed by a certified public surveyor as to their quality and weight.

In order to facilitate our mutual business, it is hoped that you would airmail us the soonest possible your proforma invoice for 2 000 tons of the above commodity with prices on CFR Genoa basis, so that we could get our client's confirmation.

Your prompt reply would be appreciated.

Sincerely yours,

Model 3: Reply to an Enquiry

Dear Mr. Bean,

We warmly welcome your enquiry of April 4 and thank you for your interest in our cushions.

We are enclosing samples and price list of back cushions giving the details you asked for. We feel confident that you will find the goods both excellent in quality and reasonable in price.

Best regards,

Yours sincerely,

Model 4: Making an Offer

Dear Sirs,

We are in receipt of your letter of Nov. 21, for which we thank you, and to which we have sent you a reply by telex this morning.

You must have noted from our telex that we are in position to make you a firm offer on 250 L/Ts Steel Tubes at £620.00 per L/T CIF Lagos, for shipment to be effected within two months after receipt of your order, and payment is to be made by sight L/C. This offer is subject to your reply reaching here within one week.

As you are aware, there has been an active demand for Steel Tubes in the market. Therefore, it is impossible for us to keep this offer open too long for it will certainly result in increased price, to which we hope you will pay attention, and meanwhile we are expecting your early reply.

Yours faithfully,

Model 5: Making a Counter-offer

Gentlemen,

Re : Bitter Apricot Kernels 1999 Crop

We are in receipt of your letter of August 14 offering us 60 metric tons of the captioned goods at RMB2 660 per metric ton on the usual terms.

In reply, we regret to inform you that our buyers in Odense find your price much too high. Information indicates that some parcels of Turkish origin have been sold there at a level about ten percent lower than yours.

We do not deny that the quality of Chinese Kernels is slightly better, but the difference in price should, in no case, be as big as ten percent.

To step up trade, we, on behalf of our buyers, counter-offer as follows ,subject to your reply being received here by August 26, our time: "60 metric tons Bitter Apricot kernels, 1999 Crop at RMB 2350 per metric ton on CIFC 2% Odense with transshipment at Copenhagen, other term as per your letter dated 14/8/99".

As the market is declining, we recommend your immediate acceptance.

Yours truly,

2. Writing Guide

(1) 应如何询盘?

When making an enquiry:

① *Tell the addressee how his name is known, introduce your firm and lines of business and express your wish to establish business relations, if it is a first enquiry.*

② *State clearly and concisely what you want and make your request reasonable, optimistic and polite. Keep your enquiry short and to the point.*

③ Use tactic versions such as "Should your prices be competitive" or "If your quotation is favorable".

(2) 询盘的要点有哪些?

Normally, a good enquiry may include the following information:

① *Minimum order quantity (MOQ).*

② *Sample availability/cost.*

③ *International standards met.*

④ *Delivery time.*

⑤ *Company brochure.*

⑥ *Full product catalog.*

⑦ *A response before a date.*

(3) 如何回复询盘?

When making reply to an enquiry:

① *Take the opportunity to make a favorable comment on your products or services.*

② *Invite your reader's attention to other products.*

③ *Use tactic versions such as "our … are rapidly becoming popular and it is difficult to meet demand, but if you place your order before …"*

(4) 如何充分利用询盘?

How to maximize the value of every enquiry you receive:

① *Reply to all enquires promptly, because buyer enquiries are valuable sales leads. Your response and the time it takes you to reply are critical to be successful. Reply today with complete information for best results. A reply should answer all the questions mentioned in the enquiry and samples should be sent to the prospective buyers as soon as possible. Of course, you may ask your receiver to share the cost by paying the postage, because sometimes sample cost is also a very heavy burden.*

② *Update your sales enquiries database. The enquiries you receive from a valuable database of clients and prospects. Use this database to follow up or offer new products.*

It is advisable for you to reply to all enquiries promptly and update your sales enquiries database so as to maximize the value of every enquiry you receive.

(5) 报价和报盘有什么区别?

A quotation is a statement of the current price of an article/ articles that you intend to sell.

An offer is a promise to supply goods on the terms and conditions stated, in which the seller not only quotes the terms of price but also indicates all necessary terms of sales for the buyer's consideration and acceptance.

(6) 报实盘应包含哪些要点?

① *Be complete, explicit and affirmative, including all the necessary terms of a transaction.*

② *Be accepted without any reserve.*

③ *Be accepted within a validity period.*

(7) 构成受盘的条件有哪些?

① *Accepted by the offeree.*

② *Explicit.*

③ *Unconditional.*

④ *Within its validity.*

(8) 在什么情况下实盘失效?

① *Be accepted beyond the validity.*

② *Be declined by the offeree.*

③ *Be made a counter-offer by the offeree.*

Section Four Selected Sentences 精选句型表达

1. Show Interest and Desires 表示兴趣和要求

(1) We are interested in/ take interest in/ are impressed by your product and wish to have the catalogues.

我方对贵方产品很感兴趣，希望能收到目录。

(2) Some of our clients express/show interest in your products and wish to have your quotations.

我方一些客户对贵公司的产品很感兴趣，并希望得到贵公司的报价。

(3) We are in the market for copper.

我们正想购买铜。

(4) We are considering buying woolen knitwear.

我们正在考虑购买贵方毛织品。

(5) We are potential buyers of the latest style blouse.

我们对贵方最新款女衬衫很感兴趣。

(6) We are ready to purchase your Maple Brand Men's Shirts in large quantity.

我公司打算大量购买贵公司的枫叶牌衬衫。

(7) We will fax you as soon as we are in the market.

我方要货即去电。

2. Introduction of Goods 表示产品享有盛誉

(1) This product is reasonable in price and excellent in quality. It enjoys a ready market in your neighboring countries and regions.

该产品价格合理，品质优良。它在你们邻近国家和地区都很畅销。

(2) We trust you will find our price reasonable and the quality of our products excellent.

我们相信你会发现我们的产品物美价廉。

(3) The material is of the finest quality.

材料品质上乘。

(4) Heavy enquiries witness the quality of our products.

大量询盘证明我们产品质量过硬。

(5) The quality of our products is well-known and universally-acknowledged.

我们产品的质量是众所周知、为人称道的。

(6) Our products enjoy great popularity in this line.

我方产品在这方面享有盛誉。

(7) Our products enjoy high reputation.

我方产品有极高的声誉。

(8) The goods are most popular with our customers.
该产品受到我方客户的极大欢迎。

(9) The goods have commanded a good market.
该产品在市场上占有很大的份额。

(10) The goods are selling fast (enjoy fast sales).
该产品销售迅速。

(11) The goods are universally acknowledged.
该产品家喻户晓。

(12) Because of the top quality, our products are the best-selling goods in the world market.
由于质量上乘，我方产品在国际市场上是最畅销的。

(13) Our goods are known for their fine quality and beautiful packing.
我方的产品以质量上乘、包装精美著称。

(14) In reference to the quality of the new product, no complaint can be made.
新产品的质量是无可挑剔的。

3. Make Enquiries 询盘

(1) Please let us know your lowest possible prices for the relevant goods.
请告知你们有关商品的最低价。

(2) Do you offer FOB or CIF?
你们报的是船上交货价还是到岸价?

(3) We'd rather have you quote us F.O.B. prices.
我们希望你们报离岸价格。

(4) How long does your offer remain valid/firm/open?
你们的报价多长时间有效?

(5) Will you let us know what your terms of payment are?
能否告知贵方付款条件?

(6) Would you please send us your lowest (keenest) quotation?
能否给我们最低报价？

(7) Please let us know your lowest possible prices for the relevant goods.
请告知你们有关商品的最低价。

(8) I'd like to have your lowest quotations, C.I.F. Rotterdam.
我想请你们报鹿特丹到岸价的最低价格。

(9) Please make us an offer within this month since we have made an inquiry for your products.

我们已对你们的产品进行询价，请在本月内给予报盘。

(10) If your prices are favorable, I can place the order right away.
如果你们的价格优惠，我们可以马上订货。

(11) Now that we've already made an inquiry about your articles, will you please reply as soon as possible?

我们已经对贵方的产品进行询价，可否尽快给予答复？

(12) We shall appreciate it very much if you would send us a copy of the price list of your products.

如贵方寄来一份产品价格单，我方将不胜感激。

(13) We hope your quotation should be based on an expanding market and be competitive.

我方希望此报盘应着眼于扩大销路且具有竞争性。

(14) We should be obliged if you would kindly quote your best price and state your best terms and discounts allowable.

请报贵方最优惠的价格、最好的条款及最低折扣，我方将不胜感激。

(15) We'd like to know what you can offer as well as your sales conditions.

我们想了解你们能供应什么，以及你们的销售条件。

(16) We are on the lookout for the following items and should be grateful if you would send samples of the same.

我们欲求购下列产品，如贵公司能寄来其样品，我们将不胜感激。

(17) Should your price be found competitive and delivery date acceptable, we intend to place a large order with you. /If your price is reasonable, quality satisfactory and delivery acceptable, we will send you large orders.

如你方价格有竞争力，交货日期合适，我们打算大量订购。

(18) We are thinking of getting a supply of Chinese tea. Please send us your best offer by cable indicating origin, packing, quantity available and the earliest time of shipment.

我方欲购中国茶，请惠电发盘，说明原产地、包装、可供数量和最早装运期。

(19) We should be grateful if you would let us have by return your lowest price for the captioned goods.

关于标题项下货物，贵方如能复函最低价，我们将非常感激。

(20) As we are likely to place large orders regularly we trust you will consider the allowance of some special concessions.

由于我方可能长期大量订货，相信你方将会做出某些特殊的让步。

(21) Your early attention to this enquiry would be appreciated.

如蒙贵公司早日办理则不胜感激。

(22) We would like to place a trial order with you.

我们期望与贵公司签订一次试订单。

(23) We ask you kindly deliver us as soon as possible, your latest price list of your sports shoes with the lowest quotations, together with an illustrated catalogue.

请贵公司尽快惠寄运动鞋的最新价目表和带有图片的商品目录，并给予最优惠的报价。

4. Rely to Enquiries 对询盘的回复

(1) Thank you for your enquiry.

谢谢你们的询价。

(2) This is in reply to your enquiry of May 10, 2011.

答复你方 2011 年 5 月 10 日的询盘。

(3) We greatly regret that the goods you inquired about are not available for the time being.
很遗憾，贵方所需要的货物暂时短缺。

(4) We regret to inform you that we have no stock of this item at present.
我方很抱歉地通知贵方此商品现在没有存货。

(5) Owing to the increased demand for this type of curtain, our stocks have run very low.
由于这种窗帘的需求急增，我方的存货短缺。

(6) We cannot take care of your enquiry at present.
我们现在无力顾及你方的询盘。

(7) Your enquiry is too vague to enable us to reply you.
你们的询盘不明确，我们无法答复。

(8) With regard to your enquiry for…, we wish to give the following in reply.
对于你方关于……的询盘，我方愿做如下答复。

(9) We welcome your enquiry of October 20, 2011 and thank you for your interest in our products.

欢迎你们 2011 年 10 月 20 日的询盘，并感谢你们对我们的产品感兴趣。

(10) We are very pleased to have received your enquiry of March 15, 2012 and enclose our latest illustrated catalogue and price list with the details you ask for.

我们很高兴收到你们 2012 年 3 月 15 日的询盘，随函附上我们最新的产品目录和价格单，上面包含你们所要求了解的详细信息。

5. Make Quotations 报价

(1) We quote you our best prices for the following goods, and shall be pleased if you can favor us with your orders.

在此就以下商品向贵公司报我方最低价，盼惠顾试购。

(2) We take the liberty to enclose herewith for your reference the newest samples and our revised catalogue and price list.

冒昧随函寄去最新的样品及最新修改的目录和价格表，供贵方参考。

(3) Thank you for your enquiry of May 5 and we are pleased to send/give/make you our best/lowest quotation for…

谢谢贵方 5 月 5 日询盘，现很高兴向贵方报……的最低价。

(4) With reference to your letter of May 10 enquiring for …, we enclose our quotation for your consideration and trust you will find our prices acceptable.

兹就贵方 5 月 10 来函询盘……，随函附上我方报价，相信贵方会感到我方报价是可以接受的。

(5) We hope that our quotation will be a satisfactory one and expect your orders.
希望我们的报价令人满意，期待接到你们的订单。

6. Make a Firm Offer 报实盘

(1) This offer is firm for orders.
此次报盘为实盘。

(2) This offer remains firms for 5 days.
此次实盘 5 天内有效。

(3) This offer will be kept open until April 10, 2012.
此报盘于 2012 年 4 月 10 日前有效。

(4) We make you the following offer, subject to your reply reaching us within 10 days.
我们做出如下报盘，以你方 10 日内回复为准。

(5) We offer you firm, as follows.
我们向你方报如下实盘。

(6) We are sorry that we are unable to entertain any counteroffer, for this offer is firm, subject to the receipt of reply by us before December 20.

很抱歉，我方无法考虑任何还盘，因为这是一个实盘，并以 12 月 20 日以前收到我方回复为准。

7. Make a Non-firm Offer 报虚盘

(1) All quotations are subject to our final confirmation.
所有的报价都以我们最终确认的为准。

(2) In reply, we make you the following offer, subject to our final confirmation.
作为回复，我们向你们报盘如下，以我方最终确认的为准。

(3) If you find the above offer acceptable, please cable us immediately for our final confirmation.

如果你方可以接受我方报盘，请及时电告我们以最终确认。

(4) Please note that our offer is subject to your confirmation reaching us here on or before May 12.

请注意我方的报盘将以你方 5 月 12 日或之前确认的为准。

(5) We are pleased to make you an offer, subject to the goods being unsold /prior sale.
很高兴向贵方报盘，此报盘在货物未售出前有效。

(6) We wish to state that our quotations are subject to alternation without notice and to our confirmation at our confirmation at the time of placing your order.

我方必须声明，我方报盘可以不事先通知随时变动，贵方订货时需以我方最后确认的为准。

8. Make Counter-offers 还盘

(1) We feel regretful for inability to accept your offer.
很遗憾我方不能接受贵方的发盘。

(2) While appreciating the quality of your bicycles, we find your prices are a little too high to be acceptable.

我们虽赞赏你们自行车的质量，但价格略高难以接受。

(3) Your price is on the high side and we have to counter-offer as follows, subject to your reply received by us on or before April 12.

贵方价格偏高，我们不得不进行如下还盘，以我方在 4 月 12 日或之前收到贵方答复有效。

(4) The price you offered is out of line with the prevailing market level, so it is beyond what is acceptable to us.

贵方价格与现行市场行情有出入，故我方无法接受。

(5) Your prices appear to be so high that to accept them would leave us with a small margin of profit.

贵方价格显得过高，如果接受我们的利润将会很微薄。

(6) To accept your present quotation would mean a heavy loss to us, not to speak of profit.

接受贵方现在的报价就意味着我们将严重亏损，更不要说利润了。

(7) Should you be prepared/ready to reduce your price by 5%, we might come to/conclude terms.

如果贵方准备降价 5%，我们则可达成一致。

(8) We would very much like to place further orders with you if you could bring down your prices at least by 10%.

贵方如能降价最少 10%，我们将很愿意继续订货。

(9) It may disappoint you to know that the price you quoted in your letter is unworkable. Information indicates that groundnuts of the similar quality are easily obtainable at a much lower figure from other suppliers.

得知贵方信中所报价格不可行也许会令你们失望。情况表明同等质量的花生可以很容易从其他供应商那里以低得多的价格购到。

(10) However you will agree that the prices offered are slightly higher if you consider the large amount of our order. Therefore we would like to ask you if you can make a further discount of 2%.

但是，如果贵方考虑我方订购量之大，就应该知道贵方的价格还是有点高，所以我方希望贵方再给 2%的折扣。

(11) Owing to the fluctuation of US dollar, we disagree with your requirement of payment by it.

由于美元的波动性较大，我们不同意使用美元结账。

(12) Your delivery date is unacceptable for us. Would you please make us prompt delivery, since we are in urgent need of this order?

我方无法接受你们的发货日期，请立即发货，我们急需这批订货。

(13) We hope that this counter offer will meet with your approval and we shall place regular orders with you on receipt of your confirmation.

希望此还盘能够得到贵公司的同意，一旦收到贵方的确认，我们将定期订购。

(14) If you can not be prepared to meet us halfway, we have to place our order elsewhere.

如果贵公司不能让步，我们只好转向别的公司订购。

(15) In view of the goods in great demand, we would advise in your interest that you accept our offer without any delay.

鉴于商品紧俏，为贵方着想，建议迅速接受我方报盘。

(16) It is hoped that you will consider our counter offer most favorably and inform us of

your acceptance at your earliest convenience.

希望贵公司从善考虑我方的还盘，如接受，请及早告知为盼。

(17) For initial orders from first-time customers our policy requires payment by irrevocable letter of credit or banker's draft on delivery. Therefore I am afraid we cannot accept your payment terms at the present time.

对于新客户的起始订单，我公司的政策是必须以不可撤销信用证或银行汇票在交货时或交货之前付款，因此恐怕目前我们无法接受贵方的付款条件。

9. Offer a Discount 给予折扣或降价

(1) Considering our long-standing friendly business relationship, we can allow you reduction of 4% in our price.

考虑到我们长期友好的贸易关系，我们同意在原价格的基础上让利 4%。

(2) In view of the long-standing trade relation between us, we made reduction of 5% this time.

鉴于我们之间的长期贸易关系，我们此次让价 5%。

(3) For the sake of future business, we'd like to have your suggestions.

为了以后的业务，我方接受贵方建议。

(4) As an encouragement of business, we'd like to grant your request to lower the price of our products.

为了促进贸易达成，我方同意贵方降低产品价格的要求。

(5) We would be willing to discuss a volume discount if your order volume is doubled.

如果贵方的订货量能翻一倍，我方将乐意与贵方讨论批量订货的折扣问题。

(6) We are prepared to allow you a 10% quantity discount if your order exceeds 200 cartons.

如果你方订单超过 200 箱，拟予以 10%的数量折扣。

(7) It is our policy not to discount our standard prices. However, we are willing to make an exception in this case as an introduction for our products.

对标准价格不打折扣，这是我方的规矩。但是，作为对我方产品的一种推广，我方愿意破例一次。

(8) We are anxious to do what we can to help you establish new business, and are prepared to allow you a special discount of 8%, if payment is made within 20 days.

我方愿意尽一切所能帮助贵方开展新的业务，所以如果贵方能在 20 天内付款，我方准备给贵方 8%的特别折扣。

(9) Considering the recent decrease in the price of raw material, we willingly adjust some of our own prices.

鉴于原材料的降价，我们将会对某些价格进行调整。

(10) We can cut the price by 10%, provided that quality of the products will be not as good as the sample we sent you.

我方同意给贵公司 10%的降价，前提是货物质量将没有样品好。

10. Decline a Counter-offer 拒绝还盘

(1) It is regretful that we have to decline your counter-offer.

很遗憾我方必须拒绝贵方的还盘。

(2) Although we are anxious to open up business with you, we regret that it is impossible for us to allow that reduction asked for, because we have already cut our prices to the lowest point after closely examining our cost calculations.

尽管我方非常渴望与贵方建立业务关系，但很遗憾我方不可能接受贵方的降价要求。因为我方在进行了认真的成本核算后已经将价格压到了最低。

(3) As your counter bid is not up to the present market level, we are sorry that we have to give you a negative reply.

由于你方还价与市价不符，非常抱歉只能给予否定答复。

(4) It is regrettable that we have to decline your counter-offer for the lack of stock at present.

很遗憾，由于目前缺货，我方必须拒绝贵方还盘。

(5) What we have quoted it really the lowest, and, as such, we regret not being in a position to reduce our price.

我们所提供的已是最低报价，因此我方不能再降价了。

(6) We have cut our price to the limit. We regret, therefore, being unable to comply with your request for further reduction.

我们已将价格降至最低，很遗憾我们不能满足贵方要求进一步让价。

(7) We regret that there is no likelihood of the price going down because the price of raw material has advanced 15%.

由于原材料的价格已上涨了15%，很抱歉，我方的价格已没有下降的可能了。

(8)Your counter-offer is beyond what is acceptable to us, as we cannot meet your requirement of payment.

由于无法满足你方对付款方式的要求，我们不能接受你方还盘。

Abstract

通过本章学习，①了解询盘、报盘和还盘的定义；②学习如何询盘、报盘和还盘；③能够区分实盘和虚盘；④熟练掌握询盘、报盘和还盘函电的书写技巧和注意事项；⑤通过熟悉标准模板掌握书写询盘、报盘和还盘函电的基本方法；⑥掌握有关询盘、报盘和还盘函电的经典句型及表达方式。

Useful Words & Expressions

1. enquire 询盘；询价；询购
2. to make an enquiry/ enquire about 发出询盘；向…询价
3. enquirer 询价者
4. enquiry 询盘
5. enquiry sheet 询价单

6．specific enquiry 具体询盘
7．general enquiry 一般询盘
8．take/have interest in…, feel/be interested in… 对……感兴趣
9．be in the market for…, be desirous of…, look/seek for… 寻购……
10．to make/send sb. an enquiry for…, enquire (for) … 对……进行询盘
11．Please state/indicate/note terms of… 请说明……的条款
12．This is in reply/response/answer to one's enquiry of… 兹复某人……的询盘
13．date/time of delivery 交货期
14．sales conditions 销售条件
15．specifications 产品规格
16．illustrated catalogue 带有图片说明的目录表
17．to make delivery 交货
18．to make prompt delivery 即期交货
19．payment terms 付款方式
20．special orders 特殊订货
21．to place a trial order with sb. for sth. 向某人试订某物
22．regular order 定期购买
23．regular supply 定期供应
24．regular customer 长期客户
25．offer 报盘；报价
26．to make an offer for/ offer for… 对……报盘(报价)
27．firm offer 实盘
28．non-firm offer 虚盘
29．Counter-offer 还盘；还价
30．offerer/ offeror 发价人；报盘人
31．offeree 被发价人；受盘人
32．offering 出售物
33．offer sheet 出售货物单
34．offer list/book 报价单
35．offer price 售价
36．lump offer 综合报盘(针对两种以上商品)
37．bid *n.* 递价；出价；递盘(由买方发出)*v.* 递盘
38．to make a bid 递价
39．to get a bid 得到递价
40．to send/forward an offer 寄送报盘
41．to get/obtain an offer 获得报盘
42．make/cable sb. an offer for… 就……商品给某人报盘；给……报盘
43．offer and acceptance by post 通过邮政报价及接受
44．to accept an offer 接受报盘

45．to entertain an offer 考虑报盘
46．to give an offer 给……报盘
47．to submit an offer 提交报盘
48．official offer 正式报价(报盘)
49．quote 报价
50．quotation 价格
51．preferential offer 优先报盘
52．cost of production 生产费用
53．be subject to 以……为条件，以……为准
54．offer subject to our written acceptance 以我方书面接受为准的报盘
55．offer subject to sample approval 以样品确定后生效为准的报盘
56．offer subject to our final confirmation 以我方最后确认为准的报盘
57．offer subject to export/import license 以获得出口(进口)许可证为准的报价
58．offer subject to prior sale 以提前售出为准的报盘
59．offer subject to goods being unsold 以商品未售出为准的报盘
60．offer subject to your reply reaching here 以你方答复到达我地为准的报盘
61．offer subject to first available steamer 以装第一艘轮船为准的报盘
62．to extend an offer 延长报盘
63．to renew an offer /reinstate an offer 恢复报盘
64．to withdraw an offer 撤回报盘
65．to decline an offer/turn down an offer 谢绝报盘
66．unacceptable 不可接受的
67．workable 可行的
68．at wide intervals 间隔时间太长
69．make headway 有进展
70．to be outbidding 高于……的价
71．price of commodities 物价
72．price list 价格目录，价格单
73．price current (p.c.) 市价表
74．the lowest/best/ bedrock/ minimum/ base / rock bottom price 最低价
75．the most favorable price 最优惠价
76．competitive price 有竞争力的价格
77．reasonable price 合理价
78．wild speculation 漫天要价
79．ceiling/ maximum price 最高价，顶价
80．to be on the high side 偏高
81．competitive capacity/power 竞争能力
82．competitive edge 竞争优势
83．a small margin of profit 利润微薄

84. average price 平均价格
85. price terms 价格条款
86. F.O.B. (Free On Board) “船上交货价”或称“离岸价格”
87. C.I.F. (Cost, Insurance and Freight) “成本加保险费、运费”或“到岸价格”
88. C&F (Cost and Freight) “成本加运费”或“离岸加运费”价格
89. F.O.B. Liner Terms F.O.B. 班轮条件
90. F.O.B. Stowed 船上交货并理舱
91. F.O.B. Trimmed 船上交货并平舱
92. F.O.B. Under Tackle F.O.B.吊钩下交货
93. C.I.F. Liner terms C.I.F.班轮条件
94. C.I.F. Ex Ship’s Hold C.I.F.舱底交货
95. F.O.B. plane 飞机离岸价(用于紧急情况)
96. acceptable 可以接受的；可以使用的
97. to pass over 转给
98. to adopt/employ/use (某种价格术语)采用某种价格
99. FOR-Free on Rail 火车交货价
100. FOT-Free on Truck 汽车交货价
101. FAS-Free Alongside Ship 船边交货价
102. Ex Factory 工厂交货价
103. Ex Plantation 农场交货价
104. Ex Warehouse 仓库交货价
105. Ex Ship 目的港船上交货价
106. Ex Dock Duty Paid 目的港码头完税交货价
107. Ex Dock Duty Unpaid 目的港码头未完税交货价
108. good quality 好质量
109. fine quality 优质
110. better quality 较好质量
111. high quality 高质量
112. fair quality 尚好的质量
113. sound quality 完好的质量
114. best quality 最好的质量
115. superior quality 优等的质量
116. choice/selected quality 精选的质量
117. prime/tip-top quality 第一流的质量
118. first-class /first-rate quality 头等的质量
119. above the average quality 一般水平以上的质量
120. below the average quality 一般水平以下的质量
121. common quality 一般质量
122. standard quality 标准质量

123．usual quality 通常的质量
124．popular quality 大众化的质量
125．uniform quality 一律的质量
126．average quality 平均质量
127．fair average quality (f.a.q.) 大路货；中等品
128．quick seller/ready seller/quick-selling product 畅销品
129．allow/offer/grant/give a special discount of …% on sth. 就……(产品)给予百分之……的特别折扣
130．bulk buying 大量购买
131．available from stock 有存货的/现货供应
132．out of stock 无存货
133．up-to-date/latest/newest price list 最新价目表
134．as specified below/as follows 如下
135．above-mentioned/before-mentioned 上述
136．under-mentioned 下述
137．offer as follows 报盘如下
138．steady demand 稳定的需求
139．ready market 现成的市场；成熟的市场
140．the taste of the market 市场偏好/需求/品味
141．be under offer, be on sale (商品)在出售中 (on sale:在售/特价)
142．market risk 市场风险
143．market survey 市场调查
144．domestic market 国内市场
145．foreign/overseas market 国外市场
146．market glut 市场饱和
147．market value 市(场)价(格)；市值
148．put sth. on the market 把……投放到市场
149．take market sharing 抢占市场份额
150．open up a new market 开拓新市场
151．welcome one' s enquiry 欢迎某人的询盘
152．give sth. your prompt attention 对某事予以即刻关注
153．enclose a catalogue and a price list 附寄目录和价格表
154．in reply to one's enquiry 答复某人询盘
155．acknowledge the receipt of 确认收到
156．be desirous of sth. 想要……
157．Letter of Credit 信用证
158．sight draft 即期汇票
159．D/P=Documents Against Payment 付款交单
160．proforma invoice 形式发票

161．consular invoice 领事发票
162．customs invoice 海关发票
163．import license 进口许可证
164．export license 出口许可证
165．cash with order 下订单时付款
166．at your earliest convenience 请尽早
167．initial orders 起始订单
168．sales confirmation 销售确认书
169．come to terms 达成协议
170．as per 按照
171．Art. No. 货号
172．Item No. 项目号；货号
173．Model No./ Type No. 型号
174．on the usual terms 按通常的(贸易)条款

Exercises

1．What should be written in the first enquiry?

2．What is a firm offer? In making a firm offer, what should be mentioned?

3．What is a non-firm offer? What's the difference between a firm offer and a non-firm offer?

4．What is a counter-offer? In a letter rejecting an offer, what are the main points to be expressed?

5．Choose the best answer to complete each of the following sentences.

(1) We have received your enquiry of 15 October____you show great interest in our electric heaters.

A．which　B．at which　C．in which　D．from which

(2) ____ will be highly appreciated if you will send us a brochure.

A．We　B．You　C．It　D．Which

(3) We are pleased to tell you that the price we quoted is our ____ price.

A．easiest　B．new　C．cheap　D．rock bottom

(4) Should your price ____ reasonable, we will place an order with you ____ the item.

A．is…for　B．is…from　C．be…for　D．be…with

(5) ____, we are airmailing you our latest quotation sheet for your consideration.

A．As request　B．At request　C．At requested　D．As requested

(6) Under the ____, it is impossible to decline our price again.

A．circumstance　B．circumstances　C．case　D．cases

(7) Marketing is ____, we have received a crowd of enquires from our customers.

A．declining　B．advancing　C．weak　D．going

(8) Our ____ catalogue and price list are sent together with the letter for your reference.

A. illustrated　B. illustrating　C. be illustrated　D. that illustrated

(9) ____ your enquiry of 6 September, we are pleased to quote as follows.

A. Replying for　B. Replying　C. Replying to　D. To be replied to

(10) Our offer will remain ____ August 31, that is, two weeks from today.

A. valid for　B. expire　C. expiration　D. valid till

(11) If you find our price ____ , please send us an email for our final confirmation.

A. acceptance　B. accepted　C. accepting　D. acceptable

(12) As soon as we have studied your catalog, we shall ____ you by fax.

A. contact with　B. be contacted with　C. contact　D. contact to

(13) We are sending you by separate airmail a complete set of samples, ____ you will find them satisfactory.

A. to hope　B. hopefully　C. in hoping　D. hoping

(14) We would make you the following offer subject to your reply ____ us not later than November 25.

A. reaching　B. arriving　C. to reach　D. to arrive

(15) Business is impossible as your price is ____ the prevailing market level.

A. out of line with　B. out of line　C. in line with　D. in line of

6. Put the following sentences into English.

(1) 一旦收到你方具体询盘，我们将立即给你们报最优惠的上海到岸价。

(2) 请报 CIF 温哥华最低价，包括我方 5%的佣金。

(3) 随函寄去我们的报价，此报价有效期仅为两周。

(4) 期待尽快收到你方的全套样品。

(5) 我们收到了你方 6 月 4 日对我们电子玩具的询价，现高兴地向你方报盘如下，供你参考。

(6) 我们的报价以合理利润为依据，不是漫天要价。

(7) 一旦收到你方具体的询盘，我们将立即给你们报出优惠的欧洲主要口岸到岸价。

(8) 关于支付条款，我们要求不可撤销的、凭即期汇票支付的信用证。

(9) 本报盘 5 日内有效。

(10) 考虑到贵方将开出大量的订单，对于我们最近的报价将允许一定的折扣。

(11) 为了开展双方间具体的业务，我们很高兴向你方报特盘，以我方最后确认的为有效报价。

(12) 我们的惯例是接受即期付款交单而不是信用证。因此，对于这笔交易和以后的交易，我们希望你能接受付款交单的支付条件。

(13) 在随附的单子上我们列出了关于包装的具体要求，请你方务必照办。

(14) 我们很遗憾不能接受你方的还价。自从我们报价给你们后，我们已按原报价与其他许多客户成交，故如你方仍有需要，请立即订购。

(15) 按照你们的要求，我们报 50 公吨大豆的实盘如下，以自本日起一周之内你方复到为准。

(16) 如果你公司能将 9 月 3 日的报价单的价格降低 3%，则我公司将乐意接受你们的报价。

(17) 你方 2 月 15 日函悉，并已转交给上海分公司。他们会直接答复你们，因为你所询问的商品是他们经营的。

(18) 敬启者：

感谢你方 4 月 28 日的询盘，很高兴向你做出如下报盘，该报盘以你方回复被我方 5 月 15 日之前接受为准，报盘如下：

1 000 打青年牌钢笔，每打 20 美元 CIF 鹿特丹，包括 5%的佣金，5/6 月份装船，凭不可撤销信用证支付，10 只一盒，100 打装一纸箱。

相信上述报盘能被你方接受，盼望你方肯定的回复。

谨上

Case Practice

客户的还盘即构成了新的报盘，以本章的导入案例为背景，根据以上新报盘，以华信公司业务员黄明的身份给加拿大 James Brown & Sons 公司写一封还盘函。要求经过仔细的核算，在利润不少于 10%的基础上进行还盘。

Chapter 4 Contract

合 同

案例导入 Case-lead-in

英国的一家公司曾向广东 MNG 公司订购了一批床单，货物到达后，觉得很满意，现在想按原订单重复订购，并给其负责人 Jenny Wang 写了一封重复订购函，其订购信函如下。

Dear Mrs. Jenny Wang,

The subject goods arrived yesterday and turned out to our entire satisfaction. As we are confident that they can find a good market here, we wish to duplicate our last order.

The relative L/C will be opened in your favor once we receive your confirmation. If possible, we'd like the goods to be delivered in October.

Best regards,

Sarah Sloan

Section One Definition and Functions of Contract
合同的含义及作用

1. Definition of Contract

After negotiations, both buyers and sellers agree with each other the terms and conditions they discussed. The buyer will write a letter to the seller to express his acceptance and readiness to place an order, and the seller usually send acknowledgement by letter after receiving an order. Once accepted and confirmed, the business is concluded.

A contract or a sales confirmation is made out, generally by the sellers, and signed by both parties. A contract is a formal agreement enforceable by law, which sets forth the rights and obligations for the parties involved in it. For smaller deals or transactions between regular business partners, a sales/purchase confirmation may be used instead of a formal contract. Though less detailed, a sales/purchase confirmation has the same legal effect.

2. Functions of Contract

The main functions of an international business contract are as follows.

(1) It is an additional proof of rights and obligations, especially vital when the deal has been reached orally.

(2) It can act as a guideline when both parties are implementing the whole deal.

A well-drafted contract spells out the rights and obligations of each party and protects you and your business to the most practical extent. It minimizes risks and protects the company in case of possible trade disputes, claims and /or legal actions. A good contract can increase your business, earn you respect, and let you make more money. A bad contract, on the contrary, can be disastrous.

Section Two Classification and Contents of Contract 合同的分类及内容

1. Classification of Contract

By level of importance, international business contracts can be divided into:

(1) Contract(合同), which emphasizes the specific ways to fulfill a specific deal.

(2) Agreement(协议书), which usually stresses the principles of the deal.

(3) Confirmation(确认书), which is used for transaction involving a small sum. It doesn't call for formal signature of both the buyers and the sellers and comes into force upon confirmation of the parties concerned.

Among the above-mentioned categories, contract is the most formal and importance one.

By content, international business contracts can be divided into 16 categories as follows.

1) Sales contract (销售合同)
2) Purchase contract (购买合同)
3) Shipping contract (运输合同)
4) Technology transfer contract (技术转让合同)
5) Compensation trade contract (补偿贸易合同)
6) Bidding contract (投标合同)
7) Agency contract (代理合同)
8) Processing and assembling contract (加工装配合同)
9) Contract for foreign labor services (涉外劳务合同)
10) Contract for international leasing affairs (国际租赁合同)
11) Contract for sino-foreign credit and loan (涉外信贷合同)
12) Contract for sino-foreign joint venture (中外合资经营企业合同)
13) Contract for sino-foreign contractual joint venture (中外合作经营企业合同)
14) Contract for retaining foreign experts (聘请外国专家合同)
15) Contract for international engineering project (国际工程承包合同)

16) Contract for sino-foreign cooperation development of natural resources (中外合作开采自然资源合同)

Among the above-mentioned categories, sales contract and purchase contract are most often used, especially sales contract.

By style, international business contracts can be divided into:

(1) Form-style contract, a printed form, which just needs filling out or ticking where necessary.

(2) Clause-style contract, which should be carefully and precisely worded.

2. Contents of Contract

Despite the diversity of contracts, the contents of a contract are more or less the same.

1) Title (合同名称)

2) Preamble (前文)

(1) Contract No. (合同号码).

(2) Date of signing (签约日期).

(3) Place of signing(签约地点).

(4) Signing parties (签约当事人).

(5) Recitals of WHEREAS clause(签约缘由).

3) Body(正文)

(1) Definition clause(定义条款):to give specific explanation to the key words repeatedly appearing in a contract, which have special meanings or easily cause misunderstanding and controversy.

(2) Specific conditions(具体条款).

① Commodity (商品名称).

② Quantity (规格).

③ Unit price (单价).

④ Total value (总值).

⑤ Packing (包装).

⑥ Insurance clauses (保险条款).

⑦ Time of shipment (装运时间).

⑧ Port of shipment and destination (装运港和目的港).

⑨ Shipping marks (运输标志，唛头).

⑩ Terms of payment (支付条款).

(3) General conditions(一般条款).

① Duration(合同有效期限).

② Termination(合同的终止).

③ Force majeure(不可抗力).

④ Assignment(合同的让与).

⑤ Inspection (检验).

⑥ Claims (索赔).

⑦ Arbitration(仲裁).
⑧ Governing law(适用的法律).
⑨ Jurisdiction(诉讼管辖).
⑩ Notice(通知手续).
⑪ "Entire Agreement" clause(完整条款).
⑫ Amendment(合同的修改).
⑬ Others(其他).
4) Witness Clause(立证结尾条款)
(1) Concluding sentence (结尾语).
① Effecting date (生效日期).
② Applicable language and text (适用文字).
③ Number of original copies (合同文本数量).
(2) Signature(签约人签名).
(3) Seal (盖印).

Section Three Cases in Detail
具体案例分析

(一) 经典案例解析

Dear Sirs,

Thank you for your letter of Feb.11, 2012 for 15 000 pieces of Women's dress.

Though the prevailing quotations are somewhat lower than our expectation, we will still accept the order on the same terms as you mentioned in view of encouraging our mutual business.

We have made out and sent you our Sales Confirmation No.0135 in duplicate and shall be grateful if you send back one copy duly countersigned.

We are pleased to learn that a letter of credit will be immediately opened in our favor. Meanwhile, in order to avoid subsequent amendments, here we would like to draw your attention to the fact that the stipulations in the relative credit should conform strictly to the terms in our Sales Confirmation.

We are appreciative of your cooperation and assure that the shipment to be dispatched after our receipt of the letter of credit will turn out to your entire satisfaction.

Yours faithfully,

Notes

1. order *n.* 订单；所订货物(后接介词 for 或 of)

We thank you for your order for 10 tons.

谢谢你方 10 吨的订单。

We are glad to place an order with you for 2 000 tea pots.

很高兴向你方订购2 000个茶壶。

We will ship our order in May.
我们将在五月份装运你方所订货物。

order　*v.* 订购

If you order immediately, we can make shipment this month.
如你方立即订购，我们可在本月装运。

2. term　*n.* 条款

terms of payment 付款方式；付款条件

trade terms 贸易术语；贸易条款

3. Sales Confirmation 销售确认书

Sales Contract 销售合同

Purchase Confirmation 购买确认书

Purchase Contract 购买合同

4. Duplicate　*a.* 复制的；副的；完全相同的
n. 复制品；副本
v. 复写；复制；使加倍

The duplicate copy of the Sales Confirmation is to be kept by us.
此销售确认书的副本由我方保存。

We intend to place a duplicate order and wonder if you could accept.
我们打算重复订购，不知你们能否接受。

in duplicate 一式两份

in triplicate 一式三份

in quadruplicate 一式四份

一式四份及以上的也常说 in four copies (in four fold), in five copies (in five fold)等。

5. duly　*adv.* 正确地，适当地；按时地，准时地，如期地=in due course/in good time

We have duly received your shipping instruction.
我们已如期收到你方的装船须知。

6. countersign　*v.* 会签(在一方已经签字的文件上签字)

to countersign a contract 会签合同

Enclosed is our contract No. 345 in duplicate, of which please return us one copy, duly countersign.
随函附上我方第345号合同一式两份，请会签并回寄一份。

7. Letter of Credit: L/C 信用证

8. in sb.'s favor 对某人有利；以某人为受益人；以某人为抬头人

The letter of credit has been opened in your favour.
此信用证的开立以贵方为受益人。

9. amendment　*n.* 修订；修改

Please send us the amendment to L/C as soon as possible.
请即寄信用证修改书。

10. stipulation　*n.* 契约；条文

We find the stipulations in your L/C different from those in our contract.
我们发现你方信用证条款与我方合同不符。

11. conform to 相一致；相符合；相吻合

Your L/C clauses do not conform to those in our S/C.
你方信用证条款与我方合同不符。

12. be appreciative of 非常感谢
13. Dispatch *v.* 发送；调遣；派遣
14. to your entire satisfaction 令贵方十分满意

(二) 一般案例表述

1. Confirming a Purchase

Dear Mr. Bakal，

Thank you for your samples and price list of Tapioca Chips. We find the prices and quality satisfactory and confirm now our purchase from you of 500 metric tons of Tapioca Chios on the following terms and conditions.

Art.No.	Quantity	Unit Price	Amount
CIF Qingdao			
TC002	200M/TS	@USDl20perM/T	USD24 000
TC008	300M/TS	@USDl50 per M/T	USD45 000

Total Value：USD69 000

Tapioca Chips are packed in plastic bags of about 20 kgs net each，two bags to a carton.

Payment is to be made by T/T .i.e. 30 percent deposit before delivery，70 percent after your faxing copy of B/L.

The delivery date will be 30 days after you receive our 30 percent deposit.

We are glad to have concluded this first deal with you. We hope it will mark the good beginning of the pleasant business relations between us.

Best wishes，

Notes

订购函可以是表格的形式，如订单(Purchase Order)、购货确认书(Purchase Confirmation)或者购货合同(Purchase Contract)，也可用商务信函。订货时，内容必须准确、清楚、讲究礼貌，对于重要的交易条款必须作出明确规定。订购信函应详细列明所要购买的货物的名称、规格、数量、价格、交货期、支付方式等内容。

2. Acceptance

Dear Sir or Madam,

Subj: Leather shoes

We accept your counteroffer of July 7th and are pleased to confirm having concluded the transaction of the captioned goods with you. Our factory has informed us that they can, at present, entertained orders of 20 000 pairs per week. Thus, you can rest assured that your order of 50 000 pairs for shipment next month will be fulfilled as contracted upon.

However, emphasis has to be laid on the point that your L/C must reach here by the end of this month. Otherwise, shipment has to be delayed.

We are now enclosing here with our Sales Contract No.37G4321 in duplicate. Please countersign and return us one copy for records. We appreciate your cooperation and trust that our products will turn out to your satisfaction.

Sincerely,

Notes

(1) 接受或确认文书实际上是买方和卖方对生意买卖的承诺。他们通过洽谈，愿意按照双方协商同意的条款签订合同。卖方所报的实盘一经买方接受，交易即告达成；或卖方所报虚盘，经买方接受后，再经卖方确认，交易也告达成；或者买方对卖方的报盘进行还盘，经卖方接受，交易也告达成；或者买方主动向卖方递交实盘或递交经本人确认的订单，两者都包括必需的贸易条款，经卖方接受后，也达成交易。

(2) 接受或确认一般需要双方多次协商之后才能达成交易，无论是买方提交订单还是卖方发出销售确认书都需双方同意签字后方能生效并执行。

(3) 通常在接受或确认交易时，还应准备订单或销售确认书。订单和销售确认书通常都有一定的条款，订单相对简单，销售确认书却非常详细，在贸易中，销售确认书常起着合同的作用，许多国家都将它作为法律仲裁的合法文件。

资料链接 Material—link

1. Standard Model

Model 1: Sending a Sales Contract

Dear Sirs,

We wish to refer to the recent exchange of cables and are pleased to confirm having concluded with you a transaction of 30 metric tons of groundnut kernels. Enclosed you will find our Sales Contract No.354 in duplicate of which please countersign and return one copy to us for our files. We trust you will open the relative L/C at an early date.

As regards additional quantities, we are working and will let you have an offer sometime next week.

Yours faithfully,

Encl.

Model 2: Sending a Sales Confirmation

20 May 2007

Kee & Co., Ltd

34 Regent Street

London, UK

Dear Sirs,

We have great pleasure in enclosing copies of faxes exchanged between us resulting in the conclusion of business for 500 Five_Ram bicycles.

We enclose our Sales Confirmation No.850 in duplicate. Please sign the bottom copy and return it to us for our files. We look forward to receiving your future enquires and orders.

Yours faithfully,

Tony Smith

Chief Seller

Model 3: Counter-Signature

Dear Sirs,

We have duly received your Sales Contract No.5623 covering 50 tons walnutmeat we have booked with you. Enclosed please find the duplicate with our counter-signature. Thanks to mutual efforts, we were able to bridge the price gap and put the deal through.

The relative L/C has been established with the Bank of China, London, in your favour. It will reach you in due course.

Regarding further quantities required, we hope you will see your way clear to make us an offer. As an indication, we are prepared to order 80 tons.

Yours faithfully,

Encl.

2. A Specimen Sales Contract

销售合同

SALES CONTRACT

卖方 SELLER:	DESUN TRADING CO., LTD. 29TH FLOOR KINGSTAR MANSION, 623JINLIN RD., SHANGHAI CHINA	编号 NO.: 日期 DATE: 地点 SIGNED IN:	SHDS03027 APR.03, 2001 SHANGHAI
买方 BUYER:	NEO GENERAL TRADING CO. #362 JALAN STREET, TORONTO, CANADA		

买卖双方同意以下条款达成交易：

This contract Is made by and agreed between the BUYER and SELLER, in accordance with the terms and conditions stipulated below.

1．品名及规格 Commodity & Specification		2．数量 Quantity	3．单价及价格条款 Unit Price & Trade Terms	4．金额 Amount
				CIFC5 TORONTO
CHINESE CERAMIC DINNERWARE				
DS1511	30-Piece Dinnerware and Tea Set	542 SETS	USD23.50	12 737.00
DS2201	20-Piece Dinnerware Set	800 SETS	USD20.40	16 320.00
DS4504	45-Piece Dinnerware Set	443 SETS	USD23.20	10 277.60
DS5120	95-Piece Dinnerware Set	254 SETS	USD30.10	7 645.40
Total:		2 039SETS		46 980.00

允许 10% 溢短装，由卖方决定

With 10% More or less of shipment allowed at the sellers' option

5．总值 Total Value　SAY US DOLLARS FORTY SIX THOUSAND NINE HUNDRED AND EIGHTY ONLY.

6．包装 Packing　DS2201 IN CARTONS OF 2 SETS EACH AND DS1151, DS4505 AND DS5120 TO BE PACKED IN CARTONS OF 1 SET EACH ONLY.
TOTAL: 1 639 CARTONS.

7．唛头 Shipping Marks　AT BUYER'S OPTION.

8．装运期及运输方式
Time of Shipment & Means of Transportation — TO BE EFFECTED BEFORE THE END OF APRIL 2001 WITH PARTIAL SHIPMENT ALLOWED AND TRANSHIPMENT ALLOWED.

9．装运港及目的地
Port of Loading & Destination — FROM: SHANGHAI
TO: TORONTO

10．保险
Insurance — THE SELLER SHALL COVER INSURANCE AGAINST WPA AND CLASH & BREAKAGE & WAR RISKS FOR 110% OF THE TOTAL INVOICE VALUE AS PER THE RELEVANT OCEAN MARINE CARGO OF P.I.C.C. DATED 1/1/1981.

11．付款方式
Terms of Payment — BY IRREVOCABLE SIGHT LETTER OF CREDIT.

12．备注
Remarks

The Buyer	The Seller
NEO GENERAL TRADING CO.	DESUN TRADING CO.,LTD.
(signature)	(signature)

3. *A Specimen Sales Confirmation*

大连文泰进出口有限公司
DALIAN WENTAI IMPORT & EXPORT CORPORATION

Tel: 86411 8277 8070

No:

Fax: 86411 8277 8078

Date:

Email:

Signed at: DALIAN CHINA

售货确认书
SALES CONFIRMATION

买方
BUYER ____________________

兹经买卖双方同意按下列条款由买方购进，卖方出售下列商品，订立本合约：

This Contract is made by and between the Buyers and the Sellers, whereby the Buyers agree to buy and the Sellers agree to sell the under-mentioned commodity.

According to the terms and conditions stipulated below:

1.

品名及规格 Commodity & Specifications	数量 Quantity	单价 Unit Price	总价 Total Amount
合同总值: Total Value:			

2. 包装：
Packing

3. 唛头:
Shipping Mark:

4. 装运口岸
Port of Loading:

5. 目的口岸
Port of Destination:

6. 装运期限: 收到可以转船及分批运之信用证 天内装出。

Time of Shipment: ○ Within days after receipt of L/C allowing transhipment and partial shipments.

7. 付款条件: 100%不可撤销即期付款及可转让可分割之信用证,并注明可在上述装运期后十五天内在中国议付有效。

Terms of Payment: ○ By 100% Confirmed, Irrevocable, Transferable and Divisible Letter of Credit to be available by sight draft and to remain valid for Negotiation in China until the 15th after the above-mentioned time of shipment.

□ BY T/T

8. 保险: 按中国保险条款,保综合险及战争险(不包括罢工险)。

Insurance: ○ Covering all risks and war risk any (excluding S.R.C.C.) as per the China Insurance Clauses.

○ To be effected by the buyer.

备注

REMARKS:

(1) 买方须于 年 月 日前开到本批交易的信用证（或通知卖方进口许可证号码），否则，卖方有权不经通知取消本确认书，或接受买方对本约未执行的全部或部分，或对因此遭受的损失提出索赔。

The Buyer shall have the covering Letter of Credit reached the Seller (or notify the Import License No.) before, otherwise the Seller reserves the right to rescind without further notice or to accept whole or any part of this Sales Confirmation not fulfilled by the Buyer, or to lodge a claim for losses this sustained of any.

(2) 凡以 C.I.F. 条件成交的业务，保额为发票的 110%，投保险别以本售货确认书中所开列的为限，买方要求增加保额或保险范围，应于装船前经卖方同意，因此而增加的保险费由买方负担。

For transactions concluded on C.I.F. basis it is understood that the insurance amount will be for 110% of the invoice value against the risks specified in the Sales Confirmation. If additional insurance amount or coverage is required, the Buyer must have the consent of the Seller before shipment, and the additional premium is to be borne by the Buyer.

(3) 品质数量异议：如买方提出索赔，凡属品质异议须于货到目的口岸起 3 个月内提出，凡属数量异议须于货到目的口岸之日起 15 天内提出，对所装货物所提任何异议属于保险公司、轮船公司、其他有关运输机构或邮递机构所负责者，卖方不负任何责任。

QUALITY/QUANTITY DISCREPANCY. In case of quality discrepancy, claim should be filed by the Buyer within 3 months after the arrival of the goods at port of destination; while for quantity discrepancy, claim should be filed by the Buyer within 15 days after the arrival of the goods at port of destination. It is understood that the Seller shall not be liable for any discrepancy of the goods shipped due to causes for which the Insurance Company,Shipping Company, other transportation organizations/or port office is liable.

(4) 本确认书所述全部或部分商品，如因人力不可抗拒的原因，以至不能履约或延迟交货，卖方概不负责。

The Seller shall not be held liable for failure or delay in delivery of the entire lot or a portion of the goods under this Sales Confirmation in consequence of any Force Majeure incidents.

(5) 买方开给卖方的信用证上请注明本确认书号码。

The Buyer is requested always to quote the No. of this sales confirmation in the Letter of Credit to be opened in favor of the Seller.

(6) 买方于收到本售货确认书后立即签回一份，如买方对本确认书有异议，应于收到后 5 天内提出，否则认为买方已同意确认书所规定的各项条款。

The Buyer is requested to sign and return one copy of this Sales Confirmation immediately on receipt of the same, objection, if any, should be raised by the buyer within five days after the receipt of this Sales Confirmation, in the absence of which it is understood that the Buyer has accepted the terms and conditions of the Sales Confirmation.

(7) 自本确认书签订后，以前有关本批交易的函电均告无效。

After the signing of this Sales Confirmation, all preceding negotiations and correspondence pertaining to the same shall become null and valid.

买方 The Buyer	卖方 The Seller

3. Writing Guide

1) 接受或确认的定义

Acceptance or confirmation is in fact an unreserved assent of buyers or sellers who, after mutual negotiations, are willing to enter into a contract in accordance with the terms and conditions agreed upon. A deal is concluded when a seller's firm offer is accepted by buyers. In cases where buyers have made counter-offers, or taken the initiative by placing a firm order or a firm bid with sellers, containing all necessary terms and conditions, sellers' acceptance concludes the deal.

2) 接受的条件

Conditions of Acceptance:

(1) *Made by offerees.*

(2) *Made on any condition.*

(3) *Made within validity of offers.*

3) 起草合同的基本原则

(1) *Terminology. A draft must choose the frequently and professionally used words and phrases to give an exact expression of what he wants to say and organize them in sentences framed to leave no room for misunderstanding.*

(2) *Precision. The language should be precise and accurate.*

(3) *Clarity. Clarity helps to avoid ambiguity, the most terrible problem in contract drafting.*

(4) *Standardization. A contract usually consists of certain parts and takes in certain forms. A drafter must follow suit, leaving little room for imagination.*

4) 销售确认的信函内容

When you send your signed S/C to your foreign buyer, your fax or email should cover the following particulars.

(1) *You are sending your signed S/C or contract by separate airmail.*

(2) *The buyer is requested to counter-sign and return one copy for your file.*

(3) *Assure the buyer of the high quality of your products and your full cooperation.*

(4) *Urge the buyer to open the covering L/C in your favor.*

Section Four　Selected Sentences
精选句型表达

1. Please let us have your signed S/C in duplicate for our counter-signing and thank you for your cooperation.

请给我们你方签好的一式两份的售货确认书供我们会签，感谢你方的合作。

2. Enclosed please find our Sales Confirmation No. HW-116 in triplicate. Please countersign and return one copy to us for our file.

随函附上我方第 HW-116 号售货确认书一式三份，请签退一份供我们存档。

3. Enclosed is our Purchase Confirmation No. 357 in duplicate. Please countersign and return one copy for our file without delay.

随函附上我们的第 357 号购货确认书一式两份，请会签后及时退回一份，供我方存档。

4. The stipulation in the covering L/C shall be in exact accordance with the terms in the S/C so as to avoid subsequent amendments.

相关信用证中的规定必须和售货确认书中的条款一致，以避免随后的修改。

5. We have duly signed our S/C and return one copy to you for your file as requested. Meanwhile, we have opened the relevant L/C and it will reach you very soon.

我们已经及时签署了售货确认书并按要求退回一份供你们备案，同时我们已经开出了相关的信用证，它很快就会送达你方。

6. We enclose a copy of Contract No. 123 duly countersigned by us for your file. Please have the goods shipped as early as possible.

随函附上我方会签的第 123 号合同一份供贵方存档。请尽快装运货物。

7. Please instruct your bank to open the relevant L/C as soon as possible so that we can arrange shipment in due time.

请通知你方的银行尽快开立相关信用证，以便我方及时安排装运。

8. We'll have the contract ready for signature.

我们将准备好合同待签字。

9. We are writing to you about the Sales Contract No. 985.

我们写信给你是想谈谈关于 985 号售货合同的事宜。

10. We invite your attention to the Sales Contract No. 852, which stipulates that shipment should be effected during July and L/C should reach us by the end of June.

请注意一下第 852 号的售货合同，上面规定货物应该在 7 月份装运，信用证要在 6 月底到达我们这里。

11. We are pleased to enclose herewith our Contract No. 256 in two original for your counter-signature. Please send one copy back to us for our file as soon as possible.

兹欣然随函附上我方第 256 号合同正本一式两份，请会签，并早日寄回一份，供我方存档。

12. It is understood that the relevant L/C is to be opened one month before the date of shipment, as is stipulated in the Contract enclosed.

贵方应该了解，正如随函附上的合同所规定的，相关信用证应在装运前一个月开立。

13. The conclusion of the dealing is certainly not the ending. It is only the beginning, and a good one, of the long and friendly business relations between us.

本次业务的完成绝非结束，而是我们双方长期友好贸易往来的一个良好开端。

14. I'm very glad that our negotiation has comet to a successful conclusion with the efforts of both sides.

我们非常高兴经过我们双方的努力，我们的谈判终于有了一个圆满的结果。

15. I know we (the seller) should draw up a contract and the buyer has to sign it.

我们知道我们(卖方)应该拟出一份合同，买方必须签署合同。

16. We both want to sign a contract, and we have to make some concessions to do it.

我们都想签合同，因此双方都要做些让步。

17. We can repeat the contract on the same terms.

我们可以按同样条件再订一个合同。

18．A few problems with supply under the old contract must be quickly resolved.

老合同中的一些供货问题必须尽快解决。

19．We ought to clear up problems arising from the old contract.

我们应该清理一下老合同中出现的问题。

20．These are two originals of the contract we prepared.

这是我们准备好的两份合同正本。

21．We enclose our Sales Contract No.45 in duplicate.

附上我们第45号销售合同一式两份。

22．The copy of our contract will be returned.

合同的副本将被归还。

23．This contract is for 250 metric tons of groundnuts at RMB1 800 per M/T C&F Copenhagen.

这是一份250吨花生的合同，价格为每公吨哥本哈根成本加运费价1 800元。

24．May I refer you to Article 5 of the General Terms and Conditions of the contract?

请您看看合同一般条款的第5条。

25．May I refer you to the contract stipulation about packing (or shipping…)?

请您看看合同中有关包装(装运等)的规定。

26．You must state the description of the goods, the quantity and the unit price in each contract.

每笔合同中都应该提到的商品的性能说明、数量和单价。

27．There is an arbitration clause in the contract. (or insurance clause, inspection clause, shipping clause…)

这是合同中的一项仲裁条款。(或：保险条款，检验条款，装运条款等)

28．We ship our goods in accordance with the terms of the contract.

我们按合同条款交货。

29．I'm sure that shipment will be effected according to the contract stipulation.

我保证我们能按合同规定如期装船。

30．We sincerely hope that both quality and quantity are in conformity with the contract stipulations.

我们真诚希望质量、数量都与合同规定相吻合。

31．All terms and conditions will be the same as those in your previous contract number C70064.

所有条款与我们过去签的第C70064号合同规定的各项条款相同。

32．The contract states that the supplier will be charged a penalty if there is a delay in delivery.

合同规定如果供货商延误交货期，将被罚款。

33．When the goods aren't up to specification stated in the contract, there is also a penalty for poor quality.

如果所交货物与合同所规定规格不符，还对质量低劣进行罚款。

34. The contract comes into effect today; we can't go back on our word now.

合同已于今日生效，我们不能反悔了。

35. Once the contract is approved by the Chinese government, it is legally binding upon both parties.

合同一经中国政府批准，对双方就有了法律约束力。

36. We have to hold you to the contract.

我们不得不要求你们按合同办事。

37. You must put their rights and interest into a contract.

你们必须把他们的权益订在合同中。

38. It's clearly a breach of contract.

这显然是违反了合同。

39. Any deviation from the contract will be unfavourable.

任何违反合同之事都是不利的。

40. The buyer has the option of canceling the contract.

买主有权撤销合同。

41. You have no grounds for backing out of the contract.

你们没有正当理由背弃合同。

42. In case one party fails to carry out the contract, the other party is entitled to cancel the contract.

如果一方不执行合同，另一方有权撤销该合同。

43. We do hope the successful result of this contract will lead to further cooperation and business between us.

我们真的希望这次合同的圆满执行能给我们带来进一步的合作和业务。

44. We hope you will seriously take the business standing into account and execute the contract.

我们希望你方严肃地考虑一下商业信用，并去执行合同。

45. You cannot cancel the contract without first securing our agreement.

如果没有事先征得我们同意，你们不能取消合同。

46. Please see to it that the stipulations in the relevant credit are strictly in accordance with the terms stated in the contract.

请注意信用证中的规定一定要完全和合同中的条款相一致。

47. Unless we receive an adequate compensation we will not agree to the cancellation proposed because the goods have already been put into production.

除非我们得到足够的赔偿，否则绝不同意你方的提议而取消合同，因为所订的货物已经开始生产了。

48. This contract will come into force as soon as it is signed by two parties.

合同一经双方签定即生效。

49. Once a contract is made, it must be strictly implemented.

合同一旦确定就应严格执行。

50．All the other terms are accepted except arbitration terms.

除了仲裁条款，其他的条款都能接受。

51．We are not in a position to make delivery of the goods under the contract.

我们无法递送该合同中的货物。

52．Earthquake is force majeure, so we have to terminate the contract.

地震属于不可抗力，我们不得不终止合同。

53．We regret to tell that we have to cancel this contract as a result of your default and reserve the right to file a claim for the loss sustained.

我们很遗憾地告诉你方，由于你方的不作为，我们只能取消合同，同时对于我们所受到的损失保留索赔权。

Abstract

通过本章学习，①了解合同的含义、作用、种类及其内容；②掌握有关合同的函电写作必须包含的基本内容；③掌握有关合同的函电写作的基本规律和注意事项；④通过熟悉标准模板掌握有关合同函电写作的基本方法；⑤熟练掌握有关合同函电经典句型的表达。

Useful Words & Expressions

1．contract 合同
2．contractor 订约人；承包人
3．contractual 合同的；契约的
4．form-style contract 表格式合同
5．clause-style contract 条款式合同
6．the preamble 合同的序言部分
7．contract No. 合同号
8．signing parties 签字方
9．right and obligation 权利和义务
10．effecting date 生效日
11．to make/place/sign/enter into a contract 签订合同
12．to draw up/draft a contract 拟订合同；起草合同
13．to get/ land a contract 得到合同
14．to countersign a contract 会签合同
15．to repeat a contract 重复合同
16．an executory contract 尚待执行的合同
17．a nice fat contract 一个很有利的合同
18．originals of the contract 合同正本
19．copies of the contract 合同副本
20．draft contract 合同草案
21．a written contract 书面合同
22．to make some concession 做某些让步

23. contract terms (or contract clause) 合同条款
24. contract provisions/stipulations 合同规定
25. contract period (or contract term) 合同期限
26. contract life 合同有效期
27. to be stipulated in the contract 在合同中予以规定
28. to be laid down in the contract 在合同中列明
29. to bring a contract into effect 使合同生效
30. to come into effect 生效
31. to go /enter into force 生效
32. to cease to be in effect/force 失效
33. to carry out a contract 执行合同
34. to execute/implement/fulfill/perform a contract 执行合同
35. cancellation of contract 撤销合同
36. breach of contract 违反合同
37. to break the contract 毁约
38. to cancel the contract 撤销合同
39. to tear up the contract 撕毁合同
40. to approve the contract 审批合同
41. to honour the contract 尊重合同
42. to annual the contract 废除合同
43. to terminate the contract 解除合同
44. to alter the contract 修改合同
45. to abide by the contract 遵守合同
46. to go back on one's words 反悔
47. to be legally binding 受法律约束
48. to stand by 遵守
49. non-payment 拒不付款
50. to secure one's agreement 征得……的同意
51. contract price 合约价格
52. contract wages 合同工资
53. contract note 买卖合同(证书)
54. contract of employment/engagement 雇佣合同
55. contract of carriage 运输合同
56. contract of arbitration 仲裁合同
57. contract for goods 订货合同
58. contract for purchase 采购合同
59. contract for service 劳务合同
60. contract for future delivery 期货合同
61. sales contract 销售合同

62. sales confirmation 销售确认书
63. purchase contract 购买合同
64. purchase confirmation 购买确认书
65. contract of insurance 保险合同
66. contract sales 订约销售
67. contract law 合同法
68. to ship a contract 装运合同的货物
69. contractual dispute 合同上的争议
70. a long-term contract 长期合同
71. a short-term contract 短期合同
72. contract parties 合同当事人
73. contractual practice/usage 合同惯例
74. contractual claim 根据合同的债权
75. contractual liability/obligation 合同规定的义务
76. contractual income 合同收入
77. contractual specifications 合同规定
78. contractual terms and conditions 合同条款
79. additional condition 附加条款
80. force majeure 不可抗力
81. contractual guarantee 合同规定的担保
82. contractual damage 合同引起的损害
83. contractual-joint-venture 合作经营；契约式联合经营
84. completion of contract 完成合同
85. execution/performance of contract 履行合同
86. interpretation of contract 解释合同
87. expiration of contract 合同期满
88. renewal of contract 合同的续订
89. for one's file/records 供某人存档
90. for one's perusal 供某人详阅
91. for one's reference/information 供某人参考
92. rest assured/be assured 放心
93. take effect from/on… 自/在……开始生效
94. upon/ on receipt of… 一收到即……
95. to one's full/entire satisfaction 令某人完全满意
96. in accordance with 按照或依据；与……一致
97. herewith 同此；随函
98. hereby 兹；特此；以此
99. in due course 在适当的时候
100. entertain a claim 接受索赔

Exercises

1. Multiple choice.

(1) Your order No. 123 was confirmed by our fax of September 15 subject to ____ of your credit within 15 days from the date.

A. arrival B. reaching C. arrive D. reach

(2) Please ____ the shipment date of your L/C to October 15 and validity to October 30.

A. amend B. extend C. establish D. expand

(3) We look forward to ____ the goods in fourth quarter.

A. the delivery of B. your delivery C. deliver D. delivery

(4) We hope the goods you ordered will arrive at the port of destination ____.

A. in good condition B. in good conditions

C. in a good condition D. in the good condition

(5) The stipulations in the relevant L/C should strictly ____ the terms set force in our Sales Confirmation.

A. in conformity with B. in accordance with

C. conform to D. conform with

(6) We agree to the amendments to the contract ____ requested in your letter of May 5.

A. as B. like C. to be D. when

(7) A sales confirmation should be countersigned by ____.

A. the seller B. both parties C. the bank D. the buyer

(8) Please see to ____ that goods should be delivered in 3 equal lots.

A. us B. it C. the L/C D. them

(9) Under the ____, we have no choice but to decline your order.

A. condition B. conditions C. circumstance D. circumstances

(10) Through our joint efforts, we have successfully concluded a ____ with your company.

A. business B. order C. trade D. deal

2. Answer the questions according to the passage.

(1) What is a sales confirmation?

(2) What are the main functions of a contract?

(3) What are the differences between a contract and a confirmation?

(4) What are the particulars in a letter of sales confirmation?

3. Put the following sentences into English.

(1) 你公司 8 月 10 日来函收悉，内附有关第 100 号订单订购 500 台缝纫机的销售确认书第 90SP-5861 号一式两份。今签退一份，请查收。

(2) 现附上我方第 101 号合同正本两份，请会签并早日寄回一份。

(3) 请尽快通知我们第 23546 号合同项下货物大约交货日期。

(4) 为了避免随后修改信用证，务请注意下列事项。

(5) 你公司 2005 年 9 月 20 日来函内附 1 000 台缝纫机订单一纸已收到。兹附寄第 346 号销售确认书一式两份，请签回一份以便存档。

(6) 关于我们向你公司订购的 1 000 台电视机，我们已收到你方的销售确认书第 4856 号。

(7) 你方 8 月 14 日的来函及随附的订单已收到。兹附寄第 235 号销售确认书一式两份，请会签一份以便存档。

(8) 请注意，信用证条款与合同条款必须严格相符，以免日后修改。

(9) 请放心，一收到你方信用证，我方将立即安排第一艘便轮装运货物。

(10) 敬启者：

兹告知已收到我们于 2008 年 9 月 1 日在青岛签订的第 112 号销售合同，现会签并确认合同条款如下。

50 公吨花生，2008 年产大路货，每公吨成本运费加保险费汉堡价 600 美元，麻袋包装，船期为 2008 年 10 月由青岛至汉堡，由卖方按发票金额的 110%投保一切险。付款条件是装船前一个月开出的不可撤销的即期信用证。装船唛头如下。

ABC
HAMBURG
NO.112

谨上

Case Practice

以本章的导入案例为背景，请以公司业务员 Jenny Wang 的名义回一封邮件，确认订单，寄送销售确认书，要求对方会签，并强调信用证条款必须与合同条款完全一致。

Chapter 5 Orders and Terms of Payment

订单及其支付条件

案例导入 Case-lead-in

加拿大 Victorian Trade Co.在收到浙江嘉兴晓栋进出口公司的报价和样品后，决定订购一批山地自行车，并随附订单。

Victorian Trade Co.
6103 Dahousie Street Toronto
B4H53A, Canada

August 12, 2008
Xiao Dong Imp & Exp. Co.
Jianxin, Zhejiang, China
Dear Sir or Madam,
Dragon Brand Bicycle

Thank you for your letter of Aug. 5 sending us your quotation and samples. We find both quality and prices satisfactory, Enclosed herewith please fin our Order No. 363.

As we are in urgent need of these goods, we hope you will make delivery at an early date.

Please send us your Sales Confirmation in duplicate as soon as possible. Thank you for your prompt attention.

Your faithfully,
Encl. As stated
W. James
(mananger)
订单:

Victorian Trade Co.
6103 Dahousie Street Toronto
B4H53A, Canada

Order Form

No. 363A

Aug. 08, 2008

Xiao Dong Imp & Exp. Co.

Jianxin, Zhejiang, China

Quantity	Description of goods	Unit Price (CIF Toronto)	Price
10	Racing Bike Standard yellow	$1 500	$15 000
10	Racing Bike Standard green	$1 500	$15 000
100	Mountain Bike blue/white	$1 000	$100 000
100	Mountain Bike pink/white	$1 000	$100 000

Total: $230 000

2% discount: 4 600

Grand Total:$ 225 400

Packing: in wooden cases

Shipment: from Jinxin not later than October 15

Payment: cash against document

Authorized by: Xiaodong Gu (mananger)

Tel.:416-288-0506 Fax:416-061-0321

E-mail: Victorian@trading.com.ca

Section One Orders and Replies
订单的下达及回复

In this task, we will discuss the definition of an order, the important elements and the difference between the first order and others and the techniques of how to write a reply to orders.

An order is a request to supply a specified quantity of goods. It may result from an offer or an enquiry with subsequent quotations. An order may be given by letter or memorandum, by telex or telegraphic message, or finally at a meeting. Usually there is no correspondence at all; instead, buyer use printed order forms and sellers use printed acknowledgements. The essential qualities of an order are accuracy and clarity. An order or an order letter should:

(1) Include full details of description, quantities and prices and quote article numbers.

(2) State mode of packing, port of destination and time of shipment.

(3) Confirm the term of payment as agreed upon in preliminary negotiations.

Sometimes, buyers will seek to protect themselves by making their order subject to certain penalties if the contracted terms should not be fulfilled. "First" orders, that is, orders from new customers, should most certainly be acknowledged by letter. The letter should:

(1) Express pleasure at receiving the order.

(2) Add a favorable comment on the goods ordered.

(3) Include an assurance of prompt and careful attention.

(4) Draw attention to other products likely to be of interest.

(5) Hope for further orders.

However, there are times when sellers cannot accept buyers' orders because the goods required are not available or prices and specifications have been changed. In such circumstances, letters of rejecting orders must be written with the utmost care and with an eye to goodwill and further business. It is advisable to recommend suitable substitutes, make counter-offers and persuade buyers to accept them.

According to commercial law the buyer's order is an offer to buy and the arrangement is not legally binding until the seller has accepted the offer. After that, both parties are legally bound to honor their agreement.

Section Two Method of Payment
支付方式

There are so many modes of payment in the international trade. Basically there are four methods of obtaining payment for export shipment.

(1) Remittance (including payment in advance and cash with order.

(2) Open account.

(3) Documentary letter of credit.

(4) Documentary collection (documents against payment, D/P or documents against acceptance, D/A).

Payment in international trade is much more complicated than that in domestic trade. The most generally used method of payment in financing international trade is the letter of credit (abbreviated to L/C), which is reliable and safe for both sellers and buyers and is accepted only when the financial standing of the importer is sound or where a previous course of business has inspired the exporter with confidence that the importer will be good for payment.

Section Three Cases in Detail
具体案例分析

(一)经典案例解析

背景介绍：客户来自意大利，订单价格及其他各项细节已经确定，可是由于付款方式的问题，订单卡住了。

Dear Water,

I'm ready to launch the 1st trial order to you in this way:

1．A706 item with monitor 7’, DVD/DivX, carry bag, battery built-in, and the normal accessories, at USD 56.5 enclosed LSCD.500 pcs DM brand, in black color; 500 pcs LEXI brand, in silver color.

2．A903 item with monitor 9’, DVD/MPEG4, TV tuner, SD/MMC/USB slot, lithium battery (as the sample tested), carry bag, at USD 97.5 enclosed LSCD. 300 psc DM brand, in black color.

3．Payment term: 100% L/C 60 days.

4．delivery: 40 days after the L/C opening.

We expect to find a good market for these goods and hope to place further and larger orders with you in the near future.

Best Regards,

Ms. Paola Esposito

Dear Paola,

Thank you for your great support to me. Regarding your order, I would like to reply you as below.

1．Will you consider larger quantity for 9’ model this time? Say 500 pcs at least would be better. As for OEM and price, it is easier for us to control. I believe you are satisfied with the performance of the sample, and believe there will be fast sale on your market. Hope you can give more support to us in this point. Can we confirm 500 pcs?

2．Payment term. To be frank, we always do with customers by 30% T/T in advance, and balance T/T before shipment for a sum of payment less than $200 000. As you know the bank charges with will be higher for L/C opening. For your coming order, the best we can do is L/C at sight. I think it is fair to both of us. Believe you can understand and confirm this point.

3．Delivery: 40 days upon L/C at sight opening.

We hope we could confirm the details together before your holiday. And begin some artworks in advance.

Awaiting your comments.

Best regard,

Water

Notes

1. trial order: 试购订单
2. launch the first trial order: 下首次试购订单
3. payment term (terms of payment): 付款条件
4. delivery: 交货时间
5. 一般有经验的国外厂商都会提供一份不同订单不同价格的报价单，试购订单一般是小批量订单，厂商对订量小的报价与大批量订单的报价，有的差距很小，有的差距很大。因此，买家在下订单时，经常会提到将会有更多更重要的后续订单，通过这种沟通方式为后来的还价做铺垫。
6. OEM是Original Equipment Manufacture（原始设备制造商）的缩写，它是指一种“代工生产”方式，其含义是生产者不直接生产产品，而是利用自己掌握的“关键的核心技术”，负责设计和开发、控制销售“渠道”，具体的加工任务交给别的企业。

7. T/T in advance:“提前电汇”(Telegraphic Transfer)，一般是买卖双方签订单后，买方提前把货款电汇至卖方账户，然后卖方才备货、发货。

8. balance: 余额

9. L/C: 信用证(Letter of Credit)

10. L/C at sight: 即期信用证

11. 由于某种产品的订单数量太少，总要努力争取更多。通过沟通或者提出一个更好的价格，客户的订单数量也许会有所增加。也因为订单数量少，不利于安排生产，工厂成本也比较高。如果能达到最低订单量以上，对于工厂和个人来说都可以创收。

12. 业务往来中，客户往往会采用对自己比较有利的付款方式，但也增加了供应商的收款风险。一般情况下，较常见和常用的付款方式有两种：第一种是即期信用证，信用证属于银行信用，双方都通过一家银行来支付和收取货款，对于双方来说，这种付款方式也比较安全；第二种是预付订金，预付订金多少要根据每个公司以及产品类型，或者和客户商谈的情况而定，但一般情况下，预付30%是比较常见的，这对于供应商来说也是一个保障，因为客户在国外，而供应商采购产品物料需要垫付高额货款，预收部分订金，大大降低了客户取消订单的可能。同样，收取余款的方式也要根据不同的情况而定，比如先付清余款再出货，或货物装船后即付，或客户见提单复印件后即付，或货物到港后即付等。一般情况下，客户必须在出货前付清余款，供应商才安排出货。

13. 客户采取远期信用证付款，对于客户的融资有利。时间越长，对客户越有利，因为客户在一定时间内，可能已经卖完所有的产品，货款也已经进账，等于是利用出口商的钱去赚钱。但对于出口商来说，资金被占用时间太长，不利于内部周转，但有利于增加业务量。

(二) 一般案例表述

1. Declining an Order

Dear Sirs,

We thank you very much for your order of Aug 3. After careful consideration on your request, however, we have come to the conclusion that we cannot but decline the said order.

In order to meet the specifications for your order we would have to install a large amount of special equipment at our plant, and this would not be possible before January next year without interrupting our normal production. This is something we cannot afford to as we will be heavily committed to orders for the rest of the year.

We regret not being in a position to accept your order, but hope that you will understand our situation. Please let us have any other inquiries of yours, as we shall be only too pleased to meet your requirements.

Yours truly,

Notes

例函中因为订单突然取消使订货人利润和精神都有损失，专诚提到“做出补偿”，这是必不可缺少的补救措施表态，以建立公司的信誉。

2. Payment Negotiation

Dear Paola,

Please kindly note that our booth number in IFA Berlin is 29.226.

For the payment term, the best we can do is L/C at sight, really. As I informed you by MSN, we always do by T/T with other customers.

Regarding your order, you place it with two models. Our boss also cares it very much. I had a hard discussion with my boss; finally she allowed the payment by L/C at sight. But normally she only accepts T/T. I really do my best to move forward the project, believe you also do your efforts to move forward.

Can I get your support?

Welcome your visit to our Berlin Show. And wish you a very happy summer vocation.

Awaiting your comments.

Best regards,

Water

Notes

1. 文中运用了比较的方法。拿其他客户的做法和该客户的做法相比较，着重突出对客户的优惠和特别支持。同样，对比的方法也可以用在价格和数量等方面的谈判上。

2. 即时沟通工具 MSN 可以快速传递某些产品信息和价格信息等。如果用于价格谈判，不是非常有效，但可以结合着使用。在谈话过程中，遇到棘手的问题不能得罪客人，可以适时地结束谈话，说明将马上处理并以邮件回复。有时候有些问题不能急着回复，因为这些问题都是很敏感，很难缠，很不好解决的问题。给自己一点时间考虑，但不能拖延，要对客户有交代，让客户知道你会怎样做，这样更容易解决问题。

3. Orders always don't come easy. 订单都是来之不易的。需要从细节方面去沟通，彼此寻找合适的平衡点去合作。

4. 邀请客户参加展销会，这也是增加客户信心和进一步沟通的最好方式。

资料链接 Material—link

1. Standard Model

Model 1: Placing an Order

Gentlemen,

Enclosed please find our order No. AB3015, for Canvas Shoes in assorted sizes, colors and designs.

We have decided to accept the 8% discount you offered and terms of payment, viz. Documents against Payment, but would like these terms to be reviewed in the near future.

Would you please send the shipping documents and your sight draft to Northminster Bank (City Branch), Deal Street, Birmingham B3 ISQ?

If you do not have any of the listed items in stock, please do not send substitutes in their place.

We would appreciate delivery within the next six weeks, and look forward to your acknowledgement.

Yours sincerely,

Model 2: Delay in Completing an Order

Gentlemen,

I am writing to you concerning your Order No. AB3523 which you placed five weeks ago. At that time we had expected to be able to complete the order within the delivery date we gave you which was July 5th, but since then we have heard our main supplier of copper has gone bankrupt.

This means that we have to find another supplier who could fulfill all the outstanding contracts we have to complete. As you will appreciate this will take some time, we are confident that we should be able to arrange to get our materials and deliver consignments to our customers by the middle of next month.

We regret the unfortunate situation over which we had no control and apologize for the inconvenience. If you wish to cancel the order it would be quite understandable, but we stress that we will be able to complete delivery by next month and would appreciate it if you could bear with us till then.

Please let us know your decision as soon as possible. Thank you for your consideration.

Yours sincerely,

Model 3: Fulfilling an Order

Dear Sirs,

order No. k1236

The above order has now been completed and sent to Zhangjiagang Docks where it is awaiting loading onto SS Eastsea which sails for Kobe, Japan on 25 July and arrives on 29 July.

Once we have the necessary documents we will hand them to Chartered Bank, your bank's agents here, and they will forward them to the Union Trust Bank in Japan.

We have taken special care to see that the goods have been packed as per your instructions, the six crates being marked with your name, and numbered 1-6. Each crate measures 6ft × 4ft × 3ft and weighs 5 cwt.

If there is any further information you require, please contact us. Thank you very much for your trial order, and we hope it will lead to further business between us.

Yours faithfully,

Model 4:Introduction to Terms of Payment

Dear Sirs,

We are pleased to receive your inquiry of 5th July and enclose our illustrated catalogue and price list.

We are confident you will be interested in our products and welcome your further inquiry.

As to our terms of payment, we usually adopt confirmed and irrevocable letters of credit in our favor, payable by draft at sight, reaching us one month ahead of shipment, remaining valid for negotiation in China for a further 21 days after prescribed time of shipment and allowing transshipment and partial shipment.

We hope the above payment terms will be acceptable to you and expect to receive your trial order soon.

Looking forward to your early reply.

Sincerely yours,

Model 5: Accepting D/P Terms

Dear Sirs,

We are in receipt of your letter of August 22. Having studied your suggestion for payment by D/A for a trial order of 120 cartons Black Tea, we regret that we are unable to entertain your request. As our usual practice goes, we require payment by confirmed and irrevocable letter of credit. That is to say, at present, we cannot accept D/A terms in all transactions with our buyers abroad. However, in consideration of our friendly relations, we are, as an exceptional case, prepared to accept D/P sight terms.

We sincerely hope that the above payment will be acceptable to you and trust you will appreciate our co-operation.

Looking forward to your early reply.

Sincerely yours,

2. Writing Guide

(1) 如何回复试购订单?

In reply to a first order, your acknowledgement should tell the buyer:

① *You are much honored.*

② *The quality of your products and your service are assured.*

③ *You also handle other similar products with the same high quality as the goods ordered.*

④ *You hope to establish a long-term business relations with him on the basis of equality and mutual benefit.*

(2) 卖方通知交货延迟的信函应说明哪些方面?

① *Apologize for the delay.*

② *Explain the reason.*

③ *Hope that the customer is not being inconvenienced unduly.*

④ *State when delivery may be expected, if this is possible.*

(3) 卖方在什么情况下会拒接订单? 在拒接信函中应说明哪些方面?

There are times when a seller does not accept the buyer's order, with any one of the following reasons.

① *He is not satisfied with the buyer's terms and conditions.*

② *The buyer's credit is suspect.*

③ *The goods are not available.*

Letter rejecting orders must be written with the utmost care and with an eye to good will and future business. When sending such letters, the seller should:

① *Regret your inability to meet the buyer's needs.*

② *Propose an alternative product, if one is available.*

③ *Hope for the opportunity to serve him another time.*

(4) 什么是汇付? 汇付的方法有几种?

When either cash in advance or cash payment before shipment is used, the buyer usually remits the payment to the seller. Remittance means the transfer of money through banks from one party to another. There are three ways of remitting the money: Mail Transfer(M/T 信汇), Telegraphic Transfer(T/T 电汇), and Demand Draft(D/D 票汇).

(5) 我国对外贸易中最常用的支付方式是什么? 这种支付方式是最安全的支付方式吗?

L/C is most commonly used by Chinese exporters because it is regarded as the safest mode of payment. In fact, the average rate of bad debts was up to 3%~5% in the first five years of the 21st century, while it was only 0.25%~0.5% in the developed countries. Furthermore, the most commonly used mode of payment is commercial credit, which accounts for 95% of all the business transactions there.

Section Four Selected Sentences
精选句型表达

1. We enclose a trial order. If the quality is up to our expectation, we shall send further orders in the near future.

我方随附试购单，如贵方产品质量达到我方期望，我方不久将有大量订货。

2. If the quality of your products is satisfactory, we may place regular orders.

如果你们产品的质量使我们满意，我们将不断订货。

3. If the quality of your initial shipment is found satisfactory, large repeats will follow.
如果贵方第一批运来的产品令人满意，随后将有大批续订。

4. We made a total of 100 000 jackets.
我们一共订了 10 万件上衣。

5. We can only supply you with 20 000 yards of pure silk.
我们只能供应 2 万码的真丝绸。

6. We want a minimum of 1 000 dozen of men's shirts and minimum of 5 000 dozen of embroidered shirts.
男衬衣至少要 1 000 打，绣花衬衣至少需要 5 000 打。

7. Can you give us an additional 200 cases?
能再增加 200 箱吗？

8. It does not pay to buy in small quantities.
小量购买不合算。

9. We place an order for additional 4 000 shirts.
我们多订了 4 000 件衬衣。

10. This year we can buy an extra 700 blue jeans.
今年我们可以多订 700 件牛仔裤。

11. We'll try our best to satisfy you with the additional 10 000 tons of coal as you asked.
你们要求增加 1 万吨煤，我们将尽量满足你们。

12. We'll increase the quantity of medicines by 300 boxes.
我们将增加 300 盒药品。

13. The maximum quantity of cotton jerseys this year is about DM25 000.
我们今年最多能订购大约 25 000 马克的棉毛衫。

14. 5 000 square meters of wool carpet is bigger than any order we've ever placed.
5 000 平方米的羊毛地毯超过了以往的订货量。

15. We have the pleasure of handing you a trial order for the various as per order sheet enclosed.很高兴向贵方试定随函附寄的订单中的各类商品。

16. We thank you for your order of …谢谢贵方……日的订单。

17. We are glad to have finalized (put through, closed, conclude) this transaction (business) with you.很高兴和贵方做成这笔生意。

18. We are obliged for your quotation of…,and enclose our official order for the following.
很高兴收到贵方……月……日的报盘，随函附上下列商品的正式订单。

19. The price quoted in your letter of …are satisfactory. Please arrange to deliver the following items at once.贵方……月……日来函所报价格合适，请立即安排装运下列正式订单。

20. Please kindly acknowledge this order and confirm that you will be able to deliver by December…请收下此订单并确认在 12 月……日前交货。

21. We shall be grateful for prompt delivery as the goods are needed urgently.
因急需此批货物，如能尽快装运，将不胜感激。

22. We enclose our order, but must point out that the falling market here will leave us little

or no margin of profit. We must ask you for a better price in respect of future supplies.

订单随附，但我方需指出,市场萧条使我方利润率日益下降，今后供货，价格定要适宜。

23．The material supplied must be absolutely waterproof, and we place our order subject to this guarantee.

产品材料必须为防水材料，我方订单以此为准。

24．While thanking you for your order, we have to explain that without supplies we have no alternative but to decline your order.

非常感谢贵方订单，需要说明的是，因无货源，我方只得取消你方订单。

25．It is regrettable to see an order dropped owing to no agreement on price; however, we wish to recommend you another quality at a lower price for your consideration.

很遗憾因价格未谈妥不能成交，但我方愿意向贵方推荐另一种质优价廉产品，望予以考虑。

26．In view of our heavy bookings, we are not in a position to commit ourselves to new orders.

鉴于我方的巨大预订量，我方不能承诺新的订单。

27．The chief difficulty in accepting your orders now is the heavy backlog of commitments. But you may rest assured that as soon as we are able to accept new orders, we shall give priority or preference to yours.

我方因订单过多无法满足贵方订购，但请相信，一旦有货源，我方会立即接受贵方订单，且给予优惠或优先供货。

28．Your order is receiving our immediate attention, and you can depend on us to effect delivery well within your time limit.

我方非常重视贵方订单，我方将在有限时间尽快发货。

29．Your order is booked and will be handled with great care. Please open the relevant L/C, which must reach hear one month before the date of shipment.

贵方订单已确立，且认真履行，请开立相关信用证，且须在装船前一个月到达。

30．The terms of payment we usually adopt are confirmed and irrevocable Letter of Credit.

我们通常采用的付款方式是保兑不可撤销的信用证。

31．We trust you will pay our draft on presentation.

我们相信你方在见到我方汇票时即照付。

32．If this change is effected, we will have to pay rather heavy expenses.

如果进行这项改变，我们将不得不付出相当大的代价。

33．Payment is to be effected (made) before the end of this month.

这个月末以前应该付款。

34．It's convenient to make payment in pound sterling.

用英镑付款较方便。

35．I've never made payment in RMB before.

我从未用过人民币付款。

36．We can't accept payment on deferred terms.

我们不能接受延期付款。

37．What's your reason for the refusal of payment?

你们拒付的理由是什么？

38．Collection is not paid.

托收款没有照付。

39．We don't think you'll refuse to pay.

我们相信你们不会拒付。

40．Only one refusal of payment is acceptable to the bank.

银行只接受一次拒付。

41．You ought to pay us the bank interest once payment is wrongly refused.

如果拒付错了，你们应该偿付我方的银行利息。

42．We'll not pay until shipping documents for the goods have reached us.

见不到货物装船单据，我们不付款。

43．We're worrying that a decline in prices might lead to refusal of payment.

我们担心市场价格下跌会引起拒付。

44．Of course payment might be refused if anything goes wrong with the documents.

如果单据有问题，当然可以提出拒付。

45．The equipment will be paid in installments with the commodities produced by our factory.

设备以我们工厂生产的产品分期偿还。

46．What is the mode of payment you wish to employ?

您希望用什么方式付款？

47．This is the normal terms of payment in international business.

这是国际贸易中惯用的付款方式。

48．We can't accept any other terms of payment.

我们不能接受其他的付款条件。

49．If you can't be more flexible, we won't accept your terms of payment.

如果你们不能灵活些，我们将不接受此种付款方式。

50．We trust you will pay our draft upon presentation.

相信你们会见票即付。

Abstract

通过本章学习，①掌握下达订单和回复订单写作的基本规律和注意事项；②学习接受订单，拒接订单，取消订单等具体信函写作方法；③了解基本的支付方式；④通过熟悉标准模板，掌握讨论具体支付方式时所使用的基本方法；⑤熟练掌握订单及其支付方式的经典句型的表达。

Useful Words & Expressions

1．new (fresh) order 新订单

2．duplicate order 重复订单

3．outstanding order 未完成的订单

4．trial order 试购订单

5．order sheet 订货单

6．place an order 下订单

7．accept an order 接受订单

8．execute an order 执行订单

9．refuse an order 拒绝订单

10．cancel an order 取消订单

11．suspend an order 暂停执行订单

12．repeat an order 续订

13．on order 已订(但尚未收到的货)

14．order form 订单表格

15．after sight 见票后

16．order with conditions attached 附条件订购

17．date of invoice 发票日期

18．full details of description 品名与规格的详细说明

19．delivery-place, date, mode of transport 交货地点，日期，运输方式

20．carriage paid, or carriage forward 运费付讫、运费已付或运费到付

21．time of delivery 交货时间

22．order of video camera recorder 订购摄录机

23．order of valves 订购气阀

24．order of cashmere sweater 订购羊绒衫

25．order of powdered milk 订购奶粉

26．order of bed sheets & pillow cases 订购床单及枕套

27．acceptance of order for furniture 接受订购家具的订单

28．offering substitute 提供代用品

29．offering rayon in place of watered silk 提供人造丝代替水洗丝

30．offering zinc oxide 99% in place of zinc oxide 99.5% 提供氧化锌 99%代替氧化锌 99.5%

31．500 pieces in total 总共有 500 件

32．rejecting ordered price 拒绝接受订单价格

33．rejecting for the reason of no supply 因无货而婉拒买方订单

34．rejecting buyer’s delivery terms 拒绝接受买方的交货条件

35．payment 支付；付款

36．to pay 付款；支付；偿还

37．terms of payment/payment terms 付款条件

38．the mode of payment 付款方式

39．payment order 付款通知

40．pay in advance 预付

41. payment in part 部分付款
42. pay in cash 付现金
43. pay by check 支票付款
44. pay in installments 分期付款
45. pay on delivery (P.O.D) 货到付款
46. down payment 付款订金
47. payment in account 账面付款
48. payment by installment 分期付款
49. payment respite 延期付款
50. payment at maturity 到期付款
51. payment on terms 定期付款
52. payment on deferred terms 迟期付款
53. Cash Against Documents on arrival of goods 货到后凭单付款
54. monthly payments of RMB ￥30 000 每月付款人民币 30 000 元
55. letter of credit at sight 即期信用证(简称 at sight L/C)
56. usance L/C, time L/C, term L/C 远期(或迟期)信用证
57. (usance/time/term)L/C at 30 days after sight; L/C available by draft at 30 days after sight; 30 days(usance/time/term)L/C 见票后 30 天议付的信用证
58. deferred payment (delay in payment) 延期付款期限
59. tight money 银根紧
60. dishonor 拒付
61. payment agreement 支付协定
62. pay order 支付凭证
63. payment by banker 银行支付
64. payment by remittance 汇拨支付
65. payment in full 全部付讫
66. clean payment 单纯支付
67. simple payment 单纯支付
68. payment for (in) cash 现金支付，付现
69. Cash With Order (C.W.O) 随订单付现
70. Cash On Delivery (C.O.D) 交货付现
71. Cash Against Documents (C.A.D) 凭单付现
72. payment in kind 实物支付
73. pay…Co. only 仅付……公司
74. pay…Co. not negotiable 付……公司，不准疏通
75. pay…Co. or order (pay to the order of...Co.) 付……公司或其指定人
76. refusal 拒绝
77. the refusal of payment 拒付
78. the bank interest 银行利息

79．decline 下降；下跌
80．something goes wrong 某事上出问题；出现差错
81．commodity 产品
82．convenient 方便的
83．flexible 灵活的；多变的

Exercises

1. Choose the best choice.

(1) We look forward to ____ a trial order.
A．receiving B．receive from you C．receipt D．receipt you
(2) We are glad that we have ____ an agreement on this matter.
A．come B．got C．reached D．arrived
(3) we have made ____ that we would accept D/P terms for your future orders.
A．clear B．it clear C．that clear D．it is clear
(4) ____ your letter of March 5，we are pleased to inform you that the L/C has been received.
A．Replying to B．Replying for C．Replied to D．Replied for
(5) We are looking forward to ____ your L/C for Order No.123.
A．receive B．receiving C．be received D．be receiving
(6) Our payment terms are ____, irrevocable letter of credit for the full invoice value.
A．confirmed B．combined C．committed D．completed
(7) We cannot ____ present entertain any fresh orders for Younger Brand Men's Shirts.
A．of B．at C．to D．for
(8) ____ is a very favorable payment term for the exporter.
A．Cash With Order B．Cash On Delivery
C．Cash Against Documents D．Payment in Advance
(9) We would appreciate you sending us a trial order, which we ____ with keen interest.
A．are waiting B．await C．await for D．are awaiting
(10) As agreed upon in our negotiations, payment ____ L/C.
A．by B．is by C．will be D．will by

2. Fill in the blanks.

(1) We shall book a trial order with you, ________ goods are competitive in price and of good quality.

(2) As we are heavily committed, we are sorry that we are not in a ________ to accept new orders.

(3) We prefer payment by D/P ________ draft at 60-day's sight.

(4) Since we are well connected ________ the department stores here, we can obtain a number of orders for you.

(5) We wish to acknowledge receipt of your letter of March 15, ________ reached us yesterday.

(6) We expect ________ place a trial order with you in the near future.

(7) We have established an irrevocable letter of credit ________ your favor with the Bank of Guangdong.

(8) Thank you ________ ordering more ________ our computer peripherals.

(9) Please make sure that the stipulations in the L/C are ________ exact accordance ________ the terms of the Sales Contract.

(10) We shall open an L/C ________ you favor ________ Barclay's Bank here ________ the extent of 15 000.

3. Answer the following questions.

(1) What should be mentioned in an order?

(2) What should be paid attention to when declining an order?

(3) What is the most generally used method of payment in financing international trade? Why?

(4) Which method is safer and better for the seller, D/P or D/A ? Why ?

4. Put the following sentences into Chinese.

(1) We allow a proper discount according to the quantity ordered.

(2) We accept your order for 1 000 sets of washing machine and will arrange shipment soon.

(3) As to terms of payment, we often require a confirmed and irrevocable Letter of Credit payable by draft at sight.

(4) In consideration of your large orders we will allow discount to the certain extent on the recent quotations.

(5) We are very happy to place an order on the following good basing on the condition that you must supply products your quotation.

(6) As agreed, the terms of payment for the above orders are letter of credit of 60 days' sight or D/P sight draft.

5. Put the following sentences into English.

(1) 如能收到贵方订单，我们将非常感谢。

(2) 请按照贵公司提供的样品，给我们寄送 600 条床单。

(3) 我们非常高兴向贵公司订购下列商品。

(4) 丝制女衬衫每件用塑料袋包好，再装入标准出口纸板箱，每箱 30 打。

(5) 应你方要求，我方破例接受即期付款交单方式，但下不为例。

(6) 我方将以托收方式开出向你方支取的即期跟单汇票。

(7) 我们只接受在签约后 3 天内电汇预付发票总金额的 20%，余下的 80%以即期信用证方式付清，要求该信用证必须在装运前 15～30 天内送达我方。

(8) 我方曾在 12 月 1 日信中告知你方，我方愿向你方试订 50 辆飞鸽牌自行车。

Case Practice

1. 以本章的导入案例为背景，请以晓栋进出口公司业务员身份，写信给 Victorian Trade Co.确认订单，并随附销售合同一式两份，要求对方会签。同时提醒对方及时开出信用证。

2. 请根据下列案例，写一封回函。

上海环宇工贸有限公司的另一业务员 Tom 的一美国客户有意求购下列产品,但其要求采用承兑交单方式支付，Tom 考虑到该客户为老客户,因此回信时便婉言谢绝承兑交单方式支付，要求客户采用付款交单方式支付。

Name of Commodity & Specs	Quantity	Unit Price	Total Value
Plush Toys	12 000pcs	US$4.70	CIFC3 New York
Art.No. KP2273 Charming Pig	13 000pcs	US$6.30	US$56 400.00
Art.No. KC2048 Long Hair Cat			US$81 900.00
			US$138 300.00

美国客商的具体联系方式是:

Ms. Georgia Jones
Marketing Manager
Potsdam Manufacturing Enterprises
145 South Airport Drive
Potsdam, New York NY, USA

Chapter 6 Letter of Credit

信 用 证

案例导入 Case-lead-in

江苏运通贸易公司根据第 121 号订单向新加坡华益商行出口 8 公吨核桃仁。5 月 6 日，新加坡华益商行开来信用证，金额计 2500 美元标题项下的 158 号信用证已收到。但是进口方信用证金额似嫌不足，订单正确的成本加保险费加运费的总值应是 2 960 美元，相差 460 美元。鉴于上述情况， 江苏运通贸易公司业务员发 email 给新加坡华益商行，要求对方修改信用证的条款，将对方信用证金额增加 460 美元。对方一俟接到信用证修改通知书当安排交货不误。

Section One Content and Classification of Letter of Credit 信用证的内容和种类

In this section, we will discuss the following aspects.

1. Definition of Letter of Credit

In international sales transaction, the seller, undoubtedly, would prefer to be paid in advance. The buyer, on the other hand, would like to make sure, before paying that

(1) the goods are actually shipped;

(2) the goods shipped meet his contractual specifications;

(3) he would prefer to take delivery before paying.

Depending on the relative bargaining power of the buyer and seller, any of these possible arrangements can be included as a term in the sales contract. If the seller is unable to determine the buyer's creditworthiness, he may insist upon "cash in advance". If the buyer wants to confirm that the goods have been shipped, the term documents against payment can be used. If the buyer insists upon taking delivery before making payment, documents against acceptance term can be used.

None of these terms are used very often. In part, this is because they imply that both sides distrust each other. To avoid this, contracting parties use a "letter of credit" (or "documentary credit", or "banker's credit" or, simply, a "credit").

So, what is a "letter of credit"?

An L/C is the written promise of a bank that acts at the request and on the instructions of the applicant and undertakes to pay the beneficiary the amount specified in the credit, provided that the terms and conditions of the credit are observed by the beneficiary.

Notes

According to UCP600, Credit means any arrangement, however named or described, that is irrevocable and thereby constitutes a definite undertaking of the issuing bank to honor a complying presentation. 根据UCP600，信用证是指一项不可撤销的安排，无论其名称或描述如何，因此构成开证行对相符交单予以承付的确定承诺。

2. Characteristics of a Letter of Credit

(1) The issuing bank undertakes to effect payment, quite independent of whether the applicant is bankrupt or is in default or not, provided the documents presented are in compliance with the terms and conditions of the credit.

(2) A letter of credit stands independent of the sales contract.

In accordance with UCP600 Article 4, a credit, by its nature, is a separate transaction from the sale or other contract on which it may be based. Banks are in no way concerned with or bound by such contract, even if any reference whatsoever to it is included in the Credit. Consequently, the undertaking of a bank to honour, to negotiate or to fulfill any other obligation under the Credit is not subject to claims or defenses by the Applicant resulting from its relationships with the Issuing Bank or the Beneficiary.

A beneficiary can in no case avail itself of the contractual relationships existing between the banks or between the Applicant and the Issuing Bank.

根据 UCP600 条款 4，就性质而言，信用证与可能作为其开立基础的销售合同或其他合同是相互独立的交易。即使信用证中含有对此合同的任何援引，银行也与该合同无关，且不受其约束。因此，银行承付、议付或履行信用证项下其他义务的承诺，不受申请人基于其与开证行或与受益人之间的关系而产生的任何请求或抗辩的影响。

受益人在任何情况下都不得利用银行之间或申请人与开证行之间的合同关系。

(3) Banks deal with documents, and not with goods, services or other performances to which the documents may relate.

银行处理的是单据，而不是单据可能涉及的货物、服务或履约行为。

(4) Banks assumes no liability or responsibility for the form, sufficiency, accuracy, genuineness, falsification or legal effect of any documents , or for the general and/or particular conditions stipulated in the document(s) or superimposed thereon; nor do they assume any liability or responsibility for the description, quantity, weight, quality, condition, packing, delivery, value or existence of the goods represented by any document(s), or for the good faith or

acts and/or omissions, solvency, performance or standing of the consignors, the carriers, the forwarders, the consignees or the insurers of the goods, or any other person whomsoever.

银行对任何单据的形式、完整性、准确性、真伪性或法律效力，或单据上规定的或附加的一般性及/或特殊性条件概不负责。

银行对任何单据中有关的货物描述、数量、重量、质量、状况、包装、交货、价值或存在与否，货物的发货人、承运人、运输行、收货人或保险人，其他任何人的诚信、行为及/或疏忽、清偿能力、执行能力或信誉概不负责。

(5) Banks dealing letter of credit business assume no responsibility for the acts of third parties taking part in one way or another in the credit transaction.

3. Advantages of a Letter of Credit

From the above description, we know a letter of credit is a conditional undertaking of payments by a bank.

(1) At the request of the buyer.

(2) Against the surrender of the stipulated documents complying with the terms and conditions of the credit.

(3) If the above requirements are met, the bank will pay to the seller, or accept the draft and make payment.

(4) The paying bank may be the issuing bank itself, or the bank nominated by it. The payee may be the beneficiary or the bank nominated by it.

So, the advantages of a letter of credit to the parties of both importers and exporters are as following.

1) From the importer's point of view

(1) Deposit a margin in the bank as a security money.

(2) Obtain shipping documents representing the title of the good after he makes payment.

(3) Stipulate any required terms in the credit to reduce risks.

2) From the exporter's point of view

(1) Receive payment against the shipping documents.

(2) When shipping the goods, no worry about difficulties in foreign exchange transfer.

4. Contents of a Letter of Credit

At present, most L/Cs are opened by telecommunication. Although the forms are different, their contents are, in the main, the same. The following details are to be found on all credits.

(1) Name and address of the issuing bank.

(2) Type of the credit. Every credit must indicate whether it is revocable or irrevocable. Whether it is a transferable credit or a confirmed credit must also be indicated in the credit.

(3) Name and address of the beneficiary.

(4) Amount of the credit and its currency.

(5) Expiry date of the credit and its place to be expired.

(6) Name and address of the applicant.

(7) L/C number and date of issue.

(8) Drawer and drawee as well as tenor of the draft. The drawer is always the beneficiary; the drawee may be the issuing bank or any other bank.

(9) Full details of the goods, including description, quantity, unit price, specification, price terms, packing, shipping mark, etc.

(10) Full details of the documents to be presented: bill of exchange (汇票), commercial invoice (商业发票), marine bill of lading (海运提单), insurance policy or insurance certificate (保险单), certificate of origin (原产地证), inspection certificate (商检证), customs invoice (海关发票), air waybill(航空运单), railway consignment note (铁路运单).

(11) Partial shipment permitted/not permitted.

(12) Transshipment allowed/not allowed.

(13) Port of shipment and port of discharge.

(14) Latest date for shipment, and the latest date for presentation of documents.

(15) Instructions to the advising bank, negotiating bank or paying bank.

(16) Other special terms and conditions.

(17) The undertaking clause of the issuing bank.

(18) The indication "This credit is subject to UCP600".

Notes

1. 开证行名包括开证地点和日期。
2. 信用证的性质中包括号码。
3. 出口方名称包括地址或通知行名称。
4. 开证文句包括开证说明受何进口商的委托开立信用证。
5. 汇票文句包括受益人应凭汇票取款，汇票的付款人是谁，金额是多少，汇票是即期还是远期。
6. 跟单文句中说明，汇票应附有哪些单据，各需几份，货物的名称、品质、数量、重量、包装和价格。
7. 开证行负责文句中明确开证行的付款责任。
8. 开证行对议付行或代付行的提示文句，要求议付行在议付或代付时应注意办理的事项。
9. 附加条款中的内容包括，如保兑条款、限制船只国籍条款，限制航程条款、履约保证条款等。

Analysis on Sample of L/C

TO: BANK OF CYPRUS LTD
LETTERS OF CREDIT DEPARTMENT
NTCOSIA COMMERCIAL OPERATIONS CENTER
INTERNATIONAL DIVISION
******
******

TEL: ******
FAX: ******
TELEX: 2451 & 4933 KYPRIA CY

SWIFT: BCYPCY2N

DATE: 23 MARCH 2009

APPLICATION FOR THE ISSUANCE OF A LETTER OF CREDIT

SWIFT MT700 SENT TO:MT700 转送至
STANDARD CHARTERD BANK
UNIT 1-8 52/F SHUN NIND SQUARE
O1 WANG COMMERCIAL CENTRE, SHEN NAN
ROAD EAST, SHENZHEN 518008 - CHINA
渣打银行深圳分行
深南东路 5002 号
信兴广场地王商业大厦 52 楼 1-8 单元
电　　话：82461688

:27: SEQUENCE OF TOTAL 序列号/电文页次
1/1 指只有一张电文
:40A: FORM OF DOCUMENTARY CREDIT 跟单信用证形式
IRREVOCABLE 不可撤销的信用证
:20OCUMENTARY CREDIT NUMBER 信用证号码
00143-01-0053557
:31C: DATE OF ISSUE 开证日
如果这项没有填，则开证日期为电文的发送日期
:31DATE AND PLACE OF EXPIRY 信用证有效期
050622 IN CHINA 050622 在中国到期:50: APPLICANT 信用证开证申请人
BCYPGB2L
BANK OF CYPRUS UK
INTERNATIONAL DEPARTMENT,
87/93 CHASE SIDE, SOUTHGATE N14 5BU
LONDON - UNITED KINGDOM.
:78: INSTRUCTIONS TO THE PAY/ACCEPT/NEG BANK 议付行
NEGO OF DOCS THRU BANK OF CHINA LIMITED CHINA IS ALLOWED.PLEASE
可通过中国银行议付，请
DEDUCT RROM YOUR PAYMENT TO BENEFICIARIES THE AMOUNT OF USD1 500
于受益人的账户中扣去 USD1 500
REPRESENTING RECORDING FEES. NEGOTIATION BANK TO OBTAIN
作为记录费。
REIMBURSEMENT FROM OUR ACCOUNT WITH REIMBURSING BANK 3 BUSINESS

DAYS FOLLOWING THEIR AUTHENTICATED TELEX/SWIFT ADVICE TO US, STATING A) OUR CREDIT NUMBER, B)AMOUNT CLAIMED, C) VALUE OF DOCUMENTS D)SHIPMENT/DISPATCH DATE AND E)THAT DOCS ARE IN STRICT COMPLIANCE WITH CREDIT TERMS. ON EXECUTION FORWARD TO US, BANK OF CYPRUS PUBLIC COMAPNY LTD,NICOSIA COMMERCIAL OPER. CENTER INTERN. DIV., 10 KYRIACOS MATSI AV. 1082 AY. OMOLOYITES, NIGOSIA, CYPRUS, ALL DOCS IN ONE LOT BY COURIER SERVICE AT BENEFICIARIES EXPENSE. 所有单据应由偿付行于 3 个工作日内通过快件形式发给我们，费用由受益人承担。

:72: SENDER TO RECEIVER INFORMATION 附言

CREDIT IS SUBJECT TO U.C.P. 2007 本信用证根据跟单信用证统一惯例 UCP600(2007 年版)开出。

I.C.C PUBL. NO.500. SUBJECT TO URR

ICC 525.COLLECT YOUR CHARGES FROM

如果提交了有不符点的单据并且被银行拒付，如果客人接受这些不符点，银行在没有收到指示之前有权把单据 REALSE 给客人。

*TRANSPORT DOCUMENTS BEARING A DATE PRIOR TO THE L/C DATE ARE NOT ACCEPTABLE. 不接受早于开证前的运输文件。

*DIFFERENCE OF USD3,363.81(T.E.30 PERCENT OF INVOICE VALUE) BETWEEN L/C AMOUNT AND INVOICES AMOUNT REPRESENTS AMOUNT PAID BY APPLICANTS DIRECT TO BENEFICIARIES OUTSIDE THE L/C TERMS WITHOUT ANY RESPONSIBILITY ON OURSELVES AND TO BE SHOWN ON INVOICES AS SUCH. L/C 跟发票上 USD3363.81 的差额(30%发票额)由申请人直接用 L/C 以外的方式给予受益人。

:71B: CHARGES

BANK CHARGES OUTSIDE CYPRUS

INCLUDING THOSE OF THE REIMBURSING

BANK ARE FOR BEN. A/C. 在塞浦路斯以外银行产生的费用包括支付行的费用由信用证收益人负担。

:48: PERIOD FOR PRESENTATION 单据提交期限

DOCUMENTS MUST BE PRESENTED WITHIN

21 DAYS AFTER B/LADING DATE,BUT

WITHIN THE VALIDITY OF THE CREDIT.在信用证有效期内，最迟在装运期后 21 天内向银行提交单据。

:49:CONFIRMATION INSTRUCTIONS 保兑指示

WITHOUT 不保兑

:53A: REIMBURSING BANK 偿付行

*TRANSPORT DOCUMENTS TO BE CLAUSED: VESSEL IS NOT SCHEDULED TO CALL ON ITS CURPENT VOYAGE AT FAMAGUSTA,KYRENTA OR KARAVOSTASSI, CYPRUS.

运输单据注明：船在其航行途中不得到塞浦路斯的 Famagusta、Kyrenta 或 Karavostassi 这些地方。

*INSURANCE WILL BE COVERED BY THE APPLICANTS.保险由申请人支付。

*ALL DOCUMENTS TO BE ISSUED IN ENGLISH LANGUAGE.所有单据由英文缮制。

*NEGOTIATION/PAYMENT:UNDER RESERVE/GUARANTEE STRICTLY 保结押汇或是银行保函。

PROHIBITED. 禁止。

*DISCREPANCY FEES USD80, FOR EACH SET OF DISCREPANT DOCUMENTS PRESENTED UNDER THIS CREDIT,WHETHER ACCEPTED OR NOT,PLUS OUR CHARGES FOR EACH MESSAGE CONCERNING REJECTION AND/OR ACCEPTANCE MUST BE BORNE BY BENEFICIARIES THEMSELVES AND DEDUCTED FROM THE AMOUNT PAYABLE TO THEM.

修改每个单据不符点费用将扣除 80 美元。

*IF THE EVENT OF DISCREPANT DOCUMENTS ARE PRESENTED TO US AND REJECTED,WE MAY RELEASE THE DOCUMENTS AND EFFECT SETTLEMENT UPON

APPLICANT'S WAIVER OF SUCH DISCREPANCIES,NOTWITHSTANDING ANY COMMUNICATION WITH THE PRESENTER THAT WE ARE HOLDING DOCUMENTS AT

IT'S DISPOSAL, UNLESS ANY PRIOR INSTRUCTIONS TO THE CONTRARY ARE RECEIVED.

如果不符点是由我方提出的并且被拒绝了，我们将作为受益人放弃修改这个不符点的权利。

THAT THE CARRYING VESSEL(S) IS/ARE:

A) HOLDING A VALID SAFETY.

MANAGEMENT SYSTEM CERTIFICATE AS PER TERMS OF INTERNATIONAL SAFETY MANAGEMENT CODE AND

B) CLASSIFIED AS PER INSTITUTE CLASSIFICATION CLAUSE 01/01/2001.

BY AN APPROPRIATE CLASSIFICATION SOCIETY

由船公司或代理出有注明 B/L 号和船名的证明书证明他们的船:

A) 持有根据国际安全管理条款编码的有效安全管理系统证书。

B) 是由相关分级协会根据 2001 年 1 月 1 日颁布的 ICC 条款分类的。

*COMMERCIAL INVOICE FOR USD11,202,70 IN 4 COPIES DULY SIGNED BY THE BENEFICIARY/IES, STATING THAT THE GOODS SHIPPED:

A) ARE OF CHINESE ORIGIN.

B) ARE IN ACCORDANCE WITH BENEFICIARIES PROFORMA INVOICE NO. HL050307 DATED 07/03/05.

由受益人签署的商业发票总额 USD11,202,70 一式四份，声明货物运输：

A) 原产地为中国；

B) 同号码为 HL050307、开立日为 09/03/05 的商业发票内容一致

:047A: ADDITIONAL CONDITIONS 附加条件

* THE NUMBER AND DATE OF THE CREDIT AND THE NAME OF OUR BANK MUST BE QUOTED ON ALL DRAFTS (IF REQUIRED).

信用证号码及日期和我们的银行名必须体现在所有单据上(如果有要求)。

:44B:FOR TRANSPORTATION TO 目的港

LIMASSOL PORT 发票中无提及

:44C: LATEST DATE OF SHIPMENT 最后装船期

090601

:045A ESCRIPTION OF GOODS AND/OR SERVICES 货物/服务描述

SANITARY WARE 陶瓷洁具

FOB SHENZHEN PORT,INCOTERMS 2 000 FOB 深圳港，INCOMTERMS 2 000

:046A DOCUMENTS REQUIRED 必须提供的单据文件

*FULL SET (AT LEAST THREE) ORIGINAL CLEAN SHIPPED ON BOARD BILLS OF LADING ISSUED TO THE ORDER OF BANK OF CYPRUS PUBLIC COMPANY LTD, CYPRUS, NOTIFY PARTIES APPLICANT AND OURSELVES,SHOWING

全套清洁已装船提单原件(至少 3 份)，做成以“塞浦路斯股份有限公司”为抬头，通知开证人和我们自己，注明

*FREIGHT PAYABLE AT DESTINATION AND BEARING THE NUMBER OF THIS CREDIT.

运费在目的港付以及注明该信用证号码。

*PACKING LIST IN 3 COPIES.

装箱单一式三份。

*CERTIFICATE ISSUED BY THE SHIPPING COMPANY/CARRIER OR THEIR AGENT STATING THE B/L NO(S) AND THE VESSEL(S) NAME CERTIFYING

FENGYI INDUSTRIAL DISTRICT, GUXIANG TOWN, CHAOZHOU CITY,GUANGDONG PROVINCE,CHINA.潮州华利陶瓷洁具厂

:32B: CURRENCY CODE,AMOUNT 信用证项下的金额

USD***7841,89

:41D:AVAILABLE WITH…BY… 议付适用银行

STANDARD CHARTERED BANK

CHINA AND/OR AS BELOW 渣打银行或以下的

BY NEGOTIATION 任何议付行

:42CRAFTS AT 开汇票

SIGHT 即期

:42A DRAWEE 付款人

BCYPCY2NO10

BANK OF CYPRUS LTD 塞浦路斯的银行名

:43PARTIAL SHIPMENTS 是否允许分批装运

NOT ALLOWED 不可以

:43T:TRANSHIPMENT 转运

ALLOWED 允许

:44A LOADING ON BOARD/DISPATCH/TAKING IN CHARGE AT/FROM…装船港口

SHENZHEN PORT 深圳

******* NICOSIA 较对应同发票上是一致的

:59: BENEFICIARY 受益人

CHAOZHOU HUALI CERAMICS FACTORY

BENE.PLEASE ACKN.RECEIPT.

CUMSTOMER'S APPROVAL.

Notes

1. 审核信用证的种类。
2. 审核开证申请人及受益人的名称、地址是否正确。
3. 审核信用证各相关日期是否合理。

(开证日期、装运期、交单期、有效期)

4. 审核信用证对所装运货物及金额的描述是否正确

(名称、规格、包装；币种、金额、数量、单价)。

5. 审核运输条款(起运/目的港、转运、运输工具)。
6. 审核单据条款。
7. 关于银行费用支付责任的审核。
8. 对空白处、边缘处加注的文字的审核。
9. 对信用证软条款的审核。

5. Classification of Letters of Credit

There are many different kinds of L/C as follows.

1) According to the attaching of documents

(1) Clean credit 光票信用证.

A clean credit is a credit against which the beneficiary of the credit may draw a bill, of exchange without presentation of documents. Payment will be effected only against a draft without any shipping documents attached thereto or sometimes, against a draft with an invoice alone attached thereto.

(2) Documentary credit 跟单信用证.

A documentary credit is universally used as a method of payment in international trade. It is a credit under which payment will be made against documents representing title to the goods and thus making the transfer of title possible.

2) According to the revocability of credit

A credit may be either revocable or irrevocable. Every credit should clearly indicate whether it is revocable or irrevocable. In the absence of such indication the credit shall be deemed to be irrevocable.

(1) Revocable credit 可撤销信用证.

A revocable credit is a credit which can be amended or cancelled at any moment by the issuing bank without prior notice to the beneficiary. However, under such a credit, if the payment, acceptance, or negotiation has been effected by the banks concerned prior to their receipt of notice of amendment or cancellation, the issuing bank will still have to reimburse them. In other words, if any bank authorized to do so has paid, negotiated, or accepted against documents presented in compliance with the terms of a revocable documentary credit, such action remains in force, provided it took place prior to that bank's receipt of notice of amendment or revocation. A revocable credit tends to be less favorable to the exporter than an irrevocable credit because it offers little security to the seller; therefore a revocable credit is generally unacceptable and rarely used.

(2) Irrevocable credit 不可撤销信用证.

An irrevocable credit is a credit which constitutes a definite undertaking of the issuing bank and can be amended or cancelled by the issuing bank only on condition that all parties concerned, that is, the issuing bank, the beneficiary and the confirming bank, if any, do agree. This credit gives the beneficiary greater assurance of payment. As a result, this type of credit is the most widely used in international trade.

According to UCP500, the credit should indicate whether it is revocable or irrevocable. In the absence of such indication the credit shall be deemed to be irrevocable.

3) According to the adding of confirmation

(1) Confirmed credit 保兑信用证.

A confirmed credit is a credit which is advised to the beneficiary with another bank's confirmation added thereto. In cases where the financial conditions in the importing country and/or the solvency of the issuing bank are in doubt, the exporter may demand that another bank, preferable in the exporting country, should undertake to honor by adding its confirmation. In this way, the exporter is assured that payment will be made by the confirming bank no matter the issuing bank is insolvent or not. Only the issuing bank can request another bank to add its confirmation.

The confirming bank usually adds on the credit such words as "This credit is confirmed by us" or "We hereby add our confirmation to this credit" and then signs thereon. It has the obligation to pay, to accept, or to negotiate a bill without recourse to the drawer and bona fide holder just same as the issuing bank.

(2) Unconfirmed credit 不保兑信用证.

A letter of credit advised to the beneficiary without adding any other bank's confirmation is called an unconfirmed credit. Usually the word "unconfirmed" is not indicated in the credit.

4) According to the method of payment

(1) Sight L/C 即期信用证.

A letter of credit calling for the presentation of sight drafts is a sight credit, under which the beneficiary (the drawer) is entitled to receive payment at once on presentation of his draft to the drawee bank or to the issuing bank if drawn on the issuing bank, once the relevant documents have been checked and found to be in order.

(2) Usance or time credit 远期信用证.

If a letter of credit specifies that drafts are to be drawn at any length of time, such as 30 days, 60 days, 90 days or 120 days, after sight, it is called a usance or time credit. Under such credit, the drafts may be drawn on and accepted by the opening bank, or the paying bank as indicated therein. In this case, the exporter issues his draft, presents it for acceptance, together with all the shipping documents, to the issuing bank or to the confirming bank or to the paying bank, as stipulated in the credit. Once the draft is accepted, this means that the accepting bank promises to pay the full amount of the draft at a specified future date. The accepted usance draft can be discounted in the discount market.

Usance credit may require no drafts at all.

Notes

使用远期信用证，必须了解客户的资信情况以及客户银行的信用，必须遵循安全收汇的原则。

(3) Acceptance credit 承兑信用证.

An acceptance credit is a credit available by acceptance, under which a bank specifically nominated therein is authorized to accept. It must be a usance credit and the draft thereunder must be a time bill drawn on the issuing bank, the advising bank, or any other drawee bank. The clause used in the credit is as follows: "This credit is available by acceptance of draft drawn on the··· bank". By accepting the draft under the credit, the accepting bank signifies its commitment to pay the face value thereof at maturity. The beneficiary will discount the accepted draft with his own bank or in local money market if he wishes to get paid immediately.

Acceptance credit is usually issued if the contract is on time basis. The beneficiary will receive payment on a specified future date. If he discounts the accepted draft in the money market, discount charges are for account of the beneficiary. This is called seller's usance credit. If the contract is concluded on sight basis, the importer may issue an acceptance or time credit for purposes of financing through discounting the accepted time draft in the discount market.

Notes

承兑信用证是指由某一银行承兑的信用证，即当受益人向指定银行开具远期汇票并提示时，指定银行即承兑，并于汇票到期日履行付款。按《UCP600》第 9 条“信用证不应要求凭申请人为付款人的汇票支付”的新规定，付款人将仅限于开证行或被指定的其他银行。这种信用证又称为银行承兑信用证(Banker's Acceptance L/C)。承兑信用证一般用于远期付款的交易。但有时，买方为了便于融资或利用银行承兑汇票以取得比银行放款利率更低的优惠贴现率，在与卖方订立即期付款的合同后，要求开立银行承兑信用证，证中规定“远期汇票即期付款、所有贴现和承兑费用由买方负担”。此种做法对受益人来说，他虽然开出的是远期汇票，但却能即期收到全部货款。

(4) Negotiation credit 议付信用证.

A negotiation credit is a credit under which a bank specifically nominated therein is authorized to negotiate or a credit which is freely negotiable by any bank.

A credit treated as negotiable is either a sight credit or a time credit, calling drafts to be drawn on the issuing bank or on any other drawee bank. A negotiation credit assures any bank negotiating the drafts thereunder that they will be duly honoured by the opening bank provided all the terms stipulated therein are complied with.

Notes

议付信用证是指开证行在信用证中，邀请其他银行买入汇票及/或单据的信用证，即允许受益人向某一指定银行或任何银行交单议付的信用证。通常在单据符合信用证条款的条件下，议付银行扣除利息和手续费后将票款付给受益人。

5) Special credits

There are numerous special letters of credit designed to meet specific needs of buyers, suppliers and intermediaries. Special credits usually involve increased participation by banks, so financing and service charges are higher than those for basic credits. The following is a brief description of some special credits.

(1) Revolving credit 循环信用证.

This is a type of credit that renews itself after its amount is drawn. To define it more clearly, it is a credit where, under the terms and conditions thereof, its amount is renewed or reinstated without any specific amendment made thereto.

To facilitate continuous repeated purchases from the same supplier a revolving credit is often used. So far as this type of credit is concerned the opening bank issues only one letter with a fixed amount available for each defined calendar period. The delivery of the goods is made in installments and at stipulated intervals. When the drawing is made by the beneficiary the original credit amount becomes again available for the next period.

(2) Transferable credit 可转让信用证.

This credit allows the supplier to transfer all or part of the proceeds of the credit to a second beneficiary, usually the ultimate supplier of the goods. This is a common financing tactic for middlemen.

(3) Back-to-back credit 对背信用证.

This is a new credit opened on the basis of an already existing nontrans ferable credit. It is used by traders to make payment to the ultimate supplier. A trader receives a letter of credit from the buyer and then opens another letter of credit in favor of the supplier. The first letter of credit is used as collateral for the second credit. The second credit makes price adjustments from which come the trader's profits.

(4) Anticipatory L/C/Red clause credit 预支/红条款信用证.

Often an exporter does not have the funds to produce products to fill current orders. A letter of credit may have already been issued by the importer in anticipation of goods being exported. If allowed by the terms of the letter of credit, the exporter may draw upon the letter to obtain funds to produce goods. Once the goods are delivered the exporter may then submit the proper documents to obtain the balance of the letter of credit. This type of interim financing is referred to as coming from a "Red Clause Letter of Credit".

Notes

预支信用证是指允许受益人在货物装运交单前预支货款的信用证，有全部预支和部分预支两种。在预支信用证项下，受益预支的方式有两种：一种是向开证行预支，出口人在货物装运前开具以开证行为付款人的汇票光票，由议付行买下向开证行索偿；另一种是向议付行预支，即由出口地的议付行垫付货款，待货物装运后，交单议付时，扣除垫款本息，将余额支付给出口人。如货未装运，由开证行负责偿还议付行的垫款和利息。为引人注目，这种预支货款的条款常用红字，故习称"红条款信用证"(Red Clause L/C)。但现在在国际贸易实务中，信用证的预支条款并非都用红色表示，其效力相同。

(5) Standby credit 备用信用证.

This credit is primarily a payment or performance guarantee. It is used primarily in the United States because U.S. banks are prevented by law from giving certain guarantees. Standby credits are often called non-performing letters of credit because they only used as a backup payment method if the collection on a primary payment method is past due. Standby credit can be used to guarantee repayment of loans, fulfillment by subcontractor, securing the payment for goods delivered by third parties. For example, an organization is seeking to bid on the construction of a dam in another country. Generally, bids on such projects require a good faith guarantee on the part of the bidder to assure the bid will be accepted if granted and that work will be done on time and in a workman-like manner. Ten percent of the bid amount is not uncommon. One of the methods of securing this guarantee is to obtain a standby letter of credit in favor of the government of the foreign country. If the bidder defaults, the foreign government is paid from the letter of credit. The bank issuing the letter then has recourse against the bidding company.

Notes

备用信用证又称为商业票据信用证(Commercial Paper Letter of Credit)、担保信用证保证信用证(Guarantee Letter of Credit)，是指开证行根据开证申请人的请求对受益人开立的承诺承担某项义务的凭证。开证行保证在开证申请人并未履行其应履行的义务时，受益人只要凭备用信用证的规定向开证行开具汇票(或不开汇票)，并提交开证申请人未履行义务的声明或证明文件，即可取得开证行的偿付。

备用信用证属于银行信用，开证银行保证在开证申请人未履行其义务时，即由开证银行付款。因此，备用信用证对受益人来说就是备用于开证申请人发生毁约时，取得补偿的一种方式。

Section Two Procedures of Letter of Credit Operations 信用证操作程序

There are many kinds of credit described as above. Generally speaking, if the buyer pays and the seller is paid by credit, it will operated by documentary credit. In this section we will take documentary credit as an example to illustrate the parties and procedures.

1. Parties to a Letter of Credit 信用证当事人

1) Applicant or Opener 申请人

The applicant or the opener is always an importer or a buyer, who fills out and signs an application form, requesting the bank to issue a letter of credit in favor of an exporter or a seller abroad. He is in duty bound to ensure that the credit is issued in compliance with the terms and conditions laid down in the sales contract within a proper or reasonable time. After the payment is effected by the issuing bank, the opener must pay the bank against correct shipping documents or refuse to pay if the documents are not in order.

2) Beneficiary 收益人

The beneficiary is the exporter or the seller in whose favor the credit is issued. If there is a discrepancy between the credit opened and the sales contract, the beneficiary may have the option to accept it as it stands or persuade the opener to have it amended so as to be in line with the contract. Once the beneficiary accepts the credit, he must deliver the goods in compliance with the contract. Then he tenders to his bank or any other bank all the relevant documents as stipulated in the credit. He is responsible not only for the correctness and genuineness of the documents but also for the goods which must conform with the contract. If the issuing bank does not pay or is in liquidation, the beneficiary can claim from the opener for the payment.

3) Issuing Bank or Opening Bank 开证行

The issuing bank is one which issues a letter of credit at the request of an applicant. It undertakes to pay to the beneficiary. If the applicant fails to pay after the issuing bank makes payment, the latter has the right to sell the goods and claim from the applicant if the proceeds are not sufficient. It is primarily liable to the beneficiary, no matter whether the applicant is in default or not.

4) Advising Bank 通知行

The advising bank is one which advises the credit to the beneficiary in accordance with stipulations on the credit. It is located in the place of the beneficiary, which is usually the issuing bank's branch or correspondent acting as an agent of the opening bank in accordance with the instructions given.

5) Negotiating Bank 议付行

Negotiating means the giving of value for draft(s) and/or documents by the bank authorized to negotiate. The negotiating bank is one which negotiates or purchases the draft drawn by the beneficiary on the issuing bank or on any drawee bank as specified in the credit. The negotiating bank naturally becomes the holder in due course of the draft after its negotiation. And so it normally has a right of recourse against the drawer, namely the beneficiary in the credit, in the event of dishonour by the issuing bank.

6) Paying Bank 付款行

The paying bank is always the drawee of a draft stipulated in the credit. Or we may say it is a bank nominated by the issuing bank to make payment under the credit. Sometimes the paying bank is the issuing bank itself.

7) Reimbursing Bank 偿付行

Reimbursing bank is the agent of the issuing bank. It honors the reimbursement claims of a paying bank or an accepting bank or a negotiating bank under a particular credit in accordance with the instructions or authorization given by the issuing bank.

Notes

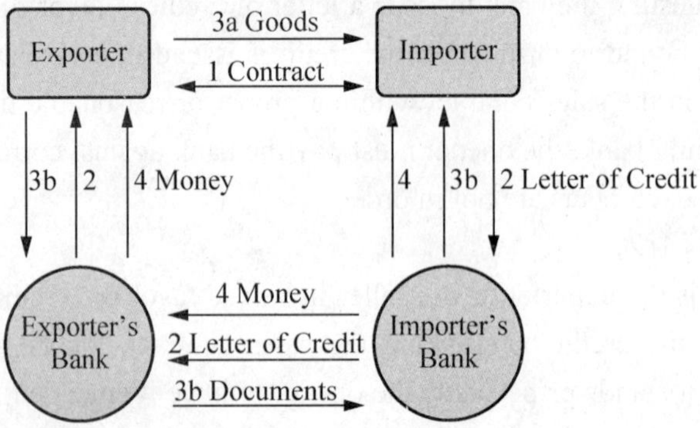

1. A purchase contract is concluded between the exporter/seller and the importer/purchaser.

2. Based on the purchase contract, the importer shall ask his bank to issue a letter of credit.

3a. The exporter ships the goods.

3b. The exporter collects documents as per L/C terms and sends the documents via his bank to the importer's bank, which shall check the documents and if they meet the terms shall deliver them to the importer.

4. The importer's bank (issuing bank) shall pay the letter of credit to the exporter and debit the importer's account.

2. Procedures of Letter of Credit Operations 信用证的程序

The documentary credit procedure involves three basic groupings of steps in the procedure: Issuance, Amendment, Utilization.

1) Issuance

Issuance describes the process of the buyer's applying for and opening a documentary credit at the issuing bank and the opening bank's formal notification of the seller through the advising bank.

(1) Contract to settlement by a letter of credit.

The buyer and seller agree on the terms of sale:

① specifying a documentary credit as the means of payment;

② naming an advising bank (usually the seller's bank);

③ listing required documents.

(2) Requesting for issuing a letter of credit.

The buyer applies to his bank (issuing bank) to open a documentary credit naming the seller as the beneficiary based on specific terms and conditions that are listed in the credit.

(3) Opening of a letter of credit.

After accepting the application, the opening bank shall stipulate L/C clauses strictly conforming to the instructions of application form and mail or telex or send by SWIFT to the advising bank named in the credit.

(4) Advising the beneficiary.

After verifying the authenticity of the credit, the advising bank shall advise the beneficiary of L/C or just transferring the L/C to him. And a copy is usually kept for file.

There are two ways of advising: one is to deliver the L/C directly to the beneficiary, attached with a signed advice note. Another one is when the addressee of the L/C is the advising bank, the advising bank shall copy word by word in its own advice note, sign, and deliver it to the beneficiary.

2) Amendment

Amendment describes the process whereby the terms and conditions of a documentary credit may be modified after the credit has been issued.

After receiving the documentary credit, the seller must examine it closely to determine if the terms and conditions (1) reflect the agreement of the buyer and seller, and (2) can be met within the time stipulated. Upon examination, the seller may find problems. If the seller still wants to proceed with the transaction, but with modification to the terms of the credit, he or she should contact the buyer immediately and request an amendment.

Amendments must be authorized by the buyer and issued by the issuing bank to the seller through the same channel as the original documentary credit. This can be an involved undertaking so any amendments should be initiated only when necessary and as soon as a problem is identified.

3) Utilization

Utilization describes the procedure for the seller's shipping of the goods, the transfer of documents from the seller to the buyer through the banks, and the transfer of payment from the buyer to the seller through the banks.

(1) The seller (beneficiary) ships the goods to the buyer and obtains a negotiable transport document (negotiable bill of lading) from the shipping firm/agent.

(2) The seller prepares and presents a document package to the advising bank consisting of documents such as negotiable transport document, commercial invoice, insurance document, inspection certificate, etc.

(3) The advising bank reviews the document package making certain the documents are in conformity with the terms of the credit and pays the seller. In the case of a credit available by negotiation, the negotiating bank (usually be the advising bank) negotiates the documents with recourse to the beneficiary. After negotiation, the negotiating bank will claim reimbursement from the issuing bank or the reimbursing bank in accordance with the reimbursement terms indicated in the credit and documents will be sent to the issuing bank.

(4) The advising bank sends the document package by mail or by courier to the issuing bank.

(5) The issuing bank reviews the document package making certain the documents are in conformity with the terms of the credit, pays the advising bank and advising the buyer that the documents have arrived.

(6) The buyer reviews the document package making certain the documents are in conformity with the terms of credit, and makes a cash payment (with a sight draft) to the issuing

bank, or signs an acceptance (promising to pay at a future date).

(7) The issuing bank sends the document package by mail or courier to the buyer who then takes possession of the shipment.

Sample of Notification of Documentary Credit

信 我 信 未 来

杭州银行

hzbank BANK OF HANGZHOU

ORIGINAL

信用证通知书

OFFICE:INTL BUSINESS DEPT **Notification of Documentary Credit**

ADDRESS:NO.419-425 JINCHENGROAD，XIAOSHANDISTRICT,HANGZHOU,CHINA Date日期 2012-03-15

TO: 致 杭州盛博物资有限公司 HANGZHOU SENBO MATERIAL CO LTD	**Our Ref No.**我行编号: AD10129631000084 **Amount** 金额: USD 59 913.12
Issuing Bank 开证行: INDUSTRIAL BANK OF KOREA (HEAD OFFICE SEOUL) SEOUL KR	**Transferred from** 转证行:
L/C No.信用证: **M04DB203NU00107**	**Issuing Date** 开证日期 : **2012年3月14日**

Dear Sirs敬启者:
We have pleasure in advising you that we have received from the A/M bank a(n).
兹通知贵司，我行收自上述银行
(√) Test Key confirmity 印押相符
Letter of credit, contents of which are as per attached sheet(s).
This advice and the attached sheet(s) must accompany the relative documents when presented.
信用证一份，现随附通知。贵公司交单时，请将本通知书及信用证一并提示。
(√) Please note that this advice does not constitute our confirmation to the above L/C nor does it convey any engagement or obligation on our part.
本通知书不构成我行对此信用证之保兑及其他责任。
( ) Please note that we have added our confirmation to the above L/C, negotiation is restricted to ourselves only.
上述信用证已由我行加具保兑，并限向我行交单。
Remarks 备注:

If you find any terms and conditions in the L/C which you are unable to comply with and/or any error(s),it is suggested that you contact applicant directly for necessary amendment(s) so as to avoid any difficulties which may arise when documents are presented.
如该信用证中有无法办到的条款及/或错误，请迳与开证申请人联系进行必要的修改，以排除交单时可能发生的问题。

本通知费 CNY 0.00
请划入我行 ________ 账户，
账号 ________。

Yours Faithfully

BANK OF HANGZHOU , XIAOSHAN SUB- BRANCH

信用证通知专用章

Section Three Cases in Detail
具体案例分析

(一) 经典案例解析

Dear Sirs,

We would like to draw your attention to our Order No.321 for 500 pieces of Blue Woolen Serge.

On 3 April, we sent you an irrevocable letter of credit which expires on 30 June.

This is our busy season and our buyers urgently need the goods. We shall therefore be very grateful if you ship the goods as soon as possible.

We must stress that any delay in shipping the order will involve us in problems with our buyers, which could affect our future business.

Your earliest reply will be highly appreciated.

Yours faithfully,

Notes

1. draw one's attention to 请……注意；提请……注意

e.g.We would like to draw your attention to the fact that the validity of the L/C is drawing near. Please do your utmost to effect shipment without further delay.

请你方注意这样一个事实，信用证的有效期已临近。请尽力完成装运，不得有进一步的延误。

2. expire *v.* 期满

expiration *n.* 期满；终止

expiry *n.* 期满；截止日期

e.g. (1) 信用证于 5 月 15 日期满。

The L/C expires on May 15.

(2) 这批货物必须在许可证期满前运到。

The shipment must arrive here before the expiration of the license.

(3) 信用证的截止日期是 5 月 15 日。

The date of expiry of the L/C is May 15.

3. be in urgent need of sth. 急需……

e.g.请尽快装运我方所订购货物，因为我方买主急需该货。

Please do your utmost to expedite the shipment of our order as our buyers are in urgent need of the goods.

4. This is a letter from the sellers. In the letter the sellers remind the buyers that the time of shipment is approaching, but they have not yet received the relative L/C. Therefore the sellers ask the buyers to open the L/C immediately so that they can make the shipment as stipulated.

5. Structure of a letter for complaint

(1) Beginning Paragraph: the reason of this letter.

(2) Paragraph Two: informing the reader of sending the L/C.

(3) Paragraph Three: asking for punctual shipment.

(4) Paragraph Four: warning in a polite way.

(5) Paragraph Five: the closing sentence of the letter.

(二) 一般案例表述

1. Urging Establishment of L/C 催开信用证

Dear Sirs,

Our S/C No. XMH20071012

With regard to 30 metric tons of Graphited Petroleum Coke under the captioned Sales Confirmation, we wish to draw your attention to the fact that the goods have been ready for shipment, but we have received neither your covering Letter of Credit nor any further information from you to date. Please note that, as agreed, the terms of payment for the above order are sight Letter of Credit established within 2 weeks upon the arrival of our Sales Confirmation.

Please expedite the establishment of the L/C in our favor, so that we are able to execute shipment within the stipulated time limit.

In order to avoid subsequent amendments, please see to it that the L/C stipulations are in exact accordance with the terms of the S/C.

We are waiting for your favorable reply.

Yours truly,

Notes

1. The covering L/C 有关信用证，covering 在此是形容词，仅用作前置定语，表示“有关的”。例如：

Please see to it that the goods we ordered are shipped as soon as the covering L/C reaches you .

注意，我方所订货物在有关信用证抵达你方时请立即装船。

2. expedite *v.* 加快，促进，发出，常用于外贸书信中，有时也用 hasten、hurry、rush 等。例如：

Please do your utmost to expedite the establishment of the L/C.

请速开出信用证。

Our end users are in urgent need of the goods, so please expedite shipment as much as possible.

我方用户急需此货，请速装船。

As we are in urgent need of the goods, could you manage to hasten the delivery? 我们急需该货，你方能否加速装运？

3. in one's favor 以……为受益人，以……为抬头

We will request our bankers to open L/C in your favor upon receipt of your confirmation of this order.

一俟受到你方关于此项订货的确认，我方便要求银行开出以你方为受益人的信用证。

We are informed that the L/C in our favor amounting to $600 000 has been opened.

我们得到通知以我方为受益人、金额为 60 万美元的信用证已开出。

We open an irrevocable Letter of Credit No.434 in favor of CITIC Trading Co. Ltd..

兹开立第 434 号不可撤销的信用证，受益人为中国国际信托投资总公司贸易公司。

4. in accordance with …与……一致，根据……，该词组可用来引导状语和表语。

Party B shall guarantee that the machines to be provided are in accordance with Party A's requirements and specifications.

乙方应保证其提供的机器符合甲方的要求与规格。

In accordance with faxes exchanged, we are glad to have sold you 50 tons walnuts.
依照双方往来传真，我们很高兴已售空你方50吨核桃。

5. see to 固定词组，表示处理、负责、注意。例如：

The transferee must see to it that the quality of the product is maintained.
接受转让一方要负责保持产品的质量。

Please see to it that the goods we ordered are shipped as soon as the covering letter of credit reaches you.
一俟收到有关信用证，请立即装运我方所订货物。

2. Request to amendment of L/C 要求修改信用证

Dear Sirs,

Re: Your L/C No. CNIMC765603

We are pleased to acknowledge receipt of your L/C No. CNIMC765603 issued by Hong Kong & Shanghai Banking Corporation against S/C XMC070126 for 20 MT FeMo.

We note from your L/C that you require the Certificate of Origin to be certified by your consul, which is unacceptable to us as there is no consul of your country here. However, it is our usual practice to have it certified by CCPIT and we therefore should be obliged if you would amend your L/C to that effect.

If your amendment could reach us by the end of this month, we would request the manufacture to expedite delivery.

Your cooperation in this respect would be highly appreciated.

Yours faithfully,

Notes

1. oblige *vt.* 强制，施恩惠于，使感激 *vi.* 施恩惠，帮忙

Kindly oblige us by realizing same as advantageously as possible. 请以尽可能有利的价格出售，我们深表谢意。

Please oblige me with a reply as soon as possible. 请尽早回复为盼。

We shall be obliged by a quotation of your lowest price for the said goods free delivered at our works.
请贵方惠寄商品目录并报价，谢谢。

2. amendment *n.* 修正，改变

amend *vt.* 修正，改变。用法：

to amend…as 将……改为

to amend…(so as)to read 将……改为。例如：

We cannot effect shipment unless you amend the assortment in your L/C according to the S/C.
除非你方按照销售确认书修改信用证中的花色搭配，否则我们无法装运货物。

Please amend your L/C to allow partial shipment and transshipment.
请修改你方信用证允许分批装运与转运。

Please amend the amount of your L/C so as to read "2% more or less".
请将信用证数量改为“可溢短装2%”。

We have amended the L/C，and we shall immediately make the shipment of the goods.
我们已将信用证修改为允许转船。

to make amendment 修改。例如：

When you find anything to the contrary in the L/C, please tell us so that we can make amendments accordingly.

若发现信用证的内容与此不符，请告知我们以便进行相应的修改。

3. to this /that effect 是介词短语，意思为“有这样或那样的内容，意思”。例如：

Notice of readiness should be tendered and accepted by Charterers or their agents within ordinary business hours to the effect that the vessel is in every respects ready and fit to deliver cargo whether in berth or not provided formalities for entering port have been passed by Port Authorities.

准备就绪通知书要在通常的办公时间递交。一旦办妥船舶进港手续，不管停泊与否，均可在上述时间内向租船人或其代理人递交通知书，内容大意是船已在各个方面准备就绪，并且适于交货。

3. Asking for Amending Terms of Shipment 修改装运条款

Dear Sirs,

Your L/C No.D 303

We are in receipt of the Letter of Credit bearing No. D 303 you established through the Barkley Bank, London on April 15th, covering our contract No. HC 54.

On perusal, we find that the port of Destination should be Belfast and no transshipment is allowed. Since there are only one or two direct steamers monthly from Dalian to Belfast, we usually have to make shipment via Hong Kong. In order to make sure that the goods will be duly delivered, which is to our mutual benefit, we request that you amend the said L/C to allow us transshipment.

In case the above amendment is not agreeable to you, you may change the port of Destination Belfast to Liverpool because there are more direct steamers available from Dalian to Liverpool.

Your kind acknowledgement will highly oblige us.

Yours truly,

Notes

on perusal. 详阅后

On perusal, we find that transshipment and partial shipment are not allowed. 在详阅后，我们发现不允许转船和分批装运。

4. Requirements of credit extended 要求信用证展期

Dear Mr. Bloch,

Re: Your L/C No. SW12GUU120/EA

30 M/T Graphited Petroleum Coke

We thank you for your L/C No. SW12GUU120/EA covering your order of 30 M/T Graphited Petroleum Coke. We regret to say that we have just received your L/C yesterday and it is impossible to effect shipment in July. As stipulated clearly in the Sales Confirmation that shipment could be made provided the relevant L/C reached us not later than the end of June.

We trust you will extend by fax the shipment date of your L/C to August 30 and validity to September 15, thus enabling us to effect shipment of the goods in question.

Your kind attention is invited to the fact that we are able to arrange to ship the consignment on S.S. Pearl sailing from Dalian on or about August 10 on condition that we receive your L/C amendment before July 30.

Yours sincerely,

Notes

1. stipulate *vt.* 规定， 保证 *vi.* 规定， 保证

stipulation *n.* 约束， 约定， 契约 ，规定， 条款。例如:

We shall make shipment within the time the contract stipulate.

我们将在合同规定的期限内装船。

According to the contract between the two parties, it stipulates that either party may withdraw at six months' notice.

根据双方之间合同规定，无论哪一方都不能提前6个月发通知来撤销合同。

This stipulation comes within the terms of your contract.

此规定合乎你的合同项目。

The period may also be extended by written stipulation between the Parties, provided the stipulation is approved by the Provider.

如经服务提供方认可，还可以通过双方的书面约定延长这一限定时间。

2. 造成出口人要求展证的原因是多方面的：主观上——货源不足，生产事故，运输脱节等；客观上——自然灾害，社会动乱或进口人未能在合同规定的期限内把信用证开到等。

在展证信中可根据责任的不同采取相应的措辞和语气，但目的都是促使进口人同意展证，从而保证合同的顺利执行。展证信涉及两个期限：装运期和有效期。展证信的中心内容：提出具体的展证要求，即要求展延多少天或展延到具体某一天，同时一定要充分说明原因和理由。

资料链接 Material—link

1. Standard Model

Model 1: Urging Establishment of L/C

Dear Sirs,

We are very pleased to have signed the Sales Contract No.5678 with you. But we have not received your L/C. We are writing you in the hope of inviting your attention to the terms about the arriving date of the L/C.

We do hope you will abide by the agreed articles and have the L/C opened before the stipulated time. On receipt of the L/C, we will make shipment immediately.

Faithfully yours,

Model 2: Advice of Establishment to L/C

Dear Sirs,

We have received your letter of December 11 in connection with your Sales Confirmation No. Y1656.

In reply, we are pleased to tell you that we have today established with the National Bank the confirmed, irrevocable Letter of Credit No. 6783 in your favor for the amount of FRF 62 000 payable by sight draft accompanied by a full set of the shipping documents.

As the season is drawing near, our buyers are in urgent need of the goods. Please arrange shipment of the goods ordered by us upon receipt of the L/C. We would like to stress that any delay in shipping our order will involve us in no small difficulty. We hope you will let us know at your earliest convenience the name of the carrying vessel and its sailing date.

Thank you in advance for your cooperation.

Faithfully yours,

Model 3 : Amendment of L/C

Dear Sirs,

While we thank you for your L/C No.112235, we regret to say that we have found some discrepancies. You are therefore requested to make the following amendments:

(1) *The amount both in figures and in words should respectively read "GBP14500"(Say Pounds Sterling Fourteen Thousand Five Hundred And Fifty Only);*

(2) *"From Copenhagen to China port" should read "from China port to Copenhagen";*

(3) *The Bill of Lading should be marked "Freight Prepaid" instead "Freight Collect";*

(4) *Delete the clause "Partial shipments and transshipment prohibited";*

(5) *"This L/C is valid at our counter" should be amended to read "This L/C is valid at your counter".*

Please confirm the amendments by fax as soon as possible.

Yours sincerely,

Model 4: Asking for Extension of L/C

Dear Sirs,

We thank you for your Letter of Credit No.BC630 issued through the Commercial Bank covering 6 000 pieces of computers.

In accordance with the stipulations of the L/C, shipment should be effected not later than August 19, and transshipment is not allowed. However, owing to the workers' strike here, there will be no direct steamer to your port until the end of August. Therefore, we have to request you to extend the date of shipment and the validity of the L/C to September 30 and October 15 respectively.

Since this is the urgent matter, please confirm the amendment by fax. Your compliance with our request will be highly appreciated.

Yours faithfully,

2. *Writing Guide*

(1) *In writing a letter of urging establishment of L/C, please be tactful:*

① *In the first letter of urging establishment of L/C, the seller should first state the fact that the goods ordered are ready for shipment but the relevant L/C has not yet been received and then express his hope that, upon receipt of this letter, the buyer will open the L/C immediately.*

② *If the first letter brings no reply, the seller should send out a second one to urge the buyer to open the L/C immediately. The second letter, though still restrained, he may express disappointment and surprise.*

(2) *In writing an amendment of L/C, please:*

① *Give the reason of the letter.*

② *Point out the problems in the L/C.*

③ *State the reasons for amending L/C.*

④ *Ask for amendment to the L/C.*

(3) *In writing extension of L/C，please:*

① *Outline the delay and the reason for it.*

② *State the new delivery arrangements and dates.*

③ *Press conformation of the extension to the L/C.*

④ *Apologize for the delay.*

Section Four Selected Sentences
精选句型表达

1．尽管我方多次提醒，贵方至今尚未开立信用证。

In spite of our numerous reminders, you haven't opened the letter of credit so far.

2．第 268 号合约项下的 800 辆自行车备妥待运已久，但至今我们尚未收到你们的有关信用证。请速开来，以便装运。

The 800 bicycles under Contract 268 have been ready for shipment for quite some time, but we have not yet received your covering L/C to date. Please open the L/C as soon as possible so that we may effect shipment.

3．通常，我方只接受保兑的、不可撤销的即期信用证。

As a rule, we only accept confirmed irrevocable letter of credit payable by draft at sight.

4．你方 456 号信用证下的货物已备妥有一段时间了，但直到现在为止，我们仍未收到关于信用证的任何消息。

The shipment under your Credit No. 456 has been ready for quite some time, but up to the present we haven't received any news of L/C.

5．装运期已临近，我们必须指出，除非你方信用证在……之前到达我处，否则我们无法在规定时间内装运。

The shipment date is approaching. We must point out that we shall be unable to effect shipment within the stipulated time unless your L/C reaches us before …

6．很遗憾，由于你方信用证迟开，我们无法在 3 月份装运货物。

We regret that we could not ship the goods by a March vessel only because of the delay of your L/C.

7．关于你方 385 号合同，我们没收到任何信用证的有关消息，信用证本应在 6 月 2 日前到达我处。

Referring to your contract No. 385, we have not received any information from you about your letter of credit which should have reached us before June 2.

8．我们很遗憾地告知贵方，我们直到今天才收到你方有关上述销售确认书的信用证。

We regret to inform you that we did not receive your L/C covering the above Sales Confirmation till today.

9．必须在信用证规定的期间向开证行或保兑行(如果有)或任何其他指定银行提交单据。

Presentment of documents must be made to the issuing bank or the confirming bank, if any, or any other nominated bank within the period specified in the credit.

10．我们很遗憾地发现有些条款与合同中的条款不符。

However, we regret to have found that there are certain clauses which do not conform to those of the contract.

11．已收到你方有关信用证，但很遗憾，里面有些内容不符，具体如下。

We have received your relative L/C, but to our regret that it contains the following discrepancies.

12．已收到你方 2 256 美元的信用证，但很遗憾地通知你方，信用证提及的……与合同内容不符。

We have received your relative L/C for US$2 256, but we regret to inform you that … mentioned therein does not agree with the contents in the contract.

13．请相应修改信用证。

Please make the amendment accordingly.

14．请通知你方银行做必要的改证。

Please advise your bank to make the necessary amendment.

15．请将 1123 号信用证修改为……

Please amend L/C No.1123 to read "…".

16。请将 100 号信用证做如下修改。

Please amend L/C No. 100 as follows.

(1) 金额提高到 50 000 美元。Amount to be increased up to US $50 000.

(2) 有效期延至 11 月 10 日。Validity to be extended to 10th November.

(3) 删除"不允许转运"。The words "Transshipment Not Allowed" are to be deleted.

17．由于供应商的延误，我们不能按信用证规定在 6 月 30 日之前发货，故请将信用证的船期和有效期分别延展 1 个月。

Owing to some delay on the part of our suppliers, we are not in a position to ship the goods before June 30 as stipulated in the L/C. Kindly extend the shipping date and credit validity for one month respectively.

18．由于……，我们希望你方将装运期和信用证有效期分别展至……(天)。

Owing to … we would appreciate your extending the shipment date and the validity of your L/C to …(date) respectively.

19．信用证有效期展至……(天)。

The validity of the L/C will be extended to … (date).

20．我们不得不要求装运期展延 15 天，相信你方不会反对。

We have to ask for an extension of 15 days for shipment, to which we trust you will have no objection.

Abstract

通过本章学习，①了解信用证的内容和基本分类； ②读懂信用证的内容和注意事项；③熟悉和掌握信用证的操作流程；④通过熟悉标准模板掌握催证、改证和展证函电的写作基本方法；⑤熟练掌握催证、改证和展证函电经典句型的表达。

Useful Words & Expressions

1．revocable L/C/irrevocable L/C 可撤销信用证/不可撤销信用证

2．confirmed L/C/unconfirmed L/C 保兑信用证/不保兑信用证

3．sight L/C/usance L/C 即期信用证/远期信用证

4. transferable L/C(or)assignable L/C(or)transmissible L/C /untransferable L/C 可转让信用证/不可转让信用证

5．divisible L/C/undivisible L/C 可分割信用证/不可分割信用证

6．revolving L/C 循环信用证

7．L/C with T/T reimbursement clause 带电汇条款信用证

8．without recourse L/C/with recourse L/C 无追索权信用证/有追索权信用证

9．documentary L/C/clean L/C 跟单信用证/光票信用证

10．deferred payment L/C/anticipatory L/C 延付信用证/预支信用证

11．back to back L/C reciprocal L/C 对背信用证/对开信用证

12．traveller's L/C(circular L/C) 旅行信用证

13．opener 开证人

1) applicant 开证人(申请开证人)

2) principal 开证人(委托开证人)

3) accountee 开证人

4) accreditor 开证人(委托开证人)

14．negotiation/negotiating bank 议付行

15．paying bank 付款行

16．reimbursing bank 偿付行

17．the confirming bank 保兑行

18．amount of the L/C 信用证金额

19．amount RMB￥… 金额：人民币……

20．documents required 单据要求

21．sight drafts 即期汇票

22．time drafts 远期汇票

23．drawn clauses 出票条款

24．signed commercial invoice 已签署的商业发票

25．in duplicate 一式两份

26．in triplicate 一式三份

27．in quadruplicate 一式四份

28．in quintuplicate 一式五份

29．in sextuplicate 一式六份

30．in septuplicate 一式七份

31.in octuplicate 一式八份

32．in nonuplicate 一式九份

33．in decuplicate 一式十份

34．expiry (expiring) date… 满期日……

35．reimbursement 索偿

Exercises

1. Multiple choice.

(1) ____ your letter of March 5,we are pleased to inform you that the L / C has been received.

A. In reply to B. Replying for C. Replied to D. Replied for

(2) Please make sure that the stipulations in the L/C ____ in exact accordance with the terms of the Sales Contract.

A. are B. is C. will be D. to be

(3) ____ the terms of payment as stipulated in the contract, please establish an irrevocable letter of credit in our favor.

A. In fact B. As a matter of fact

C. In contrast with D. In accordance with

(4) We will see to ____ that the L/C is opened within the stipulated time.

A. it B. make C. let D. them

(5) The letter of credit will be confirmed by the Bank of China , Shanghai ,that will ____ your draft on the documents at sight for the amount of your invoice.

A. accept B. pay for C. receive D. obtain

(6) We wish to call your attention to the ____ in the L/C, since there is no possibility of L/C extension.

A. variety B. validity C. possibility D. probability

(7) Not until this morning ____ your delayed letter of credit.

A. we received B. did we receive

C. we have received D. had we received

(8) Please open your L/C immediately to facilitate ____.

A. our shipping arrangement B. for shipment

C. to arrange shipment D. us to arrange shipment

(9) In reply, we have the pleasure of informing you that an L/C has been opened ____ $ 2 000.

A. at B. to C. up D. for

(10) Please ____ your L/C validity till January 23.

A. extent B. expand C. expect D. extend

2. Answer the questions according to the passage.

(1) What are the characteristics of a letter of credit?

(2) What are the contents of a letter of credit?

(3) What are the types of credits?

(4) How to reply to urge establishing an L/C?

3. Put the following sentences into English.

(1) 装运期渐近，如果能尽快开立以我方为受益人的信用证将不胜感激。

(2) 交货期日益临近，请你方尽快申请开立信用证。

(3) 请按照合约规定修改信用证。

(4) 经详阅，我们对第 276 号信用证按贵方要求进行了必要的修改。

(5) 请通知你方银行尽早对信用证进行必要的修改。

(6) 按照你方 4 月 10 日来信要求，我方已通知银行将信用证展证至 10 月 31 日。

(7) 由于我方订不到舱位，我方要求将信用证交货期和有效期分别展期到 4 月 10 日和 4 月 25 日。

4. Write a letter with the following particulars.

(1) 信用证展期电报谅已收到。

(2) 请订好舱位，务必在 8 月 15 日前发运。

(3) 已通知开证行展延装船期和有效期分别至 8 月 15 日和 8 月 30 日。

(4) 如用户对货满意，可望大量续订。

Case Practice

以本章的导入案例为背景，以业务员身份向新加坡华益商行去函，时间为 6 月 21 日。要求对方修改信用证的条款，将对方信用证金额增加 460 美元。

Chapter 7 Packing

包　装

案例导入 Case-lead-in

内地某出口公司 A 与中国香港公司 B 成交自行车 1 000 台，由 A 缮制合同一式两份，其中包装条款规定为 Packed in wooden case(木箱装)。将此合同寄至 B 方，然后由 B 签回。B 签回的合同上于原包装条款后加 C.K.D.字样，但未引起 A 公司注意。此后，B 公司按合同开证、A 公司凭信用证规定制单结汇完毕。货到目的港。B 发现系整台自行车箱装，由于自行车整台进口需多交纳 20%进口税，因此拒收货物并要求退还货款。

卖方此时才意识到 C.K.D. 是指 COMPLETELY KNOCKED DOWN(完全拆散)，只好认赔。

评析：1. 卖方忽略 C.K.D.，造成实际装载与合同不符，有不可推卸的责任。2. 卖方虽然已经结汇，但买方仍有拒收货物的权利。

Section One　Forms of Packing 包装的形式

In this task, we discuss the functions of cargo packaging, three forms of packing，some basic packaging clauses related to international trade and the techniques to write a packing letter.

Packing is of great importance in foreign trade. It may be appropriately said that packing is to goods as what clothing is to man. Except from bulk cargo and nude cargo, most cargos need to be packed in a proper way. Adequate packing prevents the goods from being damaged during transit, and a well packaged cargo facilitates handling and transportation. Packing also conveys substantial information to customers.

According to the function of packing, it can be divided into three forms: transport packing, sales packing and neutral packing.

Transport packing is also called large packing or outer packing, i.e. packing for transportation. There are many packing containers used in international market, such as carton, sack, wooden case, crate, corrugated carton, skeleton case, wooden drum, iron drum, plastic cask, gunny bag, cloth bag, paper bag, plastic bag, bundle, bale, box, can/tin, carboy, pallet and container, etc. On the outer packing, you can always find the shipping mark, indicative mark and warning mark as well as weight, measurement and place of origin.

Sales packing is also called small packing, inner packing or immediate packing, on which you can always find product code. Sales packing protects cargoes, reduces losses, aids transport, reduces cost facilitates stowage and distribution and promotes sales.

Neutral packing is the one that makes no mention at all of the name of the country producing the goods and the name of the manufacturer on the commodity and on the outer and inner packages. To make neutral packing is in order to break through trade barriers and non-trade barriers of some import countries and to meet the special needs of cross-boarder transaction.

The types of neutral packing can be divided into:

1. Neutral Packing without Brand Name 无牌中性包装

Packing without the name of origin or manufacturer, nor brand name or trade mark.

2. Neutral Packing with a Designated Brand 定牌中性包装

Packing with trade mark or brand name, but without the name of origin, nor the name of export manufacturer.

Notes

1. 运输包装,习惯上称外包装和大包装。运输包装不仅要起到防止货物运输途中受损的作用，同时，也应具备方便装卸，储存和防盗的功能。

2. 销售包装，习惯上称小包装或内包装。销售包装形式多样，用料各异，既要便于携带和使用，又要美观新颖，达到促销的目的。

3. 中性包装，它是在商品包装上既不注明生产国别、地名和厂名，也不注明原有商标和牌号的包装。中性包装分无牌中性包装和定牌中性包装。其目的是为了打破进口国所实施的关税与非关税壁垒或为了满足买方的特殊需求而采取的措施。

4. 在国际贸易中，往往因为包装材料、包装方式、包装规格、包装的文字说明和包装费用的负担引起纷争、索赔，甚至取消合同。按照一些国家的法律解释，如果一方违反了所约定的包装条件，另一方有权提出索赔，甚至可以拒收货物。包装条件是国际货物买卖合同中的重要交易条件。所以在函电写作时，对包装条款、唛头的规定要明确具体、语言表述要清晰准确。例如，运往不同国家的货物对包装上的文字说明、运输唛头的内容和语种会有特殊的要求。在磋商过程中一定要作具体的规定。

The packing clause is an important one in a contract in international trade. The exporter shall make delivery in exact accordance with the requests of packaging set forth in it. Here we take import of clothing as an example.

1. General Packing Requirements

基本包装要求

Seppa has two ways of packing goods, in cartons and hanging. What type of packing is required will be stated in the order document.

Seppa 采用两种包装方式，箱装与挂装。包装方式会在订单文件中注明。

We accept only packing according to these instructions. If any exceptions all the costs will be charged from the supplier. The charge is € 0.35 per piece.

我们只接受符合要求的包装。如有不符，供应商将承担 0.35 欧元/件的额外费用。

1) Sorting Units

包装单位

All Seppa goods shall be packed in sorting units, assortments and solid size and colour. One order can either contain only one type of sorting units (either ASS or SSC) or both types. Information regarding the sorting units will be stated in the order document.

Seppa 公司的所有货品都可以进行分类包装，其中包括配比包装以及单色单码包装。一个订单可以只存在一种分类包装形式(配比包装或单色单码包装)，也可以同时包含以上两种分类包装形式。请在订单文件中查找相对应的分类包装信息。

If the order contains both types of sorting units the packing sequence must be:

如果一个订单同时包含两种分类包装单位，包装的顺序必须依次为：

(1) Assortment (ASS = Stores).

先进行配比的包装。

(2) Solid size and colour (SSC = Warehouse).

在配比包装完毕的前提下，再进行单色单码的包装。

Both types of sorting units shall be shipped from the exporting country at the same time, if nothing else is agreed.

同一订单下的两种分类包装方式必须同时从出口国出运，除非有特殊申明情况。

SKU (Stock keeping unit)

储存单位

A unique number identifying the lowest level of an article, i.e. one article, one colour and one size.

货品最小单位的唯一标识代码，也就是一件商品只能对应一种颜色的一种尺码。

Assortment (ASS = Stores)

配比包装

A sorting unit which contains a mixture of SKU's from the same article.

包含不同颜色或尺码的分类包装。

Solid size and colour (SSC = Warehouse)

单色单码包装

A sorting unit which contains one or more pieces of the same SKU.

包含一件或几件相同颜色和尺码的分类包装。

2) Material Requirements

包装材料要求

Seppa only accepts packaging materials that are recyclable and environmental friendly.

Seppa 公司只接受可再生型及环保型的包装材料。

Plastic Bags (polybags)

塑料袋(聚乙烯制塑料袋)

Sorting units shall be packed in plastic bags. Boxes shall be avoided, should only be used when necessary to protect the contents.

每个分类包装单位需装在塑料袋中。尽可能避免使用盒子，除非货品需要以此类方式加以保护。

Plastic Quality

塑料质量

Plastic bags shall be made of polyethylene, low density (PE-LD).

塑料袋必须为低密度聚乙烯材质(PE-LD)。

All plastic material shall be marked according to DIN 6120, due to recycling. See symbol.

所有塑料制品必须按 DIN 6120 标准进行环保标记。见图例。

Plastic Thickness

塑料厚度

ASS = Stores: not exceed 40 micron.

配比：不超过 40 微米。

SSC = Warehouse: not exceed 25 micron.

单色单码：不超过 25 微米。

For hanging garments the plastic thickness should be 40 micron for all types of sorting units.

挂装：40 微米。

Corrugated Cardboard

瓦楞纸板

Export cartons shall be made of recyclable corrugated cardboard. The cartons shall be of a quality that ensures that the products are in good order and condition when they arrive at Seppa DC.

出口货品的纸板箱需为可再生型的瓦楞纸板箱。纸箱质量必须能够保证货物在运送至 Seppa 的货物分拨中心时完好无损。

Staples, strings or bands are not allowed on export cartons.

纸箱上不允许使用任何钉子、绳子、打包带(除运至仓库的天地箱)。

3) Packing Requirements

包装要求

All goods should be packed in a proper way to avoid any damages during transportation.

所有货品必须采取恰当的方式进行包装，以避免运输途中的任何可能的损害。

Packing in Plastic Bags

塑料袋包装

Size of plastic bag shall match the size of the sorting unit.

塑料袋的尺寸应按照分类包装单位的大小来调节。

Seal plastic bags around the goods, leaving no empty space.

塑料袋要封牢，袋内不可有剩余空间。

If goods need to be folded to fit Seppa export cartons they have to be folded in a proper way to avoid unnecessary creases.

如果货品必须通过折叠的方式来满足 Seppa 出口的纸箱的尺寸要求，必须以恰当的方式进行折叠以避免任何不必要的折痕及损坏。

Packing in Export Cartons

纸箱包装

Avoid empty space in export cartons.

不要在纸箱内留有空隙。

Do not exceed the maximum size on export cartons. Size limitations are mentioned below.

出口货品的纸箱尺寸不得超过规定的最大尺寸。详细尺寸要求见下。

Only sorting units with same sorting unit number are allowed in the same export carton.

同一纸箱中只允许装入同一种类同一号码的分类包装单位。

Seppa accepts only packing according to these instructions. If any exceptions all the costs will be charged from the Supplier. The charge is € 0.35 /piece.

Seppa 只接受符合要求的包装方式。如有不符，供应商将承担 0.35 欧元/件的额外费用。

2. Packing of Assortment in Export Cartons

配比的纸箱包装

Assortment (ASS = Stores) is a sorting unit which contains a mixture of SKU's from the same article.

包含不同颜色和尺码的分类包装。

The items should be sorted according to the packing list stated in the order document. Within each assortment, items shall be sorted color by color. Within one color, items shall be sorted size by size starting with the smallest size.

货品必须依照订单文件中显示的装箱单进行分类包装。在每一个配比包装内，货品必须先按照不同的颜色进行排列，而在同一个颜色中又必须按照尺寸从小到大的顺序来排列。

The sorted items are put into a plastic bag (polybag) together with a paper label, see below.

每一个分类包装单位内的货品被统一放置在一个塑料袋中，并附上一张纸质标签，如下所示。

The plastic bag shall be sealed in a way that prevents items from moving or unfolding, leaving no empty space within the plastic bag.

塑料袋的封口方式必须能保证放置袋内的货品不会移动或是(折叠状的货品)展开，袋内不可有剩余空间。

No single item should be packed individually in a plastic bag.

在配比包装情况下，不可出现一件货品单独一个塑料袋的情况。

3. Quantity Deviation

溢短装

Seppa accepts quantity deviations which are less than 5% per color. If the quantity per color varies more than 5%, supplier must contact Seppa for approval.

Seppa 只接受单个订单下单个颜色 5%范围以内的溢短装。若超出此范围，则必须通知 Seppa 或相关业务员并得到确认后方可出货。

Below instructions should be followed when there is an excess or shortage quantity in an order.

当订单出现溢短装时，需依照以下要求操作。

Orders with Assortment sorting units only (ASS = Stores).
只有配比包装(ASS = 直接运至商店的货物)。

Excess Quantity
溢装

Ordered quantity is sorted as per packing list in order document.
订单数量部分须依照订单文件上的箱单要求进行包装。

Excess quantity must be sorted as the smallest assortment containing all sizes.
超出订单数量部分，须以配比包装的方式，分配在包数最少的配比下。

Only complete assortments are accepted.
只接受配比完整的包装。

Quantity Shortage
短装

Shortage quantity shall be balanced by reducing the number of the smallest assortments containing all sizes.
少于订单数量部分，须以配比包装的方式，均衡地短装在包数最少的配比下。

Only complete assortments are accepted.
只接受完整的包装。

Orders with Solid Size and Color sorting units only (SSC = Warehouse).
只有单色单码的纸箱包装订单(SSC=仓库储存货物)。

Only complete sorting units are accepted.
只接受完整的包装。

Orders with both Assortments (ASS = Stores) and Solid Size and Color (SSC = Warehouse) sorting units.
既有 ASS 又有 SSC 的订单。

All excess /short deliveries must be balanced on the Solid Size and Color (SSC = Warehouse) part.
所有的溢短装只可均衡地配置在单色单码包装下。

Only complete sorting units are accepted.
只接受完整的包装。

An importer shall make the exporter understand his requirements for inner packing or outer packing so as to avoid the subsequent disputes, vice versa, such business letters should mention the following particulars unless both sides have reached a consensus on it before.

(1) What the packing container is.

(2) What the marking on export package looks like.

(3) What kind of directions or warnings regarding manner of handling, loading, lifting, etc . in used.

(4) Who will be responsible for faulty packing, if any.

As to reply to a packing letter:

(1) Express receipt of packing letter.

(2) Notify whether or not do as requested.

(3) If agree with customer's request, confirm details of packing; if there's disagreement, state convincing reasons.

(4) Express hope for early reply.

Section Two Marking of Goods
包装的标志

Packing must be strikingly marked. Conventionally, outer packing marks mainly include transport marks, directive marks and warning marks.

Transport marks consist of consignor's or consignee's code name;发货人或收货人的代号名称

number of the contract or the L/C; 合同号码或信用证号码

the port of destination; 目的港

numbers of the packed goods;(件号、序号)

and sometimes weight and dimensions, all of which can greatly facilitate identification and transportation. 这样易于识别货物，方便运输。

Directive marks

Directive marks are eye-catching figures and concise instructions concerning manner of proper handling, storing, loading and unloading, such as THIS SIDE UP, HANDLE WITH CARE.

指示性标志是针对一些易碎、易损、易变质的商品用醒目的图形和简单的文字提醒有关人员在装卸、搬运和存储时应注意的事项。

Examples of Directive/Indicative Mark(指示性标志)

handle with care

this way up

keep dry

keep away from heat

prevent freeze

use no hook

open here

fragile

Warning marks

Warning marks are obvious symbols or words to warn people against the hidden danger of inflammables, explosives and poisonous products, e.g. ACID—WITH CARE, EXPLOSIVE.

警告性标志是对一些易燃、易爆、有毒等危险品在其包装上清楚而明显地刷制的标志，以示警告。

Examples of Warning Mark(警告性标志):

poisonous

corrosive

radioactive

inflammable

explosive

Seppälä

IFSS　　　　Packing instructions

9.5 Summary – packing and labelling of export cartons

<table>
<tr><th rowspan="2">Type of sorting unit</th><th colspan="2">Assortments (ASS=Stores) blue or green tape</th><th rowspan="2">Solid Size & Colour (SSC=Warehouse) red tae</th></tr>
<tr><th>Large ASS:
Volume > 12 dm³ = 12 litres = 0.012m³</th><th>Small ASS:
Volume < 12 dm³ = 12 litres = 0.012m³</th></tr>
<tr><td>Poly bag material</td><td colspan="2">40 micron</td><td>25 micron</td></tr>
<tr><td>No of sorting units per export carton</td><td>Only 1!</td><td>As many as possible</td><td>As many as possible</td></tr>
<tr><td>Recommended export carton size</td><td>Adjusted to sorting unitsize</td><td>Adjusted to contents</td><td>57 x 34 x 30 cm /
22" x 13" x 12"
Adjusted to contents</td></tr>
<tr><td>Max export carton size</td><td>77 x 57 x 40 cm /
30" x22" x16"</td><td>77 x 57 x 40 cm /
30 x22" x16"</td><td>57 x 34 x 30 cm /
22" x 13" x 12"</td></tr>
<tr><td>Min export carton size</td><td>Adjusted to sorting unit size</td><td>40 x 30 x 10 cm /
16" x 12" x 4"</td><td>40 x 30 x 10 cm /
16" x 12" x 4</td></tr>
<tr><td>Max export carton weight</td><td>15 kg = 33 lbs</td><td>15 kg = 33 lbs</td><td>15 kg = 33 lbs</td></tr>
<tr><td>Export carton with contents</td><td>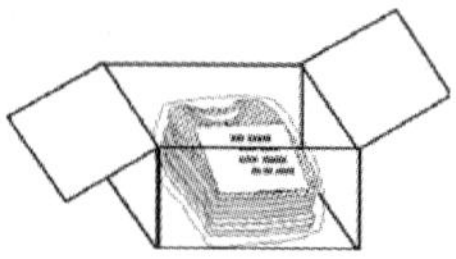</td><td>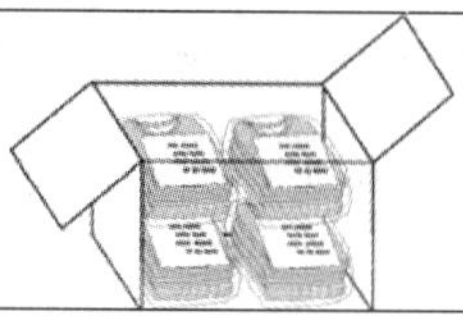</td><td>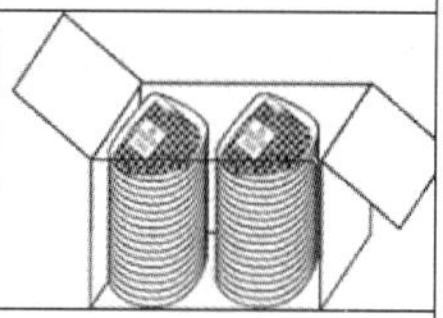</td></tr>
<tr><td>Label contents - sorting unit</td><td colspan="2">Paper label inside plastic bag. Example:
<table>
<tr><td>Company</td><td>Seppälä Oy</td></tr>
<tr><td>Order number</td><td></td></tr>
<tr><td>Assortment</td><td>1</td></tr>
<tr><td>Number of assortments</td><td>80</td></tr>
<tr><td>Assortment description</td><td>White S/1 M/2 L/2 XL/1</td></tr>
</table></td><td>No label needed.
Price tag must be visible.</td></tr>
<tr><td>Label contents – export cartons</td><td colspan="2">Sticker label on outside of carton. Example:
<table>
<tr><td>Company</td><td>Seppälä Oy</td></tr>
<tr><td>Address</td><td>Tikkurilantie 146 , 01530
Vantaa , Finland</td></tr>
<tr><td>Order number</td><td>3023175</td></tr>
<tr><td>Assortment number</td><td>3</td></tr>
<tr><td>Number of sorting units in this carton</td><td>1</td></tr>
<tr><td>Export carton sequence number / Total number of export cartons</td><td>101 / 180</td></tr>
<tr><td>Assortment description
Colour / pieces and size</td><td>Black S / 2 M / 4 L / 3 XL / 1</td></tr>
</table></td><td>See label contents - Warehouse</td></tr>
<tr><td>General</td><td colspan="3">• Only sorting units with same type of sorting unit number are allowed in the same export carton.
• Avoid empty space in export cartons. Transport costs are based on volume.</td></tr>
</table>

Section Three Cases in Detail
具体案例分析

(一) 经典案例解析

Dear Sirs,

Re: Our Order No. 226

Further to our telephone conversation on 22 regarding the packing of the above order for Smart Choice, we would like to propose the following.

1. Our clients would like to have the products packed in window packing for inner packing so that the products can be seen directly. They believe it will help to promote the sales.

2. They prefer wooden cases to cartons for outer packing. They fear that cartons are not strong enough for ocean transportation. They might be easily damaged through rough handling. They are more susceptible to pilferage and damage by moisture.

3. Please indicate HANDLE WITH CARE and mark our initials SJP in triangle, under which the port of destination and our Order No. should be stenciled on the outer packing.

Please let us know if you can do as requested.

Yours faithfully,

Notes

1. Further to our telephone conversation on 22 regarding the packing of the above order for Smart Choice, we would like to propose the following.

就我们 22 日商谈的关于“明智选择”产品的订单包装问题，我们想提出以下几点意见。

pack *v.* 包装

注意 packing，package 与 packaging 的区别。

例如：买卖合同的内容除依照本法第十二条的规定以外，还可以包括包装方式、检验标准和方法、结算方式、合同使用的文字及其效力等条款。

Besides those specified in Article 12 of this Law, a sales contract may also contain such clauses as manner of packing, inspection standards and method of settlement and clearance, and the language adopted in the contract and its authenticity.

原文中的“包装方式”，不能译成 package manner，而应译为 manner of packing。这两个意思相近的词，中译英时应特别注意。

package 意为 parcel of things, packed together 即“包、包裹”。从词性出发，package 是名词，所以就是指实实在在的包裹。例如:

一捆信件，a package of letters

20 支装的一包香烟，a package of 20 cigarettes

packing (不可数名词)意为 process of packing (goods)，包装货物的过程，打包，打行李等意。从词性来看，packing 是动名词，它包含有动作的成分，就是 the way of packing，或者 how to pack，所以实意是打包装。从回复客人的邮件看，当然是要告诉客人两种不同的打包方式，而不是两个不同的包裹，显而易见要用 packing。

e.g. packing machinery 意思是用于包装的机械，如在火车站给行李打包用的打包机。

package machinery 是用于制造包装材料的机械，如生产瓦楞纸盒的机械。

Carefully remove the computer from its foam packing.

packaging 是可销售产品的包装材料，目的是保护产品或鼓励人们购买，多为纸质的(尤其是美国英语中)，例如：

It's the same old stuff in better packaging.这个是老东西换上新包装而已。

2. Our clients would like to have the products packed in window packing for inner packing so that the products can be seen directly. They believe it will help to promote the sales.

我们的客户希望商品内包装是橱窗包装，以便于商品能直接被看见。他们相信这有助于推销商品。

have sth. packed in 将商品包装在……

sth. be packed in

3. They prefer wooden cases to cartons for outer packing.

他们偏好用木箱而非纸板箱做外包装。

prefer 偏好

prefer A to B 宁愿要 A 不要 B

prefer doing A to doing B

prefer to do A rather than do B

prefer that

prefer not to do something

4. Please indicate HANDLE WITH CARE and mark our initials SJP in triangle, under which the port of destination and our Order No. should be stenciled on the outer packing.

请标明"小心轻放"字样，并且在外包装上刷上一三角形，内刷我公司首字母 SJP，其下刷目的港及我方订单号。

mark *v.* 刷唛

stencil *v.* 印刷

(二) 一般案例表述

1. Labels and Gift Box Revise and Confirmation

Dear Paola,

Attached is the rating label for your translation. Thank you.

Best regards,

Water

Hi water,

Check the Italian translation for the rating label. Please , insert the model code on the rating label of 7', too.

Looking forward to receive the rating label revised before you proceed to printing it.

Rgds,

Ms. Paola Esposito

Dear Paola,

Thank you. I will send back for your confirmation tomorrow morning.

Good night.

Best regards,

Water

Hi Water,

Find the gift box art work attached. You can download the print file from this link:

http://www.duem.it/clienti/pdvd950tv.zip

Please, insert the barcode and send me the full gift box for my last approval.

My B. Rgds,

Ms. Paola Esposito

Dear Paola,

Thank you. Well received the gift box for 9' and 7' (DPN brand and in black color). We will revise as per your request.

But now about the one in Silver color? I think you got it now, I sent you here again.

I would like to mention as below.

(1) 7', the LOGO "DVD", I wish to revise it with your standard LOGO. I will send you the silk printing for confirmation soon.

(2) 9'model, DPN logo, the position you placed is on the speaker net, that position cannot allow to be real silk printing, as the sample you got on hand. If you are sure it is just for the gift box design, it would be OK.

Please let me know. I don't need to revise it, so don't worry!

Please find the attached file for 7' and 9' rating label. We re-made it, could you check it and advice?

And please confirm me the SPEC sheet as attached. We have to confirm the functions with you. As I have to arrange for production as per that file.

By the way, I got your L/C advice today from our bank. Thank you.

Looking forward to your reply soon.

Best regards,

Water

Hi Water,

Please, read my BLUE reply below and revise the rating label attached. Find the shipping mark attached!

Rgds,

Ms. Paola Esposito

Dear Paola,

Thank you for your kind reply. I would like to revert as below.

I already got the SPEC confirmation. But one question please, about the serial number.

As there are two different colors, I have to instruct our factory to make it clear; I would like to fix the serial number like this,

(1) DPM PDVD650, in black color, it is beginning from SH65000 to SH65505.

(2) LX PDVD650, in silver color, it is beginning from SH65506 to SH66006.

Please let me know it is OK or not.

Regarding the shipping mark, as it includes main mark and side mark, please find the attached file for my understanding, is it OK?

Regarding the revise artwork, I would send back for your confirmation soon.

Awaiting your comments.

Best regards,

Water

Hi Water,

Check my BLUE reply.

Rgds,

Ms. Paola Esposito

Dear Paola,

Here is the rating label for 7' and 9'. Please advise.

Best regards,

Water

Hi Water,

They are OK, you can proceed to printing. Thanks for your kind cooperation.

B. Rgds,

Ms. Paola Esposito

Dear Paola,

Well understand the rating labels are confirmed.

Thank you.

Best regards,

Water

Dear Paola,

This is Water, I would like to enclose the gift box for your reference. Revised already. Please kindly confirm it back to me.

Thank you.

Best regards,

Water

Hi Water,

It's Ok, proceed with all gift boxes.

Rgds,

Ms. Paola Esposito

2. DVD Player Artwork Design Revise and Confirmation

Dear Water,

Is it possible to use these pictures (with some small changes) for our order?

Best regards,

Dmitry Umrikhin

Dear Dmitry,

Thank you for the gift box design. It looks cool.

We could do as per your request. But can you send us the photo of the model? If we use the photo from the image you sent to me, it is not good for mass production. Because of its low quality.

Or could we use the similar photo to replace? Also you can send me the photos you need for our reference.

And if you got the AI or CDR format about the gift box, that would be fine. And we just need to make some small changes.

Awaiting your comments.

Best regards,

Water

Dear Water,

Sorry, we don't have AI or CDR format. That was the reason why I ask you to do, if a jpg picture is suitable.

Yes, you can use your model's picture. I hope, the model will be nice.

Best regards,

Dmitry Umrikhin

Dear Dmitry,

Thank you for you replies.

OK, we will source some photos for background of the gift box.

By the way, can you send me the word file of Russian wordings? It can help us to finish the design and can save time I think.

Awaiting for your reply.

Best regards,

Water

Dear Dmitry,

Please refer to the attachment for the user manual of small size 10201.

Best regards,

Water

Dear Dmitry,

Please refer to the attachments for

1．BRAND 10201 front and rear panel silk printing.

2．BRAND 10202 front and rear panel silk printing.

Please reply with you comments.

Best regards,

Water

Dear Dmitry,

How are you doing?

1．Have you checked the SPEC sheet? Please kindly advise back with your comments.

2．How about the artworks?

Please feel free to reply.

Best regards,

Water

Dear Water,

Thank you very much for your kind support!

The SPEC sheet and the artworks will be checked today.

Best regards,

Dmitry Umrikhin

Dear Dmitry,

Please refer to the attachment for 10201/02 RC silk printing. Please kindly confirm back soon.

And about the gift box design, can you send me the Russian language translation in word format?

As per your draft, the functions are as attached. But the model 10201/02, no optical output, please offer me the translation properly.

Awaiting your reply soon.

Best regards,

Water

Dear water,

Please arrange following amendments to the player's panel.

10201 front panel:

Please add DIVX, MP3, JPEG signs.

Please make BRAND logo 2 times bigger.

Could you please add a smile picture (as shown attached)?

10202 front panel:

Please add a MPEG4 sign.

Please add POWER inscription near the POWER button.

Best regards,

Dmitry Umrikhin

Dear Dmitry,

Please refer to the attachment for the revised panel silk printing. And kindly confirm soon.

Thank you.

Best regards,

Water

Dear Water,

Please find attached the confirmed panels for 10201 and 10202.

Best regards,

Dmitry Umrikhin

Dear Dmitry,

Thank you for your kind confirmation. Well received the files.

Best regards,

Water

Notes

包装设计涉及的内容一般较多，可能出现反复修改的情况，也极容易出错。在制作和确认的过程中要特别细致，领会客户的意思，制作出客户满意的设计。在一定的时间内，完成制作和确认，因为这将直接影响生产部分制订生产计划表。通常生产部门除了需要生产物料备齐之外，还需要收到一整套确认的包装设计才能安排生产。

资料链接 Material—link

1. Standard Model

Model 1:Negotiating Terms of Packing and Stipulated Marks 磋商包装条款、指定唛头

Gentlemen,

We have carefully studied your offer dated November 21 together with the samples. We find both quality and prices satisfactory and are pleased to give you an order on the understanding that the packing of the ordered goods can meet our requirements.

The shirts should be packed with polythene wrappers for each,10 dozen to one cardboard carton with stenciled shipping marks as follows:

K.H.C

HAMBURG

NOS. 1-100

As you probably understand that your shirts will be in competition with many others in our market. An eye-catching wrapping ready for window display will certainly help us push the sales.

We hope that you will accommodate us in this respect and send us your Sales Confirmation in duplicate.

Please let us know whether you can arrange this for us and, if so, on what terms.

Yours faithfully,

Model 2: Asking for Improving Packing 改善运输包装

Dear Mr Li,

We have received your letter of March 10 with pleasure. Totally speaking, your suggestion about packing is very good. But we believe wooden case is not necessary because it's too heavy.

We believe waterproof carton is a better choice because cartons are comparatively light and compact. So you can use cartons to instead. Each carton contains 10 bags.

We hope you will accept our opinion and appreciate your cooperation.

Yours faithfully,

Model 3 : Amending Terms of Packing 修改包装条款

Dear Daniel,

We acknowledge with thanks receipt of your letter of April 16 enclosing Contract No. 07ST0406 in duplicate but wish to draw your attention to the fact that the packing clause in it is not clear enough. The relative clause reads as follows: wooden cases, strong enough for long-distance transportation. In order to avoid subsequent trouble, please see to the ordered goods will be packed with cartons covered with waterproof cloth, each weighing 1 000Lbs—measurement 36″ ×36″ ×24″ .

This will apply to all shipments unless otherwise instructed.

Please let us know whether these specifications can be satisfied by you and whether they will lead to an increase in your prices.

We hope to receive your favorable news soon.

Best Regards,

2. *Writing Guide*

(1) 提及收到对方来函(报价、货物或者订单)，并说明写信的目的——包装要求、通知装运唛头或要求修改包装条款。

(2) 具体说明包装条件、包装唛头或要求修改的条款，如果有必要，向对方说明理由，包装条款、唛头的规定要明确具体，语言表述要清晰准确。

(3) 要求对方尽快给予答复。

Section Four　Selected Sentences
精选句型表达

1. You will know that our packing has been greatly improved and we are sure that they will meet with the satisfaction of the clients.

你将知道我们的包装已经改良，我们相信它们可以让客户满意。

2. The dimension of the cases is 17cm high, 30cm wide and 50cm long with a volume of about 0.026 cubic meter. The gross weight is 23.5kg.

箱子尺寸为高 17 厘米、宽 30 厘米、长 50 厘米，体积约 0.026 立方米，毛重 23.5 公斤。

3. They save shipping space and facilitate the storage and distribution of the goods. 他们节

省运输空间，便于储存和货物分发。

4. In addition to the gross, net and tare weights, the wording " Made in the People's Republic of China " is also stenciled on the package.除毛重、净重和皮重外，"中华人民共和国制造"也要在包装上加上钢印。

5. We have made a number of improvements in packaging and presentation. Please set your mind at ease.

我们已经在包装和介绍上做了一些改进，请提出宝贵意见。

6. Our containers are in complete conformity to the specification laid down by the International Standardization Organization.

我们的集装箱与国际标准化组织规定的规格完全相符。

7. We refer carton packing to wooden case packing.

我们希望用纸箱包装，而不是木箱包装。

8. Our cartons for canned food are not only seaworthy , but also strong enough to protect the goods from damage.

我们罐装食品用的纸箱不仅适合海运，而且坚固，足以防止货物受损。

9. Cartons are not likely to be mixed with wooden cases while in transport or storage, so that the rate of breakage is lower than that of wooden cases.

纸箱在运输和储存时不能和木箱混在一起，这样破损率比与木箱在一起要低。

10. Shirts packed in such cartons are not so susceptible to damage by moisture as those packed in wooden cases.

装衬衫的这种纸箱没有木箱包装的那么易于受潮破损。

11. We want the machine to be packed each in wooden case supported with soft materials to ensure that the machines thus packed will not shift inside the cases.

我们希望机器能用衬有软材料的木箱包装来保证机器免于移位。

12. Please see to it that each carton is properly sealed, with a fireproof lining inside.

请确认每箱都用防火内衬材料来适当地密封。

13. We need these goods to be packed in special packing materials even though they may cost us more.

我们需要用特殊的材料包装货物，尽管它们成本更高。

14. We would like to have the screws packed in double gunny bags.

我们希望用麻袋包装螺丝。

15. In order to avoid any possible damage in transit, we would ask you to pack the goods in strong but small wooden cases.

为了避免运输中任何可能的受损，我们要求你们用坚固而小巧的木箱包装货物。

16. We refer special cartons of 30cm×60cm with two or three dozen to each carton because it's convenient and easy to handle.

我们要求用 30cm×60cm 的特别纸箱，每箱两打或三打，因为这样便于搬运。

17. You'd better pack them in cartons of 10kg each instead of wooden cases of 6kg.

你们最好用每 10 公斤一箱的纸箱取代每 6 公斤一箱的木箱来包装。

18．As you know , oil painting is a highly inflammable commodity , and extra precautions are necessary. We should like you to have the goods packed in strong metal cartons, each containing 40 tins.

您知道，油画是一种易燃商品，很有必要特别谨慎。我们要求您用坚固的金属箱包装，每箱装 40 幅。

19．Is your normal packing still ten dozen per carton?

你们的正常包装仍是每箱 10 打吗？

20．We hope that the beer is packed six bottles in a box which should be beautiful, durable and easy to carry.

我们希望啤酒 6 瓶一箱，这样会美观、耐用并易于搬运。

21．The packing must be able to withstand rough handling.

包装必须经受得住野蛮搬运。

22．When packing, please take into account that the boxes must be able to withstand rough handing and transport over very bad roads.

包装时请考虑到盒子必须经受得住野蛮搬运以及崎岖道路的运输。

23．Please give special attention to the packing, or the good could be damaged in transit.

请特别注意包装，否则货物在运输过程中会被损坏。

24．Greater care must be given to packing, as any damage in transit would cause us heavy losses.

请倍加关注包装，因为运输中任何的损坏将会导致我们严重损失。

25．Please ship the goods in strong packing to ensure good condition on arrival.

请用坚固的包装运输以确保安全抵达。

26．The packing must be in line with local market preference.

包装必须与当地市场偏好相吻合。

27．A large number of the bed spreads we ordered from you last year were found soiled when they reached us. I hope you will take necessary precautions in packing this consignment.

去年向你方订购的大量床垫到达我们时被发现玷污，我希望你们要特别注意包装。

28．Your packing must be seaworthy and can stand rough handling during transit.

你们的包装必须适合海运且在运输途中经得起野蛮搬运。

29．We hope that the goods should be packed in a manner which ensures their safe arrival at the destination and facilitates their handling in transit.

我们希望这批货物包装的风格能确保货物安全抵达目的地且在运输中便于搬运。

30．The wooden cases used to pack the goods should be securely strapped.

包装货物用的木箱要用包装带加固。

31．The packages should be marked with the same numbers as given on the order sheet.

包装应由订单上列明的相同数字标记。

32. As regards markings, please note that the port of destination, Shanghai, should be clearly stenciled on each case with the case number for easy identification.

对于标记，请注意目的地——上海，每箱上用比较明显的数字加盖钢印。

33．As these machines are precision instruments which cannot stand rough handling, the wording “Handle with Care” should be also marked on each case.

由于这些机器是精密仪器，经不起野蛮搬运，故每箱应注明“小心轻放”字样。

34．Please see that the cases are marked “Fragile” or “Handle with Care”.

请注意木箱上标明“易碎品”或“小心轻放”。

35．Port of destination, package number, gross and net weights, measurement and shipping mark shall be stenciled conspicuously on each package.

每箱上应显著地标明目的地、包装号、毛净重、尺寸和唛头。

36．For dangerous and poisonous cargo, the natural and the generally adopted symbol shall be marked conspicuously on each package.

对于危险和有毒货物，每箱上应显著地标明约定俗成的符号。

37．Please mark the packages with the same lot numbers as given on the order sheet in order to avoid being mixed up.

请根据订单对包装做同批标记以免混淆。

38．Every package shall be marked “CCD” in diamond and the package number.

每个包装上应标明菱形的“CCD”和箱号。

39．Please mark the bales with your company’s initials in a diamond.

请用贵司第一个字母以菱形方式标记货物。

40．Correct and distinct marking for the outside containers is absolutely necessary.

正确而清晰的外箱标记是绝对有必要的。

41．Our packing is strong enough to withstand bumping and rough handling under normal conditions.

我们的包装足够坚固，正常情况下经得起碰撞和野蛮搬运。

42．The cases used for packing our transistor radios are light but strong.

我们电子收音机包装用的木箱轻巧坚固。

43．The export cases used to pack the goods are strong enough to protect the instruments.

包装用的出口木箱坚固，足以保护设备。

44．The cartons lined with plastic sheets are waterproof.

内衬塑料袋的纸箱可以防水。

45．We plan to use cardboard boxes with iron straps for reinforcement.

我们计划用铁带加固的硬纸盒。

46．Our strip scissors are packed in boxes of one dozen each, 200 boxes to a wooden case.

我们的磨剪一打一盒，200 盒一木箱。

47．We’ll pack them 10 dozen to one carton, gross weight around 25kg a carton.

我们要将它们打包成 10 打一纸箱，每箱毛重约 25 公斤。

48．Our export fruit knives are packed in boxes of 100 dozen each.

我们的出口水果刀以 100 打为一盒进行包装。

49．The packing of our men’s shirts is each in a polybag, 5 dozen to a carton lined with waterproof paper and bound with two iron straps outside.

我们男式衬衫的包装为每一个聚乙烯袋一件，5 打一纸箱，内衬防水纸，外加两条铁带加固。

50．Our cotton prints are packed in cases lined with draft paper and waterproof paper, each consisting of 30 pieces with 5 colors for on design.

我们的花布

51．The cigars are packed 5 pieces to a small packet, 20 packets to a carton,144 cartons to a cardboard container.

雪茄 5 只一小包，20 包一箱，144 箱一纸板箱。

52．These cartons are well protected against moisture by plastic lining.

这些纸箱内衬塑料布防潮效果很好。

53．All the goods will be packed according to the special way you require.

所有货物根据你方要求的方式包装。

54．As requested, the shirts will be packed in waterproof material.

根据要求，衬衫将用防水材料包装。

55．We plan to use cardboard or plastic cartons for the outer packing.

外包装我们计划用纸板或塑料箱。

56．Your goods will be packed in wooden cases with tin-lining and iron hoops.

你们的货物将用内衬锡纸外加铁箍的木箱包装。

57．The goods we packed in new and sound jute bags, each containing about 200 pounds.

我们将货物装进新而结实的麻袋里，每袋 200 磅。

58．The cartons are well protected against moisture by polythene sheet lining.

纸箱内衬聚乙烯袋，防潮效果很好。

59．If the goods are packed in cartons, any traces of pilferage will be in evidence, therefore the insurance company may be made to pay the necessary compensation for such losses.

如果用纸箱包装，任何偷窃痕迹都很明显，因此保险公司很容易进行赔偿。

60．Such packing has also been accepted by our insurance company for WPA and TPND.

这样的包装保平安险和盗窃和提货不着险已被保险公司接受。

61．The cartons are comparatively light, and therefore easy to handle.

纸箱相对轻便，因此易于搬运。

62．It is our usual way to pack these goods in cartons.

我们通常用纸箱包装这些货物。

63．Cartons are quite fit for ocean transportation, and they are extensively used in our shipments to other continental ports to the entire satisfaction of our clients.

纸箱非常适合海运，它们广泛用于我们其他大陆港口的运输，客人完全满意。

64．Cartons are more convenient to handle in the course of loading and unloading.

纸箱在装卸时便于搬运。

65．We would like to inform you that we used to pack our scissors in wooden cases but after several trial shipments in carton packing, we found our cartons just as seaworthy as wooden cases.

我们想通知你，我们用木箱包装剪刀，但经过几纸箱包装试运后，我们发现我们的纸箱和木箱一样适合海运。

66. Cartons are less expensive, lighter to carry and cost lower freight.

纸箱相对便宜，轻易搬运且运输费用低。

Abstract

通过本章学习，①了解包装函电的作用；②了解包装的基本形式分类；③了解包装标志的基本内容；④掌握包装来往函电写作必须包含的基本内容；⑤掌握包装来往函电写作的基本规律和注意事项；⑥通过熟悉标准模板，掌握磋商包装条件、装船唛头、改善运输包装和修改包装条款等类型函电写作的基本方法；⑦熟练掌握包装函电经典句型的表达。

Useful Words & Expressions

1. skin packing 吸塑包装
2. blister packing 起泡包装
3. neutral packing 中性包装
4. skin packing 吸塑包装
5. hanging packing 挂式包装
6. catch sb.'s eye 引某人注目
7. mark 唛头
8. unlabelled packing 无牌的包装
9. in bulk 散装
10. in loose packing 散装
11. nude packing 裸装
12. bulk pack 整批包装
13. consumer pack 零售包装
14. large packing 大包装
15. inner packing, external packing, end packing 小包装
16. shrunk packaging 压缩包装
17. foam-spray packaging 喷泡沫包装
18. gift-wrap 礼品包装
19. bag, sack 袋
20. jute bag 麻袋
21. polythene bag, plastic bag 塑料袋
22. polythene net 尼龙绳网袋
23. zippered bag 拉链袋
24. case, chest 箱
25. box 盒
26. wooden case 木箱
27. carton 纸箱

28．container 集装箱
29．rate 板条箱
30．fibre board case 纤维板箱
31．packet 小包
32．bale 包
33．bundle 捆
34．tin , can 罐头
35．basket 篮，篓，筐
36．bamboo basket 竹篓
37．bottle 瓶
38．wooden keg 小木桶
39．hogshead 大桶
40．iron drum 铁桶
41．cylinder 铁桶
42．barrel 琵琶桶
43．drum 圆桶
44．waterproof paper 防水纸
45．cellophane 玻璃纸
46．kraft paper 牛皮纸
47．canvas 帆布
48．fibreboard 纤维板
49．nylon strap 尼龙腰子
50．plastic strap 塑料腰子
51．adhesive tape 胶带
52．stuffing material 填料
53．nylon plastic 尼龙丝
54．fermented plastic 泡沫塑料
55．paper scrap 纸屑
56．saw dust 木屑
57．tar paper 沥青纸
58．wax paper 蜡纸
59．slushing compound 润滑油
60．tarpaulin 油布、防水帆布
61．Indicative Mark 指示性标志
1) upward 向上，由下往上
2) This Side Up 此端向上
3) Handle With Care 小心轻放
4) Keep Upright 请勿倒置
5) Use No Hooks 请勿倒挂

6) Not to be tripped 请勿倾倒
7) Keep in a dry place 在干燥处保管
8) Keep in a cool place 在冷处保管
9) Keep away from boilers 远离锅炉
10) Keep away from heat 请勿受热
11) Keep away from cold 请勿受冷
12) Keep Dry 防湿
62. Warning Mark 警告性标志
1) Explosive 爆炸品
2) Fragile 易碎品
3) Inflammable 易燃品
4) Inflammable Gas 易燃气体
5) Inflammable Solid 易燃固体
6) Inflammable Liquid 易燃液体
7) Dangerous When Wet 遇水燃烧品
8) Poison 毒剂
9) Poison Gas 毒气
10) Spontaneously Combustible 自燃物品
11) Organic Peroxide 有机氧化物
12) Oxidizing Agent 氧化剂
13) Radioactive 放射性物品
14) Corrosive 腐蚀性物品

Exercises

1. Fill in each of the blanks with a word from the list below.

on	from	for	to
downward	in	due to	against
within	upward	with	at
up	onto		

(1) As the goods will be checked up ____ the customs, the boxes must be a type which can be easily opened and fastened.

(2) The freight charges from works to Shanghai are totally US$4 ,000 ____ this consignment, excluding container hire, which will be charged ____ your account.

(3) Our titanium baskets are packed ____ boxes of ten each, and forty ____ a wooden case.

(4) Lot number as given in the contract must be marked ____ the plastic woven bags.

(5) The crates are lined ____ waterproof material and the lids are secured by nailing.

(6) The machines must be well protected ____ dampness, moisture, rust and shock.

(7) The bags, should be fairy good in quality and suitable for ocean transportation, ____

which the name of the goods, weight, country of origin.

(8) Every 100 dozen should be packed in a wooden case marked TM and numbered ____ No.1

(9) The best we can do is to ship the whole quantity of 50 tons ____ one lot ____ the contracted time of shipment.

(10) Any damage ____ the packing has never occurred ____ the way of transportation.

2. Answer the questions according to the passage.

(1) What is the function of packing?

(2) What are the kinds of packing according to its function?

(3) How to make a complaint?

(4) How to reply to a reasonable complaint?

3. Put the following sentences into English.

(1) 每批货物我们都会特别小心的。

(2) 此种物品易碎，请以耐用包装来装箱。

(3) 外包装打包还是使用木箱，由买方选择。

(4) 请确保此包装牢固，足以承受粗鲁的搬运。

(5) 我们通常把每件男衬衣装入一个盒子里，半打装一箱，10 打装一个木箱。

(6) 请把每台电视机装一纸板箱，每 4 台装一适合于出口的木箱。

(7) 绿茶 100 克装一听，50 听装一纸箱，2 纸箱装一板条箱。

(8) 我们要求内包装小巧而精美以有助于销售，外包装轻便而坚固以易于搬运。

(9) 敬启者：

感谢你方 8 月 1 日来信，经商榷，我们决定采用内衬防潮纸的纸箱包装，因其轻便，更易于搬运。

请在纸箱上标明毛重、净重及尺码，并请在一个椭圆形(ellipse)内刷上我公司名称缩写，椭圆形下面指明箱号和目的港。因货物易受潮，因此外包装上还应刷上“保持干燥”等警告性标志。

敬请谨遵我方指令，按时装运。

Case Practice

以下面的案例为背景，请以公司业务员的名义撰写一封关于包装的邮件。

我方是××公司，从事家具产品的进口业务。

2011 年 5 月，我方从××竹制家具有限公司购买了一批竹制品家具。由于合同中包装条款不够清晰，我方公司于 5 月 18 日递函就包装问题提出了一些要求。

1. 木箱包装，一套一箱。同时箱子内要求垫有塑料泡沫以免货物受压。

2. 外包装上要刷上本公司的名称缩写，其中包括目的港和订单号。此外，还请用三角形标明“勿压”等指示性用语。

我方已在合同中就上述内容做了注脚，并请拉斯维卡公司及时汇签后退还一份给我方。

Chapter 8 Insurance

保　　险

案例导入 Case-lead-in

安徽芜湖艾莉格斯服饰有限公司是一家大型服装生产公司，产品主要出口到欧洲、北美和澳洲。该公司从事女式针织衫、无袖上衣、女式棉衣、女式休闲裤、儿童服装、马甲、工作服、运动套装和箱包等的生产和设计。

2011 年 7 月 22 日，美国 Edward &Sons Cotton Trading Co.,Ltd.同其签约，决定以 CFR 条件进口 1 000 包棉布，于 2011 年 8 月 25 日致函中方企业，要求其代为投保，下面是其要求投保的信函。

Edward &Sons Cotton Trading Co.,Ltd.
56 Green Street
New York
Wuhu Ailigesi Garments Co.,Ltd.
ANHUI
CHINA

Dear Sirs,

<u>Re: Our Order No. 2005 for 1 000 Bales of Cotton</u>

We wish you to refer to our Order No. 2005 for 1 000 bales of cotton, from which you will see that this order is placed on a CFR basis.

As we desire to have the shipment insured at your end, we would appreciate it if you will arrange to insure the captioned goods on our behalf against All Risks and War Risk for 110% of invoice value, i.e. USD 10 020.00.

We shall of course refund you the premium upon receipt of your debit note or, if you like, you may draw on us at sight for the amount required.

We sincerely hope our request will meet with your approval.

Yours faithfully,
Edward &Sons Cotton Trading Co.,Ltd.
Manager

Section One　Essentials of Business Letters of Insurance 保险商务信函要点

1. What Is Insurance(什么是保险)

Insurance is a form of risk management primarily for the purpose of hedging against the risk of a contingent loss. It is the equitable transfer of the risk of a loss, from one entity to another in exchange for a premium. The company selling the insurance is the insurer, receiving the premium determined by the insurance rate. Thus the insurer's underwriting performance is measured in its combined ratio which is a reflection of the company's overall underwriting profitability. Insurance companies also earn investment profits on "float". "Float" or available reserve is the amount of money, at hand at any given moment that an insurer has collected in insurance premiums but has not been paid out in claims. Insurers start investing insurance premiums as soon as they are collected and continue to earn interest on them until claims are paid out.

2. Why Is Insurance Important (为什么保险重要)

Any kind of insurance is used to help protect consumers when certain things happen. People think it is very important because it protects the insurers' assets. As insurance companies are held responsible for deciphering what coverages each individual needs it is very important to make sure that your valuables are properly insured in the unfortunate event of a storm or otherwise.

For the business of exporting goods overseas, shipping items-no matter if it's by land, air or sea-comes with certain, often uncontrollable risks. It is therefore a good idea to obtain insurance from a certain insurance corporation who can help to protect you and your business from loss due to situations overseas that are out of your control, such as an unexpected political or social uprising or any other catastrophes.

3. Types of Cargo Insurance 货物运输保险的基本分类

Irrespective of transport modes, there will be many risks involved in cargo transportation during transit. Thus, exporters or importers need to cover their goods with insurance companies against different risks.

Cargo transportation insurance can be classified into ocean marine cargo insurance, overland transportation insurance, air transportation cargo insurance and parcel post insurance.

The ocean transportation cargo insurance mainly includes ocean transportation cargo insurance, ocean transportation cargo war insurance, ocean transportation frozen cargo insurance and ocean transportation wood-oil bulk insurance.

The overland transportation insurance chiefly consists of overland transportation cargo insurance, overland transportation cargo war insurance and overland transportation frozen cargo insurance.

The air transportation cargo insurance is make up of air transportation insurance, air transportation all risks and air transportation cargo war risks.

The parcel post insurance refers to parcel post risks, parcel post all risks and parcel post war risks.

4. Patterns of Business Letters of Insurance(保险信函的模式)

Beginning: (1) Refer to the captioned goods under the order or contract specified.

Body: (2) Make a brief introduction about the insurance and the practice in effecting insurance followed on your part.

(3) Show such information as the amount insured, coverage, premium, extra premium and extra risks etc.

Closing: (4) Hope and expectation.

5. Layout of Business Letters of Insurance(保险信函的布局)

(1) Putting personal information of the addresser at the upper left and that of the addressee at the lower left.

(2) Showing the information that the letter asking for insurance by the other party has been received.

(3) Providing the information concerned about insurance in detail.

(4) Expressing the desire to win order from the other party with service of good quality in the end paragraph.

6. Tips to Be Considered in Making Business Letters of Insurance (保险信函写作的注意要点)

(1) It's important to understand the insurance clauses in the contract clearly and precisely.

(2) In case the insurance is effected on our side, such information as subject matter, insurance coverage, insurance amount, insurance premium, insurance rate, the insurer and the insured, etc. of different insurance companies should be taken into account for a better choice of insurance companies.

Section Two Cases in Detail
具体案例分析

(一) 经典案例解析

Asking for Insurance Arrangement
(Letter1)(要求投保)

Dear Sirs,

Re: Our Order No.113, Your Sales Contract No. 90 Covering 400 Cases Pottery.

We wish to refer you to our Order No.113 for 400 cases of pottery, from which you will see that this order was placed on CFR basis.

As we now desire to have the shipment insured at your end, we shall be much pleased if you will kindly arrange to insure the same on our behalf against All Risks for 110% of the invoice value, i.e. USD3 300.

We shall of course refund the premium to you upon receipt of your debit note or, if you like, you may draw on us at sight for the same.

Yours faithfully,

Reply to an Insurance Arrangement (Letter 2)
(对要求投保的回复)

Dear Sirs,

Re: Your Order No. 113, Our Sales Contract No. 90 Covering 400 Cases Pottery.

We thank you for your letter of June 30, requesting us to effect insurance on the captioned shipment for your account.

We are pleased to confirm having covered the above shipment with the People's Insurance Company of China against All Risks for USD3 300. The policy will be sent to you in a day or two together with our debit note for the premium.

For your information, this parcel will be shipped on s/s "Fengqing", sailing on or about the 10th next month.

Yours faithfully,

Notes

1. place order
2. on…basis 以……为基础
3. have sth. insured against…将……投保……险
4. at your end 由你方
5. at sight 即期
6. Kindly *adv.* 劳驾，请

例句：Kindly shut the door. 劳驾把门关上。

7. on one's behalf 代表某人，还可以说成"on the behalf of"
8. refund 退还
9. upon receipt of 收到
10. debit note 借记通知单
11. draw on sb. 向……开立(汇票等)
12. effect insurance on the goods 对商品投保
13. captioned 标题项下的
14. for one's account 由谁负担费用
15. cover…(货物)with…(保险公司)against…(险别)
16. s/s 是 steamed ship 的缩写
17. Letter 1 是买方在 CFR 条件下要求卖方对标题项下的货物进行投保的信函表达。一般说来，国际贸易中最常见的 3 种术语是 FOB、CFR 和 CIF。

FOB(Free on Board)

在我国，习惯把 FOB 称作"离岸价"，因其不准确性而渐受淘汰。采用这一价格术语是指卖方在合同

规定的装运港把货物装到买方指派的船上，并负责承担货物在装运港越过船舷前的一切费用和风险。关于FOB的适用范畴，按2000年《通则》的规定，FOB只适用于海运和内河船运，也就排除了空运和铁路运输使用该术语的可能性。

CIF(Cost Insurance Freight)

CIF 在我国习惯叫做“到岸价”，这种叫法也不精确。采用 CIF 这种术语，在其后面应注明目的港，例如 CIF 青岛。

CIF 条件是指卖方负责租船定舱，按期在装运港将合同规定的货物装上运往约定目的港的船上，办理保险手续，并负责支付运费和保险费。至于有关风险和责任的划分则同 FOB 条件一致，即卖方仅负责货物在装运港装上船以前发生的风险。

CFR(Cost and Freight)

CFR 又称离岸加运费价、运费在内价。

CFR 后面注明的也是目的港，如 CFR 香港。

CFR 是介于 FOB 和 CIF 之间的一种价格术语，它是由卖方负责运输安排，但买方负责保险。除此之外，其他的风险、费用划分及权利义务大体与 CIF 相同，也是一种象征性交货合同。

CFR 由于是由买方办理保险，故卖方一等货物装上船，就须立即向买方发出装船通知，以便买方办理投保。如果由于卖方疏忽致使买方未能投保，则卖方必须承担运输途中的风险。

18. structure of a letter for asking for insurance arrangement and reply to an insurance arrangement

正规的商业信函一般应该有主题行(subject line)或者提示人行(attention line)，在称呼下面空两行缮打，置于信函中央，它有助于保证该信及时交给确切的收信人或部门。

(1) Beginning Paragraph: referring to the terms and agreed by the two parties.

开篇段落会再次提及双方的协议条款。

(2) Transitional Paragraph: expressing the desire to have goods insured and illustrating the coverage and the amount insured.

中间的主要内容：表达希望对方投保的愿望、投保的险别和投保金额。

(3) Ending Paragraph: hoping for an early solution.

结尾：保费的支付方式。

(二) 一般案例表述

1. Asking for Insurance Arrangement (Letter3)(要求投保)

Dear Sirs,

We wish to refer you to our order No.123 for 200 “Phoenix” brand bicycles, from which you will see that this order was placed on a CFR basis.

As discussed in our telephone conversation, we would like to leave insurance arrangements to you. So we shall be pleased if you could have the goods covered against All Risk on our behalf for 110% of the invoice value, i.e. $7 000. The premium is to be charged to the consignee and will be paid by them on presentation of the documents by your agents in Shanghai.

We sincerely hope that our above request will meet with your approval.

Yours faithfully,

2. Asking for Insurance Arrangement (Letter4)(对要求投保的回复)

Dear Sirs,

In reply to your letter of January 23 asking us to effect insurance on the above order, we are pleased to inform you that we have covered the shipment with the People's Insurance Company of China against All Risk for $7 000. The policy is being prepared accordingly and the debit note for the premium will be presented by our agents in Shanghai to the consignees in a week or two.

For your information, we are making arrangements to ship the bicycles by s/s. "Eastwind" which is due to sail for your port on or about February 4.

Yours faithfully,

3. Asking for Extra Insurance(Letter5)(要求投保附加险)

Dear Sirs,

Please refer to our Order No. A135 for 10 000 M/T Rock Phosphate, from which you will certainly note that this order is placed on CIF basis.

Now we would like to remind you to have the shipment insured in due course. Please see to it that the above-mentioned goods should be shipped before October 20 and that the shipment should be covered WPA for 130% of the invoice value. We know that according to your usual practice you insure the goods only for 10% above the invoice value; therefore the extra premium will be for our account.

We sincerely hope that our request will meet with your approval and await your reply with keen interest.

Sincerely yours,

4. Asking for Extra Insurance(Letter 6) (要求投保附加险)

Dear Sir or Madam,

As regard to your fax dated 14th ,Oct. 2003 covering the commodities for A.R. under Contract 2133, we hereby want to keep you informed that the AJC of 3FCL shipping to Iraq will need to add the War Risk at the proportion of 0.3% of the total invoice value, and goods packed in plastic bags of 4FCL to Baltimore will additionally cover the F.P.A..

Of course, please note that the remain goods are still covered against the original insurance terms stipulated in the contract.

Your faithfully,

5. Clarification of Insurance Terms(Letter 7)(解释保险术语)

Dear Sirs,

Re: Your L/C No. TK309

We thank you for your letter of December 6 and your L/C No.TK309 for RMB25 000 issued by the Bank of Singapore, advised through the Bank of China, Hong Kong.

On going through the stipulations of your credit, we regret to find that in addition to FPA and War Risk, you require insurance to cover TPND and SRCC which were not agreed upon by both parties during our negotiations at the First Beijing International Fair. Under the ordinary circumstance, no loss or theft of such merchandise as mild steel flat bars is likely to occur during transport or after arriving at its destination. Therefore, it is our practice to cover FPA for such commodity. Since you desire to have your shipment insured against TPND, we can arrange such insurance at your cost.

With regard to SRCC, we wish to state that the People's Insurance Company of China, from now on, accepts this special coverage and will fall in with the usual international practice.

We hope you will see your way to arrange with your bank for an amendment to your L/C to increase the amount in order to cover the extra premium under advice to us.

We assure you that as soon as your amendment reaches us, we shall of course, make the necessary arrangement for the shipment.

Yours faithfully,

6. Clarification of International Insurance Practices(Letter 8)(解释保险惯例)

Dear Sirs,

We have received your letter of June 20 in regard to insurance. Now we would like to inform you of the following.

Normally we cover insurance WPA and War Risk in the absence of the definite instructions from our customers. If you desire to cover All Risks, we can provide such coverage at a slightly higher premium. As to the insured value, our general practice is to insure at invoice value plus 10%. Any additional premium for insurance coverage over 110% of the invoice amount, is so required, shall be for buyer's account.

Risk other than All Risks and War Risk can also be covered here, and the extra premium will again be borne by the buyer.

We hope the above information will serve your purpose.

Yours faithfully,

资料链接 Material—link

1. Standard Model

Model 1: Advising Insurance Rate(通知保险费率)

Dear Sirs,

We have received your letter dated 14th July and are pleased to note that you would like to insure with us a shipment of Glassware from Tianjin to New York by sea.

We would advise that the rate now being charged by us for the proposed shipment against All Risks including War Risk is 1% subject to our own Ocean Marine Cargo Clauses and Ocean Marine War Risk Clauses, copies of which are enclosed herewith for your reference.

If you find our rate acceptable, please let us know the details of your shipment so that we may issue our policy accordingly.

We are looking forward to your early reply.

Yours faithfully,

Model 2: Making Claims against the Insurance Company(向保险公司提出索赔)

Dear Sirs,

We are the holder of the insurance policy No.123 issued by your company on 1 000kg of chemical fertilizer shipped by s/s"…". We regret to inform you that during the voyage the ship encountered bad weather and the above consignment incurred heavy loss. We have arranged for the surveyor to investigate the extent of the damage and shall forward his report together with our claim as soon as possible.

Please let us know what particulars you need from us when we submit our claim.

Yours faithfully,

Model 3: Asking for Modifying the Insurance Clauses(修改保险条款)

Dear Sirs,

We refer to your L/C No.123 covering…, which we have just received.

Please note for this article we do not cover Breakage. You have to, therefore, delete the word "Breakage" from the insurance clause in the credit. Furthermore, we wish to point out that for such articles as window glass, etc. even if additional Risk of Breakage has been insured, the cover is subject to a franchise of 5%. In other words, if the breakage is surveyed to be less than 5%, no claim for damage will be entertained.

We trust that the position is now clear, please fax the amendment at once.

Yours faithfully,

2. *Writing Guide*

There are a great number of risks involved in international trade.Therefore, most risks will be covered by buyers or sellers prior to the actual business transactions happens. Before we have goods involved insured, we should take the following questions into account.

1) *Who Should Be Responsible for Insuring*

Generally speaking, who should be responsible for insuring depends on the trade terms in the sales contract. Under the term of CIF，the seller is up to make insurance, whereas under the condition of FOB and CFR, the buyer is obligated to insure the specified goods. Under some circumstances, even the contract is signed on the basis of FOB and CFR, at the request of the buyer, the seller can also effect insurance on the buyer's behalf. However, the risks and expenses concerned are for the buyer's account.

E.g. The buyer should effect the insurance for his own account.

We would like to effect insurance on your behalf.

2) *The Coverage*

In the selection of coverage, some factors should be considered:the nature of goods, packing, shipping route, port and the function of goods etc..The premium varies with coverage. It's generally understood that the extra premium should be borne by the seller in case of additional risks needed.

E.g. Insurance is often effected for the 110% of invoice value against All Risks.

The premium rate is 0.25%.

In case additional risks are needed, the extra premium should be collected.

3) *The Amount Insured*

According to UCP600, the amount insured should be 110% of the CIF or CIP value if it's not particularly stipulated in the Letter of Credit. However, the amount insured exceeding 110% of the CIF or CIP value are not unusual.

E.g. We have insured the 1 000 cases of beer for the 110% of the invoice value against All Risks.

We can effect the insurance for the 150% of the invoice value to your satisfaction, but the premium difference caused by increasing the amount insured by 40% of the invoice value should be on your account.

4) *The Choice Of Insurance Company*

E.g. For transactions concluded on CIF basis, we usually effect insurance with the People's Insurance Company of China against All Risks , as per Ocean Marine Cargo Clauses of the People's Insurance Company of China dated 1st January ,1981.

5) *Try not to Use Two Kinds of Languages*

One is the language difficult to understand, the other is the language full of technical or special words.

6) *Avoid Useing CLICHÉ*

But true jargon or commercial jargon can be used if necessary because it helps to make the meaning clear and easy to understand.

Section Three Selected Sentences
精选句型表达

1．Insurance is to be covered by the buyer.

由买方投保。

2．It is the general practice that the insurance is to be covered in the same currency as in the Letter of Credit.

按惯例，投保币种应和信用证规定的币种一样。

3．If you desire us to insure against a special risk, an extra premium will gave to be charged.

如果你方想要我方投保其他特殊的险别，则须支付额外的费用。

4．We shall cover the shipment for 10% above the invoice value.

我们按发票金额加成 10%投保。

5．We shall arrange insurance on your behalf.

我们将代你方投保。

6. We have covered insurance on 1 000 cases of Qingdao Beer for 110% of the invoice value against risks.

我们已将 1 000 箱青岛啤酒按发票金额的 110%投保一切险。

7．Have insured at your end.　让你方为所订货物投保。

8．We have insured the goods against WPA. 我们已经给这些货物投保水渍险。

at invoice value plus 10%按发票价值另加收 10%

for 110% of invoice value 按发票金额的 110%

for 10% above invoice value 在发票价值上加收 10%

9. His account with the Bank of China had been debited with the sum of $5 for half-yearly bank charges.

中国银行把一笔 5 美元的账记入他的账户的借方，作为半年的银行手续费。

debit an amount to one's account 把一笔金额记入某人账户的借方

debit one's account with an amount 把一笔金额记入某人账户的借方

10. We shall cover insurance for 110% of the invoice value in accordance with your request.

根据你方要求，我们将按发票金额的 110% 投保。

11. We shall cover WPA and against War Risk according to the usual practice.

我们将按一般惯例投保水渍险和战争险。

12. The insurance policy covers us against Breakage.

保单给我们保了破碎险。

13. As the contract stipulates that insurance should cover 110% of the invoice value, if you desire to cover insurance for 130% instead, the extra premium should be for your account.

由于合同规定按发票金额的 110%投保，如你方要求按 130%投保，额外保费应由你方负担。

14. Our insurance coverage is for 110% of invoice value up to the port of destination only.

我方按发票金额的 110%投保仅至目的港。

15. Kindly note that the insurance covers F.P.A. and War Risks only. Should additional insurance coverage be required, the extra premium incurred would be for the buyers' account.

请注意，保险只包括平安险和战争险。如果要求投保附加险，所需额外保险费将由买方支付。

16. W.P.A. coverage is too narrow for a shipment of this nature. Please extend the coverage to include TPND.

对这种性质的货物只投保水渍险是不够的，请加保偷窃提货不着险。

17. We have covered insurance on 1 000 cases of beer for 110% of the invoice value against all risks.

我们已将 1 000 箱啤酒按发票金额的 110%投保一切险。

18. If you desire us to insure against a special risk, an extra premium will have to be charged.

如你方想投保特殊险别，将向你方收取额外保费。

19. This risk is coverable at a premium of 0.25%.

该险别的保险费是 0.25%。

20. The insurance company insures this risk with 5% franchise.

保险公司保这种险有 5%的免赔额。

21. After loading the goods on board the ship, you must go to the insurance company to have them insured.

货船装船后，你方必须找保险公司为货物投保。

22. We can serve you with a broad range of coverage against all kinds of risks for sea transport, such as Free of Particular Average (F.P.A.), With Particular Average (W.P.A.), All Risks and Extraneous Risks.

我们可以承保海洋运输的所有险别，如：平安险、水渍险、一切险和附加险。

23. W.P.A. plus Risk of Breakage suit your consignment.

贵方货物适合于投保水渍险及破碎险。

24. The premium is calculated according to the premium rate or rates for risks to be covered.

保险费是根据投保险别的保险费率计算的。

25. They will undertake to compensate you for the losses according to the risks insured.

他们将根据所投保的险别，对损失负责赔偿。

26. We are able to cover all kinds of risks for transportation by sea, land and air.

我们可以办理海运、陆运和空运的所有险别。

27. We won't have such a risk included, as it is not stipulated in the Ocean Marine Cargo Clauses.

我们不能投保此项险别，因为海洋运输条款中没有包括这一险别。

28. Do you cover risk other than W.P.A. and War Risk?

除了水渍险和战争险外，你们还投保其他险吗？

29. As a rule, the extra premium involved will be for buyer's account.

按常规，额外保险费应由买方负责。

30. Please note that our insurance coverage is for 110% of the invoice value only.

请注意，我们的保险范围只是发票金额的 110%。

31. How long is the period from the commencement to termination of the insurance?

保险责任的起讫期限有多长？

32. We adopt the warehouse-to-warehouse clause that is commonly used in international insurance.

我们采用国际保险中常用的“仓至仓”的责任条款。

33. According to international practice, we do not insure against such risks unless the buyers call for them.

按照国际惯例，我们不投保这些险别，除非买主要求投保。

34. Breakage is a special risk, for which an extra premium will have to be charged.

破碎险是一种特别险，需收取额外保险费。

35. Because they aren't delicate goods and not likely to be damaged on the voyage.

因为这些不是易碎易损的货物，航行中不大可能被损坏。

36. Insurance: To be covered by the Seller for 110% of the total invoice value against All Risks, as per and subject to the relevant ocean marine cargo clauses of the People's Insurance Company of China, dated January1, 1981.

保险由卖方按发票金额的 110%投保一切险，以中国人民保险公司 1981 年 1 月 1 日有关海洋运输货物保险条款为准。

37．The insurance shall be limited to 60 days upon discharge of the insured goods from the seagoing vessel at the final port of discharge. 被保险货物在最后装卸港卸离海轮后，保险责任以 60 天为限。

38．We shall cover W.P.A. for 110% of the invoice value. 我们将按发票总金额的 110%投保水渍险。

39．How long is the period from the commencement to termination of insurance? 保险责任的起讫期限多长？

40．To cover All Risks, the insurance company shall be liable for total or partial loss on land or sea of the insured goods within the period covered by the insurance.

对投保"综合险"，投保货物在承保期内，不论在海上还是在陆上遭受的全部或部分损失，保险公司均予以赔偿。

41．The insurance company is responsible for the claim, as far as it is within the scope of coverage.

只要在保险责任范围内，保险公司就应赔偿。

42．If we conclude the business on CIF basis, what cover will you take out for the goods?

我们这批货如果以 CIF 条件成交，你方负责投保哪些险别？

43．We generally insure W.P.A. on CIF. basis. 按到岸价交易，我们一般投保水渍险。

44．I should point out that our prices were calculated without insurance for any special risk.

我应该指出，我们的价格没有把特殊险计算在内。

45．Special risks such as TPND, Leakage, Breakage, and Freshwater, can also be covered upon request.

特殊险别，如盗窃提货不着险、漏险、破损险、淡水险等，可根据要求另保。

46. The insurance premium to breakage is 3%. We can cover the Risk of Breakage for you if you want.

破碎险的保险费率是 3%。如果你方想投保破碎险，我方可以代为办理。

47．Our insurance coverage is for 110% of invoice value up to the port of destination only.

我方以发票金额的 110%投保仅至目的港。

48．According to the international practice, we do not insure against such risks unless they are called for by the buyers. 按照国际惯例，我们不投保这类险别，除非买主要求投保。

49．Insurance of the goods shall be covered by us on 110% of the CIF value.

货物的保险将由我方以 CIF 价的 10%投保。

50．We adopt the warehouse to warehouse clause which is commonly used in international insurance.

我们采用国际保险中惯用的"仓至仓"的责任条款。

51．Kindly note that the insurance covers F.P.A. and War Risks only. Should, additional insurance coverage be required, the extra premium incurred would be for the buyers' account.

请注意，保险只包括平安险和战争险。如果要求投保附加险，所需额外保险费将由买方支付。

52．Please insure the goods at our cost against damage in transport.

请对货物在运输途中的损失投保，费用由我方承担。

53. We have concluded the business on an FOB basis, so the insurance should be effected by you.

这批货是以 FOB 条件成交的，所以应由你方投保。

54. We generally insure our export shipment with the People's Insurance Company of China.

通常我们向中国人民保险公司为我们的出口商品投保。

55. The insurance company will compensate you for the loss.

保险公司将赔偿你方损失。

56. I suppose the additional premium for the special coverage should be on the buyer's account.

我认为特别险所附加的保险费应由买方负担。

57. Please give us the policy rates for F. P. A. coverage.

请给我方平安险的保险费率。

58. This kind of additional risk is coverable at 2%.

这种附加险的保险费是 2%。

Abstract

通过本章学习，①了解保险的基本分类；②了解常见的保险条款及保险险别，了解保险相关知识，通过学习能正确区分险别；③掌握不同内容的保险来往函电写作的基本技巧；④通过熟悉标准模板掌握保险函电写作的基本方法；⑤熟练掌握国际商务函电写作里面关于保险的经典句型的表达和常用专业词汇和术语。

Useful Words & Expressions

与保险本身有关的术语

Insure 保险；投保；保证

Insurance 保险

the amount insured 保险金额

underwriters 保险商(指专保水险的保险商)；保险承保人

insurance company 保险公司

insurer 保险公司；保险人

insurance underwriter 保险承保人

insurance applicant 投保人

insurant, the insured 被保险人；受保人

insurance coverage, risks covered 保险范围

PICC (People's Insurance Company of China) 中国人民保险公司

premium rate 保险费率

insurance premium 保险费

premium rebate 保险费回扣

premium tariff 保险费率表
extra premium 额外保险费
insurance claim 保险索赔
insurance broker 保险代理人；保险经纪人
insurance agents 保险代理人
insurance declaration 保险声明书；保险通知书
insurance endorsement 保险批单
insured cargo /goods 投保货物
average 海损
Particular Average (P.A) 单独海损
General Average (G.A) 共同海损
Marine Losses 海损
partial loss 部分损失
total loss 全部损失
insurance policy
保险单，俗称大保单，正规保单——保险单除载明投保各项内容外，还列有保险公司的责任范围及双方的权利义务。
insurance certificate
保险凭证，分保单，俗称小保单——简式保单，对双方的权利义务未加叙述，常用于双方订有预约保单的情况下。

与保险险别有关的术语
Types of International Cargo Transport Insurance 国际货物运输保险种类
air transportation insurance 航运运输保险
marine insurance 海运险；水险；海上保险
ocean marine cargo insurance 海洋运输货物保险
overland transportation insurance 陆上运输保险
parcel post insurance 邮包保险

Insurance Clauses 保险条款
1．China Insurance Clauses 中国保险条款(CIC)(made by PICC)
Ocean Marine Cargo Clauses 中国海洋运输货物保险条款 (OMCC)
2．Institute Cargo Clauses 协会货物保险条款 (ICC)
1) ICC(A)
2) ICC(B)
3) ICC(C)
4) Institute War clauses-Cargo
5) Institute Strike clauses-Cargo
6) Malicious Damage Clause 恶意损害险条款

Types of Basic Coverage 基本险别
insurance Free of (from) Particular Average (F.P.A.) 平安险(单独海损不赔)
insurance With Particular Average (W.P.A.) 水渍险
insurance against all risks 一切险

Additional Risks 附加险别

1. 一般附加险(General Additional risks)

(1) 短量险(Risk of Shortage)。
(2) 淡水雨淋险(Fresh Water Rain Damage, FWRD)。
(3) 混杂、沾污险(Risk of Intermixture and Contamination)。
(4) 渗漏险(Leakage)(渗漏损失或变质)。
(5) 碰损、破碎险(Clash and Breakage)。
(6) 串味险(Taint of Odour)。
(7) 受热、受潮险(Sweat and Heating)。
(8) 钩损险(Hook Damage) (吊钩或手钩)。
(9) 锈损险(Risks of Rust)。
(10) 包装破裂险(Breakage of Packing)。
(11) 偷窃、提货不着险(Theft, Pilferage and Non-Delivery, TPND)。

2. 特别附加险(Special Additional Risk)

(1) 黄曲霉素险(Aflatoxin)。

(2) 舱面险(on deck)(集装箱类传统装于甲板的货物无须投保就可获得保险保障，保险人一般不愿意接受在一切险基础上加保)。

(3) 交货不到险(Failure to Deliver)。

(4) 进口关税险(Import Duty)。

(5) 拒收险(Rejection)。

(6) 货物出口到香港(包括九龙)或澳门存仓火险责任扩展条款(Fire Risk Extension Clause, FREC—for storage of cargo at destination Hong Kong, including Kowloon, or Macao)。

3. 特殊附加险(Specific Additional Risks/Coverage)

(1) 战争险(War Risk)。
(2) 罢工险(Strike Risks)。
(3) 战争险的附加费用险(Additional Expense-War Risk)。

Exercises

1. Multiple choice.

(1) I'd like to have the insurance ____ for 130% of the invoice value.

A. cover B. covered C. covering D. to cover

(2) Your L/C calls for an insurance amount for 180% of the invoice value. ____ , we would request you to amend the insurance clause.

A. The case is like this B. The case being it

C. Such is the case D. Such being the case

(3) Need we insure the shipment against Leakage Risk?

Yes, you ____ .

A. must B. need C. should D. can

(4) The Pacific Insurance Company ____ the liability if you had covered W.P.A.

A. will take B. would have taken

C. has taken D. is going to take

(5) Lloyd's, an association of London underwriters, developed from a small seventeenth-century London coffee house, ____ underwriters at that time met to do business.

A. that B. which C. where D. in that

(6) We are pleased to confirm ____ the above goods against All Risks for $5 500.

A. have arranged B. having assured

C. to have ensured D. having insured

(7) Damage ____ the goods was caused by heavy rain ____ transit.

A. of, in B. to, in C. for, during D. on, during

(8) PICC stands ____ the People's Insurance Company of ____ .

A. for, Clause B. like, China

C. by, Cargo D. for, China

(9) On inspection of the consignment unloaded ____ the port of discharge, we found ten bundles ____ .

A. by, losing B. from, missed

C. at, missing D. on, lost

(10) We thank you for your letter of March 25, requesting us to effect insurance on the captioned goods for your ____.

A. cost B. amount C. account D. expense

(11) Insurance is to be ____ by the buyer if a transaction is concluded on FOB or CFR basis.

A. covered B. done C. made D. taken

(12) Since the premium varies with the extent of insurance, extra premium is for buyer's account, ____ additional risks be covered.

A. if B. as C. must D. should

(13) We now desire to have the consignment ____ at your end.

A. assured B. ensured C. insured D. insurance

(14) We'd like to have the insurance ____ for 110% of the invoice value.

A. covering B. cover C. to cover D. covered

(15) Damage ____ the goods was caused by heavy rain ____ transit.

A. for, during B. on, during C. of, in D. to, in

(16) We shall arrange insurance ____ your behalf.

A. in B. by C. on D. for

(17) Insurance was originally applied to losses ____ sea.

A. in B. on C. over D. at

(18) W.P.A. is one of the ____.

A. basic risks B. additional risks

C. special additional risks D. general additional risks

(19) In insurance, the party who insures others against possible loss or damage and promises to effect payment in case of loss or damage is called the ____.

A. insured B. consignee C. insurer D. consignor

(20) Under the trade term CFR, the ____ must contract for the cargo transport insurance.

A. buyer B. seller C. consignee D. carrier

(21) Since the premium varies with the extent of insurance, extra premium is for buyer's account, ____additional risks be covered.

A. must B. if C. should D. as

(22) Please insure against All Risks as W.P.A is too narrow a ____.

A. risk B. insurance C. amount D. coverage

2. Translate the following sentences into Chinese.

(1) Please quote us your lowest W.P.A. rate for US$20 000 on sewing machines from Hong Kong to Qingdao/up to the port of the destination.

(2) We wish to cover the consignment against All Risk from our warehouse at the above address to the port of Montreal.

(3) In the absence of definite instructions from our clients, we generally cover insurance against W.P.A. and War Risk; if you desire to cover F.P.A., please let us know in advance.

(4) Since the premium varies with the extent of coverage, extra premium is for buyer's account, should additional risks be required.

(5) The franchise for the additional Risk of Breakage on such fragile articles is 5%. In other words, if the breakage is surveyed to be less than 5%, no claims for damage will be entertained.

(6) We are enclosing the requested endorsement (to the policy).

(7) We thank you for your instructions to arrange the shipment of fans. We take it that you wish us to insure the goods against the usual risks, for the value of the goods plus freight. Unless we hear from you to the contrary, we shall arrange this.

(8) Please let us know the premium at which breakage is coverable by the insurers on your side/at your end.

(9) If any other risks are to be insured against, please let us know by the end of this week, so that we can adjust our insurance charges accordingly and effect shipment without delay. If higher percentage is required, we can do as requested provided you bear the extra premium.

(10) We wish to know whether you can issue a special rate for the promise of regular monthly shipments.

(11) F.P.A. covers total losses resulting from both natural calamities and accidents, and partial losses caused by accidents.

(12) We have covered insurance on 1 000 cases of beer for 110% of the invoice value against All Risks.

(13) If you desire us to insure against a special risk, an extra premium will have to be charged.

(14) This risk is coverable at a premium of 0.25%.

(15) The insurance company insures this risk with 5% franchise.

(16) After loading the goods on board, you must go to the insurance company to have them insured.

(17) We can serve you with a broad range of coverage against all kinds of risks for sea transport, such as Free of Particular Average (F.P.A.), With Particular Average (W.P.A.), All Risks and Extraneous Risks.

(18) W.P.A. plus Risk of Breakage suit your consignment.

(19) The premium is calculated according to the premium rate or rates for risks to be covered.

(20) They will undertake to compensate you for the losses according to the risks insured.

(21) We are able to cover all kinds of risks for transportation by sea, land and air.

(22) We won't have such a risk included, as it is not stipulated in the Ocean Marine Cargo Clauses.

(23) Do you cover risk other than W.P.A. and War Risk?

(24) As a rule, the extra premium involved will be for buyer's account.

(25) Please note that our insurance coverage is for 110% of the invoice value only.

(26) How long is the period from the commencement to termination of the insurance?

(27) We adopt the warehouse-to-warehouse clause that is commonly used in international insurance.

(28) According to international practice, we do not insure against such risks unless the buyers call for them.

(29) Breakage is a special risk, for which an extra premium will have to be charged.

(30) Because they aren't delicate goods and not likely to be damaged on the voyage.

(31) Please insure for us the goods detailed below against All Risks.

(32) As to the goods sold on CIF basis, we would say, our company will insure against All Risk and War Risk for 110% of the invoice value. If you want to insure broader coverage, the extra premium involved will be for buyer's account.

(33) When the goods are delivered to the consignee's warehouse at the destination named in the policy, the insurance shall terminate.

(34) The principal perils which the basic marine policy of the PICC insures against under its Ocean Marine Cargo Clauses are F.P.A., W.P.A. and All Risks.

(35) It should be noted that the cover is limited to 60 days upon discharge of the insured goods from seagoing vessel at the final port of discharge before the insured goods reach the consignee's warehouse.

(36) In the absence of your definite instruction, we shall effect insurance W.P.A. according to our usual practice.

(37) We wish to know whether you can issue a special rate in return for the promise of regular monthly shipments.

(38) We have drawn on you for this amount at sight through the Bank of China.

(39) We are pleased to confirm having covered the above shipment with the People's Insurance Company of China against All Risks for $ 3 000. The policy will be sent to you in a day or two together with our debit note for the premium.

(40) We have the pleasure of informing you that shipment of bicycles under contract No. 123 will be effected by S.S. Peace which is scheduled to leave here on July 2. Please arrange insurance for this cargo.

3. Translate the following sentences into English.

(1) 按到岸价交易，我们一般投保水渍险。

(2) 由于此次交易是以 FOB 条件成交的，投保应由贵方负责。

(3) 为了安全起见，我方建议贵方为这批货物投保一切险和战争险。

(4) 本函附寄了有关包装和货物价值的一些材料。如果贵方能报从港口到港口一切险的保险费率，本公司不胜感激。

(5) 请为我们的皮革制品投保偷窃提货不着险、玷污险、淡水雨淋险以及水渍险。

(6) 我们已向中国人民保险公司将 100 公吨羊毛按发票金额的 110%投保一切险，保险费用为 3%。

(7) 将由我方按照到岸价的发票金额 110%办理该货的保险，如果需要，额外增加保险的费用将由买方承担。

(8) 我们对此货品投保一切险和战争险。

(9) 这份保单给我们投保了渗漏险。

(10) 我们已经安排了适当的保险。

(11) 请将装运给我们的货物投保水渍险和兵险。

(12) 请按发票价的 110%投保。

(13) 至于第 345 号合约项下的 300 架缝纫机，我们将自行办理保险。破碎险的保险费率是 1%，如你方愿意投保破碎险，我们可以代为办理。

(14) 至于索赔，我们的保险公司只接受超过实际损失 5%的部分。

(15) 请告知你们的价格是否包括偷窃及提货不着险。

(16) 如果没有你们的明确指示，我们将按一般惯例投保水渍险和兵险。

(17) 很遗憾，我们不能接受这一索赔，因为你们的保险没有包括“破碎险”。

(18) 在你们惯常用的 CIF 价格条件下，所投保的是哪些险别？

(19) 我们常从保险公司那里定期拿到一笔可观的保险回扣。

Case Practice

以本章的导入案例为背景，请以公司业务员 Tom 的名义回一封邮件，说明已经向中国人民保险公司为上述货物投保了一切险和战争险，投保金额为 10 020.00 美元。保险单正在准备之中。本周末将会把保险单和收取保险费的索款通知一并寄给他们。并告诉他们，你们正在安排 QUEEN 号货轮装运该 1 000 包棉布。该轮船将于 9 月 10 日左右从美国旧金山港起航。

Chapter 9 Shipment

装　运

案例导入 Case-lead-in

杭州某公司向卖方订购 6 吨经过加工的聚乙烯，订单号 4567，该批货原定于下月底才能装运。当时订购这批货时，买方认为存货足够用至 12 月份。然而，最近市场对这种聚乙烯的需求量变大，市场变化大以至于买方想修改合同条款，同卖方磋商要求卖方立即安排装运，并表达了进一步合作的愿望。

Section One　Shipping Instruction and Shipping Advice 装运须知和装运通知

Transport is an important part in the international trade. The effectuation of the transport signifies the exporter's fulfillment of the obligation to make delivery of the goods.

It is indispensable to import and export business.

Transport allows goods to be conveyed from one place to another. Without transport, international trade would not be possible.

There are many modes of transportation in international trade, such as seaway transportation, airway transportation, roadway transportation and railway transportation.

Seaway transportation is a widely accepted mode of transport and a majority of international trade is conveyed by maritime transport. Basically, there are two types of ocean freight according to the assorted shipping vessels used, that is, liner business and tramp business.

Airway transportation plays a more important role in international conveyance of cargo for its many advantages over maritime transport, such as high speed, low risks, and simplified documentation system, elimination of storage and capital tie-up. Of course, employment of air freight is still restricted due to its many weak points, such as limited carriage capacity and high expense.

Roadway transport, dissimilar to the other modes of transport, has its own distinctive features. Normally road vehicle can provide a door-to-door service without intermediate handling. Road transport has a spacious flexibility in that should circumstance demand a change in routing or a blockage of shipping service. It can also provide a reliable service with high quality.

Railway transportation is a mode of transportation through which the cargo is conveyed through railway. It is not affected by bad weather; therefore, normal operation through the whole year is guaranteed. This mode of transport benefits from its large transport capacity and high transport continuance.

The seaway transportation is undoubtedly the most economical mode of transportation in international trade particularly when bulk commodities are involved, with advantages of easy passage, large capacity and low cost. That's why today 98% of world trade on volume term is conveyed by sea transport.

However, it is slow, vulnerable to bad weather and less punctual if compared with roadway or airway transport.

If a transaction is concluded on CIF basis, the exporter need to book shipping space or charter a ship. Of course, this complex process shall usually be handled by a professional shipping and forwarding agent. The exporter shall send a Shipping Instruction to the shipping company through the agent before goods are loaded. After goods are loaded on board, the exporter shall inform the foreign importer of particulars covering the shipment by sending a Shipping Advice.

The seller should let the buyer know as soon as the shipment is effected, by sending the buyer the shipping advice together with a set of shipping documents which normally covers the following details.

Importer's address
Invoice No.
Purchase order No.
L/C No.
Date and number of the Contract
Name of the carrying vessel
Beneficiary and date of this advice
Date and number of Bill of Lading
Names of commodities and their quality and value
Name of the shipping port/loading port
Estimated Time of Departure (ETD)
Name of the destination port
Estimated Time of Arrival (ETA)
Number of containers
Terms of payment
Freight
Documents enclosed

Notes

1. **FOB** (Free on Board, named port of shipment)船上交货(指定装运港) It means that the seller fulfils his obligation to deliver the goods when they have passed over the ship's rail at the named port of shipment. This means that the buyer has to bear all expenses and risks of or damage to the goods from that point.

CFR (Cost and Freight, named port of destination)成本加运费(指定目的港) It means that the seller shall undertake the cost and freight necessary to carry the goods to the named port of destination, but the risks of, losses of, or damage to the goods, as well as any additional costs due to events occurring after the time the goods have been delivered on board the vessel, are transferred from the seller to the buyer when the goods pass the ship's rail at the port of shipment.

CIF (Cost , Insurance and Freight, named port of destination)成本加保险费、运费(指定目的港) It means that the seller has the obligation to procure marine insurance against the risks of, losses of, or damage to the goods during the carriage.

2. Bill of Lading: It is the most important shipping document. It is a contract between the shipper and the shipping company. It is a receipt for the consignment.

Section Two　Terms of Shipment
装运条款

Terms of Shipment，as the compulsory part of a contract, involve time of shipment, port of loading and destination, means of conveyance and shipping document, etc.

Time of shipment refers to the time limit for loading the goods on board the vessel at port of shipment (if shipment is made by sea).

Port of loading is the port of departure.

Port of destination is the destination that the goods are finally designated to.

Means of conveyance covers direct shipment, transshipment and partial shipment.

Partial shipment

If possible, the seller may choose to make several partial shipments of the contracted goods at different times. "Partial shipments allowed" should be stated in the L/C as well as in the contract.

Transshipment

If there is no steamer directly from the port of loading to the port of destination, transshipment is necessary. In order to avoid dispute that might arise in the future, the seller should first get the buyer's permission for transshipment and then, "Transshipment is allowed" should be stated in the L/C as well as in the contract.

Here are examples about terms of delivery instructions and documentation.

The Documents and Delivery Information Requested by Seppa

Please find below the instructions we request you to follow strictly to ensure us the fluent customs clearance in Finland as well as control during transport.

请严格遵循以下要求，以确保 Seppa 订单出运流程的快速、顺利。

Delivery By Air Freight
空运货物

• Commercial invoice, packing list and photocopies of certificates of origin must be sent along with the Air Waybill.

清关所需的副本发票、箱单、正本产地证须同空运提单一起由货代随机发出。

• Originals of certificate of origin must be sent to Seppa's Import department by courier two weeks before delivery of the goods at the latest.

如没有随机，则产地证正本须在出运前两周快递至 Seppa 进口清关部门。

• Commercial invoice and packing list in addition to the copy of Air Waybill have to be sent to Seppa's Import department by fax or email immediately after delivery of goods.

一旦确认出运，请在出运当天将副本的发票、箱单、产地证、空运提单、出运记录发送传真或电子邮件至 Seppa 进口清关部门。

• The consignment and the relevant documents must be addressed to Seppa Oy instead of a bank or forwarding agent.

所有对应文件上显示的地址必须为 Seppa Oy，不可用银行或货代信息替代。

• Seppa's order numbers need to be written clearly in every document and on every carton.

Seppa 订单号必须正确标示在所有相关文件及箱唛上。

Delivery by Truck (仅供非中国大陆及港澳台地区参考)
陆运货物

• Commercial invoice, packing list and original EUR.1/ATR-certificates, if required, must be given to the forwarder for delivering along with the consignment.

• Commercial invoice and packing list must be sent to Seppa's Import department by fax or email immediately after delivery of goods.

• The consignment and documents have to be addressed to Seppa Oy instead of a bank or forwarding agent.

• Seppa's order numbers need to be written clearly in every document and on every carton.

Delivery by Sea
海运货物

• Copies of invoice, packing list and Bill of Lading in addition to the originals of certificate of origin must be sent to Seppa's Import department by courier one week after shipment of goods at the latest.

清关所需的副本发票、箱单、正本产地证须同海运提单一起，在船开后一周之内，快递至 Seppa 进口清关部门。

• Originals of invoice and packing list, full set of Bill of Lading and photocopies of certificate of origin need to be sent to the bankers thus that Seppa receives them one week before arrival of the goods at the latest. (仅适用于 L/C 或 D/P 付款)

Please Issue The Documents As Follows.

在同一船次上出运的订单，配比号为 6、7、9 的货品，须做一套出运文件(包括提单、产地证)；其余配比号的货品，则须做另一套出运文件(包括提单、产地证)。为明确，请把发票、箱单按订单号单独做。

• One separate Bill of Lading to cover the assortments 6, 7, 9 and another separate Bill of Lading to cover all the other assortments.

• One separate commercial invoice for the assortments 6, 7, 9 and another separate commercial invoice for all the other assortments.

• One separate packing list including net and gross weights for the assortments 6, 7, 9 and another separate packing list for all the other assortments.

• One separate certificate of origin to cover the assortments 6, 7, 9 and another separate certificate of origin to cover all the other assortments.

The supplier is responsible for complying with the relevant rules of origin in the EU.

供应商须保证所做的文件能使货物在目的港正确无误地清关，否则由此所造成的问题将由供应商承担。

Section Three　Cases in Detail
具体案例分析

(一) 经典案例解析

Dear Sirs,

Thank you for your inquiry of April 30th. The shipping containers we provide are of two sizes, namely 20ft and 30ft respectively.

They can be opened at both ends, thus making it possible to load and unload at the same time. For carrying goods liable to be spoiled by damp or water they have great advantages of being both water-tight and air-tight.

Containers can be loaded and locked at the factory, if necessary. Pilferage is therefore impossible.

Being temperature-controlled, our containers are provided for any cargo that needs a special care. This lends its full benefit in shipping.

There is also a saving on freight charges, when separate consignments intended for the same port of destination are carried in one container, and an additional saving on insurance because of lower premium charged for container-shipped goods.

We enclose a copy of our tariff and look forward to receiving your instructions.

Yours faithfully,

Notes

1. Containers　　集装箱；容器；货柜
2. Spoil　　损坏糟蹋；溺爱；猎物；废品
3. water-tight　　防水的；密封的
4. air-tight　　密封的；不透气的

5. Pilferage　　小偷小摸；盗窃；行窃偷窃
6. Premium　　奖金；保险费；溢价；升水
7. shipping containers　　集装箱
8. at both ends　　两面
9. lends its full benefit　　利用(或发挥)其优点
10. a copy of our tariff　　费率表副本一份

11. 本信函向客户提供集装箱相关信息，对于此类内容必须尽量写得详细，以便客户了解具体情况，更有利于贸易往来。

12. "namely 20ft and 30ft respectively"、"They can…" "making it possible … at the same time"、"… if necessary."、"There is also …" 等对集装箱进行具体描述的句子不仅仅包含集装箱的规格尺寸，具体作用等，还描述了采用集装箱在保险方面的好处等，言简意赅，描述清晰准确。体现了"完整性"，"具体性"、"清晰性"以及"体谅性"原则，为客户的选择提供详情，给客户留下深刻印象，同时赢得好感。

13. 首段的"Thank you for"以及尾段中的"look forward to"体现了"礼貌性"原则，首尾呼应，给对方留下良好印象。在贸易往来中，秉持礼貌性原则，有利于树立良好的企业形象，赢得更多客户。

14. 本文是一篇涉及对外贸易装运中集装箱选择的信函。在集装箱日益成为现代外贸交易运输主体时，集装箱的选择也对买卖双方利益产生一定的影响。文中从我方拥有的集装箱尺寸、优点、特色、费率四个方面详细介绍了我方所能提供的集装箱，详细、具体而且全面、到位。

首先，在第一段中对对方的询盘给予感激，并且顺势向对方提出了我方所能够提供的集装箱尺寸为20英尺和30英尺两种。

在第二段中我方站在对方的立场充分向对方说明了我方集装箱所具有的优点："both water-tight and air-tight。"

在第三段中向对方说明我方集装箱还在码头时就可以锁住，有防止偷窃的额外优点，进一步向对方阐述我方集装箱的优点。

第四段又进一步说明我方集装箱优点："our containers are provided for any cargo that needs a special care"。

第五段从费率方面说明了我方集装箱的优点，即费率低。

(二) 一般案例表述

1. Confirm Shipping details

Dear Water,

How are you? Our forwarder's information as below.

Com: DALLTD.

Contact person: Ms. Daisy Chan daisy@dal.com

Ship by sea to our agent in Finland

Com: Net Logistic

Add: Eskolantic 1, 4 floor 00720 Helsinki, Finland

Contact person: Ludmila Suominen

Tel: +358 20 755 82

Mob: +358 40 867 92

Fax: + 358 20 755 82

E-mail: ludmila.suominen@netlogistic.com

Arrival port-Kotka (port Mussalo)

Water: Well understand.

Please, put the following data into the papers covering orders.

The Invoice and Packing List should be made for: WMT LTD Rm.1501, One Peking, 1 Peking Road, Tsimshatsui, Kowloon, Hong Kong

Water: Well understand. But no need contact person? Before sending to courier, I will send to you for confirmation first.

Please, put in the B/L Cinsignee, Notify party-according to our instructions.

Water: OK, will do as per your instructions.

Please, don't put in papers "Acmra, ACM, Acpower, Rostkkiy Dmitry" etc.

Water: Well understand.

Shipping mark. WMT.
If any questions, please let me know.
Best regards,
Irina

Dear Irina,

Thanks for your kind information about forwarder. I will contact with her accordingly. I think I already knew her, as you asked DAL to send the samples before. By the way, have you got the samples we sent to you? In fact the new samples, also sent by DAL Daisy I guess.

First, please find my reply in your e-mail in Blue. Here below I would like to make sure the points with you together.

A: Regarding the shipment details. In order to make it more clear, I would like to make sure with you again as below.

Delivery terms: FOB Shenzhen, FREIGHT COLLECT-right
Consignee: TO ORDER-the same notify party
Notify Party: right
Net Logistic
1, 4 floor 00720 Helsinki, Finland
Contact: Ludmila Suominen
Tel: + 358 20 755 82
Fax: + 358 20 755 82
Port of discharge: Kotka
Place of delivery: Kotka
Description of goods: (please explain to me, as some countries is quite strict to this kind of product) charger

If you have something to remind me, please keep me informed.

B: Shipping Mark.

Will you have your own shipping mark? "WMT" for main mark only? And how about side mark?

We would suggest the following. Please advise your comment.

main mark OK

WMT

C/No.:

side mark OK

QTY:

N.W:

G.W:

MEAS:

And for your reference, the package should be: 40PCS/CTN, Gross weight:: 3.5kg, Net weight: 3.00kg. Measurement: 41.3cm×29.8cm×26.5cm

Look forward to hearing from you.

Best regards,

Water

Notes

如果是信用证付款，信用证上会明确地陈述所有关于出货的细节。一般情况下，在租船订舱或者交单时无须再向客户咨询，只需要根据信用证陈述的要求去做即可。如果不是信用证付款，在出货之前，必须向客户了解并核实出货的细节要求。因为这些文件关系到客户在当地是否可以清关，或者是否容易清关，这也是文件的基本要求。

Dear Water,

Thank you for your e-mail. Also, please find my reply in your e-mail in Blue.

Contact person in the invoice and PL not necessary. For us will be better if you will make telex release. Is it possible?

Irina

Notes

邮件回复的特点。通常回复客户的邮件是新写一个文本，在新的文本里回复客户的问题，或者表达沟通的信息。但是，由于问题点太多，回复时为避免重复陈述的麻烦，在原邮件里直接回复问题也是常见的，这样的回复清楚明了，也节省时间。回复邮件的字体颜色和原邮件的字体颜色不同即可，一般以蓝色为主。也可以在回复的内容前加入自己的名字，这样让客户更清楚地知道哪些是你的回复，明白要确认的东西，直接肯定。如果有疑问，可以提出让对方回答。

Dear Irina,

Thank you very much for your kind reply.

Well understand. Then we will do telex release for you.

I'm looking forward to hearing from you.

Best regards,

Water

Notes

一般情况下，发货人通过银行交单或将提货单寄给收货人。因为提货单是货物所有权的凭证，收货人只有拿到正本提单后才可以提货。由于电放后发货人将不再掌握货权，因此在办理电放前一定要确认发货人能够安全收款，否则极易造成钱货两空的局面。

电放就是凭电子的、电传的或者传真件放行的意思。提单文件电放在贸易中也是常见的一种操作方式。因为这种方式快捷、便利，但只适用于在货款已安全入账的前提下操作。电放文件适用于航程较短的国家，比如日本、韩国只有两天左右的航程，如果通过银行寄送，文件尚未到达货物已经到港，为了不影响收货，电放文件更为合适，收货人凭文件传真件即可提货。另一种情况是客户直接要求电放，因为电放文件可以为某些国家的客户清关提供便利，这样也省去寄送文件的一些费用。

Dear Irina,

How are you doing?

I would like to inform you that the goods will be ready of shipment on April 30th. Could you arrange the balance payment for Pro forma Invoice # GW080402-01 accordingly?

I already sent the booking to Daisy. I think she will confirm the details with you then.

Looking forward to hearing from you.

Best regards,

Water

Notes

如果是 T/T 付款，应提前通知客户货物完成的时间和出货时间，以便客户安排验货和支付余款。安排余款时，有些客户要求提供签章的商业发票，根据实际要求制作文件即可。另外，也需要提前联系客户的货代公司了解船期，以免延误。

向客户提供问题之外的信息，比如已经和客户的货代取得联系，或者已经安排订舱等。主动让客户了解订单的进展情况，让客户放心，这也是体现服务的一种方式。

Dear Water,

Thank you for your e mail. We shall pay balance in the near future.

Irina

Dear Irina,

Thanks for your information about payment in the near future. We are waiting for your bank receipt then. By the way, I already booked space with Daisy this morning.

As the shipment from Hong Kong will be easier for our customs clearance, can we do FOB HK? And I consulted with Daisy also, she said they can receive goods from HK too. If OK to you, namely we can choose FOB Shenzhen as well as FOB HK. And please note that no cost up.

Look forward to your reply soon.

Best regards,

Water

Dear Water,

FOB HK-OK.

Irina

Notes

邮件标题是一封邮件主要内容的体现。在撰写邮件时，往往需要明确标题，或者根据邮件内容修改标题，这样收件人在查找邮件时可节省时间，也更容易了解邮件的主要内容。

文中，主要的内容是更改交货港，标题可以写成 Change FOB Shenzhen to FOB HK.这样就方便接收邮件的人阅读和了解。

因为香港是自由贸易港，相对于大陆的一些港口，对于某些公司来说操作更为方便。但是从大陆到香港需要支付额外的运费，所以在订单谈判时，需要明确交货港。如果需要更改，需要和客户商量。

Dear Irina,

Well understand. Thanks. We will arrange well for you and inform you the details accordingly.

Best regards,

Water

Dear Water,

How are you? We have prepared payment. On Monday-Tuesday money will be on your account. Please see attachment.

Irina

Dear Irina,

Thanks for your kind arrangement. I will check and arrange shipment accordingly.

Best regards,

Water

Notes

T/T 付款在一般情况下，3 个工作日即可入账。如果有银行汇款回执单(通常称为银行水单)，更容易查询汇款情况。即使款项尚未入账，也可以查到账款的具体情况。所以在客户转账后，通常都会要求客户提供银行水单。特别是在收取订金的时候，因为收到银行水单之后，可以说账款已经打出，正常情况下，工厂是确认客户的订金到账之后才安排备料及生产，但这个时候工厂可以提前备料，或者准备订单的设计材料等，这样有利于保证交货时间。

Dear Water,

How are you? Did you receive money?

Irina

Dear Irina,

Today we may get it. And I will keep you informed.

Your forwarder has offered the S/O to us. We will catch the vessel on May 6th.

Best regards,

Water

Notes

客户关心的问题要肯定回复，做到让客户放心。这样既体现了公司的服务水平，也体现了自己的工作效率。客户的满意度提高了，对公司形象和个人形象的提高都是非常有好处的。让订单操作顺畅，是更多订单的前提保障。

Dear Irina,

How are you doing?

Please find the attachment, B/L copy for reference. Hope you can confirm me soon.

Looking forward to your early reply.

Best regards,

Water

Dear Water,

We confirm it is OK. Please go ahead.

Irina

Dear Irina,

Herewith enclosed the original B/L for your record. We have telex released for you.

Best regards,

Water

Notes

在正本提单出来之前，一般都有副本供确认。除了提单之外，还需要同时向客户提供其他出货文件，如商业发票、装箱单等客户要求的文件。因为客户可能对产品描述等有一定的要求，不能出现什么文字、需要包括哪些内容等，所以，向客户提供提单和其他出货文件确认也是关键的一步。

2. Confirm Shipping Documents Draft

Dear Water,

Please, when you issue all shipping documents, before sending to the bank, send a copy to me for my approval.

Thanks for your cooperation.

Best regards,

Paola

Dear Paola,

Thank you for your kind e-mail. Sure I will send you the PI and other DOCs for your confirmation before sending to bank.

Thank you.

Water

Dear Paola,

Good morning. Herewith I wish to enclose the revised PI for your check first. Please advice.

Could you confirm with UPS about the shipment date? I wish to send the goods to UPS before Nov.12th which is the vessel closing date as UPS told me. Therefore we could catch it for shipment.

Looking forward to hearing from you soon.

Best regards,

Water

Hi Water,

The PI is correct now! I inform UPS to manage your shipment soon.

Hi Piera, Hi Carl,

Mr. Water, from Zhejiang company, PO153, is ready to send you the goods before Nov.12th, try your best to arrange this goods for vessel on 12th. Thanks for your cooperation.

Looking forward to receiving confirmation asap.

My B. Rgds,

Paola

Dear Paola,

How are you doing? This is Water. I use my alternative e-mail to contact you because my business e-mail is broken today.

We have sent the goods to UPS today. Please kindly check the attached photos for your reference.

Thank you.

Best regards,

Water

Hi Water,

Thanks for your e-mail. Please, start to send all shipping documents copy by e-mail before you send them to the bank so I can check!

Thanks for your attention and support.

Rgds,

Paola

Dear Paola,

Here is the shipping DOCs for your reference, including CI, PL and B L. Please kindly advise back soon.

By the way, the LSCD license is under application and the C/O too. Will send you the copy for reference later.

Looking forward to hearing from you soon.

Best regards,

Water

Dear Paola,

Reminder!!!

Could you kindly confirm the attached shipping DOCs soon? As I have to confirm with UPS to issue the original B/L.

Thank you for your kind attention.

Best regards,

Water

Notes

客户没有及时回复邮件，需要提醒客户确认文件。只需要转发原邮件，并在邮件中标注 reminder 或者 friendly reminder，显得更客气一些。另外，在平常的客户联系中也可以这样写，第一次提醒可以用 first reminder，第二次用 second reminder，超过两次，就需要再写一封邮件探明客户处于什么状态，或者直接打电话联系。在邮件中，如果需要强调客户确认的内容，可以再陈述一次。提醒的单词用不同的颜色标出，说明这是提醒客户要重视的。

Hi Water,

For the B/L:

The notification has to be for:

SMG

Interporto Campano Lotto H, G1 80035-Nola, NA, Italy

For the Invoice:

You have to correct the Invoice with right amount (USD 85.235,50) as the revised PI sent to me. Send me them again for my approval before sending all documents to the bank.

Don't forget to insert certificate copies (CE, Rohs, LSCD) and lab test, certificate of origin.

Looking forward to hearing from you very soon.

Rgds,

Ms. Paola Esposito

Dear Paola,

Thank you for your kind reply. For your comments, I would reply you as below.

As your L/C stipulate the notify is the same as applicant, and your applicant is:

SMG

VIA E. CORCIONI 30 81031 A VERSA

OK, it's our legal registered office.

It is not the notify you said to me here. I think we have to do as per L/C.

We will offer other DOCs as per your L/C request.

OK.

By the way, I think we have to revise the shipper name and address. It should be as per the L/C. Will revise it the same as beneficiary in L/C, I will send you the copy later.

I will wait for your copies.

Look forward to your confirmation soon.

Best regards,

Water

Hi Water,

Check my red reply below.

Rgds,

Ms. Paola Esposito

Dear Paola,

Thank you for your kind reply.

Revised B/L, please check as attached.

C/O and LSCD license, please check as attached.

Hope it is OK now and kindly confirm soon please.

And please excuse all the trouble in conveniences caused. Believe in future we could do better for you.

Best regards,

Water

Hi Water,

Now it's OK, please, send the original shipping documents to the bank asap.

Thanks for your cooperation. Surely, in future we will cooperate better.

B.Rgds,

Ms. Paola Esposito

Notes

在和客户合作的过程中，无论是哪一个步骤都有可能出现状况，杜绝状况的发生是我们应该做的，但是如果状况发生了，我们要积极地面对，要和客户形成有效的沟通。特别是以 L/C 付款而且是远期信用证，风险更大，在文件处理方面需要更加细致。

解决问题后，适当地向客户表达歉意，并表达将来的合作态度，让客户形成愉悦的心理感受，从心底感受到我们真诚的服务，从而使以后的合作更加密切。

资料链接 Material—link

1. *Standard Model*

Model 1: Urging Shipment 催促装运函

Dear Mr. Wang,

Re: Shipment of the Canned Mushroom under S/C No.56

We are writing to call your kind attention to the shipment of the canned mushroom under Sales Contract No.56. The date of shipment is approaching, but up to now, we haven't got any information from you regarding the progress of the preparation of the goods.

As you know, this transaction is on a FOB basis. It is our duty to book the shipping space. Only after knowing when the goods will be ready for shipment, can we book the shipping space in time with the suitable shipping line.

Please notify us when the goods will be ready for shipment as soon as possible.

Yours sincerely,

Model 2: Replying Letter 回复催促装运函

Dear Mr. Spear,

Re: Shipment of the Canned Mushroom under S/C No.56

Thank you for your letter of Sep.18 enquiring about whether the goods under Sales Contract No.56 are ready. We would like to inform you that the goods are being packed and will be ready for shipment on Sep.26, 2008.

Please book the shipping space and inform us of the name, voyage of the vessel, the name and address of the shipping line you will nominate and the departure time of the vessel so as to enable us to contact the agent of the shipping line in our area for loading the goods.

We look forward for your early reply.

Yours sincerely,

Model 3 : Shipping Instructions to the Seller before Shipment 致卖方装运须知函

Dear Mr. Wang,

Re: Shipment of the Canned Mushroom under S/C No.56

Thank you for your letter dated Sep.22 informing us that the captained goods will be ready for shipment on

Sep.26. We have confirmed the booking with Hyundai Merchant Marine Shipping Co. for 3 20-foot equivalent units.

The name of the vessel on which the shipping space is booked is Hyundai Star (Voyage No. 009E). The estimated departure time of the vessel from Yantai Port is Sep.28.

Please contact the Daya Freight Forwarding Co., Ltd., the agency of Hyundai Merchant Marine Shipping for specific arrangements of the shipment. The contact information of Daya Freight Forwarding Co., Ltd. is listed below:

Address: Room 806, Qili Mansion, Chaoyang Street, Yantai City

Tel: 0535-6228292　　Fax: 0535-6228293

Please fax us the shipping advice as soon as the shipment is executed.

Yours sincerely,

Model 4 :Shipping Advice to the Buyer After Shipment 致买方的装运通知函

Dear Mr. Spear,

Re: Shipment of the Canned Mushroom under S/C No.56

I would like to inform you that the 20 metric tons of canned sliced mushroom under Sales Contract No.56 have already been shipped on board the vessel you nominated.

The vessel departed from Yantai Port on September 28 as scheduled. No changes are made concerning the name and voyage of the vessel. The estimated arrival time of the vessel to Los Angeles, USA is Oct. 18.

In compliance with your request, related shipping documents including shipped on board Bill of Lading, Commercial Invoice, Packing List, Certificate of Insurance and Certificate of Origin will be sent to you by DHL tomorrow.

We hope the goods will reach you in time and turn out to your entire satisfaction.

Yours sincerely,

Model 5 :Sending Document of Shipment 寄发装运单据函

Dear Sirs,

Thank you for your letter of August 1 enquiring about the shipment of your order under L/C No.CQYW708265.

Please accept my apology for the delay which has been caused by the unavailability of shipping space from Bombay to London.

The matter was, however, in hand and your consignment was shipped yesterday on board S.S. Prince which is sailing directly to London. I enclose one set of shipping documents comprising:

1．*One non-negotiable copy of the B/L.*

2．*Commercial Invoice in duplicate.*

3．*One copy of the Certificate of Quantity.*

4．*One copy of the Insurance Policy.*

I'm glad that we have been able to execute your order as contracted. I trust the goods will reach you in time for the winter selling season and prove to be entirely satisfactory. I will personally ensure that you receive our prompt and careful attention at all time.

Yours sincerely,

2. *Writing Guide*

1) 有关装运的信函写作目的

Pressing earlier shipment, amending terms of shipment, sending shipping advice and dispatching shipping documents.

2) 装船指令写作技巧

(1) *Receipt of the contract.*

(2) *Detailed requirements for the shipping marks.*

(3) *Expectation of goods.*

3) 装运函件要点

Opening：*receipt of cable and thanks.*

Body：(1) *Mentioning goods under the order and contract*

(2) *Informing shipment and detailed request*，*if it is a letter of pressing earlier shipment.*

(3) *Discussing terms of shipment or asking for amendment to terms of shipment*，*suggesting other terms of shipment and giving reasons, if it is a letter of asking for amendment to terms of shipment.*

(4) *Sending packing instruction*，*if it is a letter of packing request.*

(5) *Asking for partial shipment and transshipment and giving the reason*，*if it is a letter of partial shipment and transshipment.*

Ending: Expectation of an early reply and cooperation.

Section Four　Selected Sentences
精选句型表达

1．It is now over two months since we sent the order for Tape Recorders, yet we are still awaiting delivery. You should know that the delivery date is very important to us.

你知道我们磁带录音机的订单已经发了两个多月了，我们仍在等货送达，抵达日期对我们而言十分重要。

2．Please take the matter up at once and see to it that the goods are delivered without further delay.

请立即处理此事，要知道货物送达不得延误。

3．Please get the goods dispatched with the least possible delay.

请发货，尽量避免延误。

4．I wonder if you could check the order I placed with you last month. It hasn't arrived yet.

我想知道你方是否检查了上月发给你方的订单，它仍没送达。

5．Please do your utmost to hasten shipment.

请尽最大努力发货。

6．We are much in need of the goods. Please expedite shipment as soon as possible.

我们急需该货，请尽可能安排发货。

7. We wish to call your attention that up to the present moment no news has come from you about the shipment. Our users are in urgent need of the machines and are pressing us for an early delivery.

我们希望你能注意到，直到目前还未收到你发货的任何消息，我们的消费者急需该机器，请尽早为我们发货。

8. As our customers are in urgent need of the contracted machines, we hope you can assure us of an early shipment.

由于我们的顾客急需合同中的机器，我们希望你方能确保早日发货。

9. I want to know why our alloy inserts haven't arrived yet. Our customers are in urgent need of them.

我想知道为何我们的合金镶块还未送达，我们的顾客急需它们。

10. We hope that there will be no delay in shipment any longer.

我们希望发货不再延误。

11. This order is so urgently required that we must ask you to make the earliest possible shipment.

该单如此急需，我们必须要求你方尽早发货。

12. We shall appreciate it very much if you will effect shipment as soon as possible, thus enabling the goods to arrive here in time to catch the brisk demand.

若早日发货，将不胜感激，这样货物可以及时抵达以迎合活跃的需求。

13. We hope you will send the air-conditioners as soon as possible, for the hot season is rapidly approaching.

我们希望你能尽早将空调发出，因为炎热的季节马上到来。

14. The goods we ordered are seasonal goods. So it will be better to ship them all at once.

我们所订的货物为季节性产品，故尽早发货为佳。

15. In order to be in time for the season, early shipment is of utmost importance to us.

为了赶上销售旺季，对我们而言，早点发货尤为重要。

16. We might refuse the shipment if it doesn't arrive on time.

若货未及时到达，我们可能拒绝发货。

17. We must insist on delivery within the time contracted and reserve the right to reject the goods if we fail to receive the goods before this week.

如果本周不能收到货物，我们必须坚持根据合同时间发货并保留拒收货物。

18. We regret to say that unless you are able to give us an assurance of delivery within the next two weeks, we shall be obliged to cancel the order.

我们遗憾地告知你方，除非你们保证在接下来的两周内发货，否则我们将被迫终止订单。

19. If shipment is too late, we'll be forced to withdraw the contract.

如果发货太迟，我们将被迫撤销合同。

20. If you still delay delivery , I'll have to cancel the order.

若你们仍延迟发货，我们不得不取消订单。

21. If you can't effect delivery within the stipulated time, we will have to lodge a claim against you for the loss and reserve the right to cancel the contract.

若你们不能在规定的时间内发货，我们不得不要求你们赔偿并保留撤销合同的权利。

22. If you fail to deliver the goods according to the agreed time, you should indemnify us for all losses and corresponding expenses.

若你们不能根据协议时间发货，你方应该赔偿我们的损失及相关的费用。

23. If there is still no information from you about the expedition of shipment by the end of this month, we'll be forced to cancel the contract and reserve the right to lodge a claim against you for the loss.

若本月末仍未获悉贵方发货的消息，我们将被迫撤销合同并保留追究贵方给我方造成的损失的权利。

24. We wish to point out that if you fail to effect shipment within the time specified, we shall not be able to fulfill the contract with our client.

我们要说的是若你们不能在规定的时间内发货，我们将无法与我方客人履行合同。

25. We would like to emphasize that any delay in shipping our booked order will undoubtedly involve us in no small difficulty.

我们要强调的是我们的订单的任何延误将毫无疑问造成到我们不小的困难。

26. Your failure to deliver the goods within the stipulated time has greatly inconvenienced us.

你方未在规定的时间内发货给我们造成极大的麻烦。

27. Any delay in shipment would be detrimental to our future business.

任何发货延迟将危及我们未来的业务。

28. We trust you will see that the order is shipped within the stipulated time, as any delay would cause us no little financial loss.

我们相信你方明白那个订单必须在规定时间内发货，因为任何延误将会导致我们损失惨重。

29. As you know, June is the right season for the goods, so if they arrive later than June, we will miss the selling season.

你知道，六月是该货的旺季，若迟于六月到达，我们将错失销售季节。

30. Should you delay the shipment any longer, the fireworks might become useless to us.

一旦你延迟发货，烟花可能对我们毫无用处。

Abstract

通过本章学习，①了解装运的基本分类；②掌握装运来往函电写作必须包含的基本内容；③掌握装运来往函电写作的基本规律和注意事项；④通过熟悉标准模板掌握装运函电写作的基本方法；⑤熟练掌握装运函电经典句型的表达。

Useful Words & Expressions

1. advice of shipment 装运通知
2. anticipate shipment 提前装运
3. accept forward shipment 接受远期装运
4. cash against document at port of shipment 在启运港凭单据付现
5. cash on shipment 装货付款
6. consign for shipment 托运
7. country of shipment 启运国
8. current shipment 近期装运
9. day of shipment price 装运日价格
10. delay in shipment 延迟装船；延期装船
11. delay shipment 延期装运
12. delayed shipment 延期装运
13. early shipment 提早装船
14. goods awaiting shipment 备运货物
15. immediate shipment 立即装船
16. inland shipment 内陆运输
17. installment shipment 分批装船；分期装运
18. knocked-down shipment 分运费
19. light-weight shipment 轻量货运输
20. notice of shipment 装船通知
21. on deck shipment 舱面装货；货装舱面
22. one shipment 一次装运
23. pallet shipment 托盘装运
24. parcel shipment 包裹运输
25. part shipment 分批装运
26. partial shipment 部分装运；分批装运
27. penalty for late shipment clause 延迟装运罚款条款
28. port of shipment 装运港；载货港；起运港；发货港
29. received for shipment 收货候装
30. received shipment 备运
31. report of shipment 装运报告
32. shipment advice 装船通知
33. shipment by cheapest route 以船运费最低的航线装运
34. shipment by steamer 以船舶装运
35. shipment index 交货指数
36. shipment not in accord with the sample 来货与样品不符
37. shipment outward 寄销

38. shipment price 交运价格；发送价格
39. short shipment 短缺载货
40. split shipment 分批发货
41. standard shipment 标准装运
42. terms of shipment 装运条件
43. time of shipment 交货时间；交运时间
44. underdeck shipment 舱内装货
45. untimed prompt shipment 不限期即期交运

Exercises

1. Multiple choice.

(1) We shall advise you by cable as soon as the goods ____ .

A. will ship B. will be shipped C. ship D. are shipped

(2) We have received your letter of the 1st March ____ us to effect shipment as soon as possible.

A. to ask B. that ask C. asking D. for asking

(3) The shipment ____ Contract No. 333 has arrived here duly.

A. against B. by C. for D. in

(4) The additional charges are ____ your own account.

A. for B. at C. of D. on

(5) According to the shipping ____, it will be impossible for us to ship the goods in October.

A. schedule B. timetable C. plan D. scheme

(6) ____ this trial order prove satisfactory to your customer, we can ____ you that repeat orders in increased quantity will be placed.

A. if, assure B. if, ensure

C. should, assure D. should, ensure

(7) We have the pleasure to inform you that the shipment has gone ____ per S.S. Victoria and hope that it will arrive at the ____ in perfect condition.

A. to, port B. as, destination

C. shipping, warehouse D. forward, destination

(8) Please ____ us your freight rate and let us have any information of your ____ .

A. tell, your shipment B. offer, sailing

C. quote, sailing D. offer, vessel

(9) The shipment time is June or July at our _____ and the goods will be shipped in one ____ .

A. option, lot B. option, consignments

C. choice, shipment D. decision，cargo

(10) Your prompt attention to shipment is ____ desirable ____ all parties concerned.
A. the most, for　　B. most, with　　C. most, to　　D. least, with

2. Answer the questions according to the passage.

(1) How many modes of transportation are there in international trade? And what are they?
(2) Which mode of transportation is a more important way in international trade? Why?
(3) When sending a Shipping Advice to the buyer, what is often enclosed?

3. Put the following sentences into English.

(1) 我们没法取得舱位，所以要求转运。(obtain shipping space)
(2) 另一种方法就是我们将货物分批装运。(alternative)
(3) 开往你地的轮船非常少，我们很难在直达轮上订到舱位。(few and far between，direct liner)
(4) 第E493号合同和第2864号信用证项下3 000台彩电到目前为止仍未收到任何装船消息，这给我们带来很大麻烦。(involve in)
(5) 关于第90号合同项下小麦装运事宜，我方用户坚持要求第一批5吨货物于10月底前装运，否则将提出索赔。关于第二批5吨货物，我公司正努力说服他们接受11月底装运而不要坚持12月交运。由于货物必须在年底前到达欧洲，无法接受12月份装运。

如贵方确实不能提前交货，是否能向国内其他方面进货，我们一直努力设法解决这一问题，但却无法说服用户不处罚金而接受第一批货推迟交货。

希望尽快确认第一批5吨货物将按合同规定于10月底前交货。

Case Practice

以本章的导入案例为背景，请以公司业务员Daniel的名义缮制一份买方催促卖方尽快发货的信函。详细地阐明催促卖方尽快发货的原因，即近来这种聚乙烯的需求量大增。表明一收到上述货物，我方将能更准确地判断我方的需求，并将相应地向贵方订货。

Chapter 10 Complaints and Adjustments

申诉与理赔

案例导入 Case-lead-in

宁波益佳玩具进出口公司是一家拥有自营进出口权的外贸型生产企业，有着15年的OEM生产历史，产品资源丰富，品类繁多，主要客户有迪斯尼、沃尔玛、肯德基、可口可乐等。公司依托于常年生产高标准外贸订单的质量控制体系、雄厚的设计开发能力，为不同的客户提供最适合的产品和服务。公司目前拥有工人150余人，专业设计师8人。公司主要提供以下产品和服务。

企业促销赠送类玩具产品；

婴幼儿专用的毛绒产品系列(玩具、毯子、枕头等)；

家居系列毛绒产品(餐巾盒套、毛绒凳子、卡通镜框等)；

各种款式的有声和无声的动物毛绒玩具。

2007年 5月2日公司收到一个客户电子邮件形式的投诉。

Frank ,

We have problems that need to be solved!

(1) *The bottom of the can falls off ! It needs to be attached harder in the bottom to avoid all the magnets to fall out . Get back to me how we are going to solve this problem. See pictures of the problem.*

(2) *The Santa samples have arrived and all of them are in the wrong colour ! They should be in the same colour as the first can of sample we got but they aren't ,and this colour isn't acceptable . The colour has to be dark red ,not light red as the news samples are.See picture.*

Please confirm the solution for these problems ASAP !

We won't take the goods if these problems can't be solved!

BR ,

Daniel

Section One　Types of Complaints
申诉的种类

In this task, we discuss the types of complaints and the techniques to write complaints.

There are two kinds of complaints being frequently made by buyers:

(1) The genuine complaint, which arises from one of the following situations.

① The wrong goods may have been sent.

② The quality may not be satisfactory.

③ The goods may have been delivered damaged or late.

④ he prices charged may be excessive, or not as agreed.

(2) There is the complaint made by buyers who find fault with the goods as an excuse to escape from their contracts, either because they no longer want the goods or because they have found that they can get them cheaper elsewhere.

If a complaint has to be made by buyers, the matter should be investigated in detail, and these details should be laid before the party charged. When making a complaint, plan your letter as follows.

(1) Begin by regretting the need to complain.

(2) Mention the date of the order, the date of delivery and the goods complained about.

(3) State your reasons for being dissatisfied and ask for an explanation.

(4) Refer to the inconvenience caused.

(5) Suggest how the matter should be put right.

A complaint may result from wrong delivery, unsatisfactory quality, damaged goods or being overcharged, etc.

If a complaint has to be made, your letter should:

(1) Express your regret.

(2) Inform the receiver of the subject matter, such as order/contract number and its date.

(3) Tell him directly why you are not satisfied.

(4) Give your suggestions and hope for an early reply.

Section Two Adjustments
理赔的方式

It is very normal for dealers to meet trade disputes. There are many ways in the settlement of an international trade dispute. Normally, amicable settlement or conciliation is the first choice because it saves time and cost while maintaining good business relations. If amicable settlement does not lead to a satisfactory result, the parties concerned may seek for arbitration in which the arbitration award shall be final and binding to both parties. It is more flexible compared with a legal suit.

Replies to complaints should always be courteous, even if the complaint is unfounded; the sellers should not say so until they have good and reliable grounds on which to repudiate the claim.

Suppose you are the seller, the following rules are to be noted when dealing with a complaint, and it also means adjustments.

(1) The first thing that has to be decided is whether the complaint is justified. If so, you

have to admit it readily; express your regret and promise to put matters right.

(2) If the complaint is not justified, point this out politely and in an agreeable manner. It would be a wrong policy to refuse the claim offhand.

(3) If you cannot deal with a complaint promptly, acknowledge it at once. Explain that you are looking into it and that you will send a full reply later.

(4) All complaints should be treated as serious matters and thoroughly investigated. There is no need for the sellers to go into a long story of how the mistake was made and a short explanation may be useful.

Section Three Cases in Detail
具体案例分析

(一) 经典案例解析

Dear Sir,

Thank you for your delivery of table cloth which we ordered on October 12th. To our regret, on inspection, we found that the goods do not conform to the samples. We wish to invite your attention to the following points whether you agree to our proposal.

(1) The colors of the cloths are different to your original sample.

(2) The finish is unsatisfactory.

We are returning two of these by separate mail and would like you to replace the whole in correct color immediately, as we are in urgent need of them. Concerning the airfreight, we agree to pay the extra costs for airfreight. However, your costs for packing and insurance must have been lower for air cargo and we request you to ask this fact into consideration and bear some part of the airfreight charges.

We think that we may be able to dispose of them and await your reply as to whether you agree to our proposal.

Yours faithfully,

Notes

1. complaint 抱怨；控诉
2. dispatch 发送；派遣
3. inspection 检查；检验
4. conform 一致；(使)遵守
5. airfreight 空中货运(费)

6. 本文是客户的一封申诉信，抱怨卖方(出口商)产品的质量不佳，但还不是索赔。一般说来，客户提出索赔时必须附有检验单位的证明书，然后才能提出索赔、要求理赔。申诉的目的虽然同样是为了换货或者赔偿，但还处于索赔的准备阶段，也就是说，如果客户得到补偿，他就不再进一步办理索赔手续。因此，卖方必须给予申诉与索赔同样的重视，并且要慎重处理。

7. Structure of a letter for complaint

(1) Beginning Paragraph:referring to the terms agreed by the two parties.

开头：提及双方的协议条款。

(2) Transitional Paragraph: the reasons of complaining and the solution you hope.
中间的主要内容：写抱怨的原因和你希望的解决方式。

(3) Ending Paragraph: hoping for an early solution.
结尾：希望早日得到解决。

8. to our regret 我们表示道歉；对不起；让我们遗憾的是……

Much to my regret, I am unable to accept your invitation.
我不能接受您的邀请，深表歉意。

9. on inspection 通过检查，相当于 when inspected

10. debit sb. with sth. 计入(某人账户的)借方

11. conform to /with 与某物一致；符合；相似

12. as we are in urgent need of them 因为我们急需用这些货物

13. request you to ask this fact into consideration 敬请贵方考虑这一事实

(二) 一般案例表述

1. Missing Goods

Dear Paola,

Good morning.

Have you got the goods? And how about the DOCs? Hope everything is going well.

Looking forward to hearing from you.

Best regards,

Water

Hi Water,

Just today I got the goods and they are missing 12pcs from the carton box closed:

7'portable 6pcs USD 33 900

9'portable 6pcs USD 58 500/USD 92 400

Rgds,

Ms. Paola Esposito

Dear Paola,

Thank you for your kind feedback.

For the case you mentioned, could you let me know more information? If the following situation happened, please state us clearly. We must check and solve properly.

(1) How many cartons you received for each item? (7' and 9')

(2) The carton is blank?

(3) Or it is less than 5pcs in 6 cartons? Namely every carton is 4pcs or 3pcs or 2pcs or only 1pc, but not 5pcs.

If possible, please show me some photos. I will check with our factory carefully, too. Hope we could find out what the real situation is.

Looking forward to your comments soon.

Best regards,

Water

Dear Water,

Now I cannot show the pictures more since you know we have just 1 day to arrange the goods for our customers, you know the goods shipped by delay from China and it arrived here just 3 days before the Christmas holidays.

Anyway, I have the report from the warehouse, the pieces missing from first No.1-12 master box! Some master box missed 1 piece or 2 pieces!

Rgds,

Ms. Paola Esosito

Dear Paola,

Merry Christmas to you. Thank you for your kind feedback.

I understand what you told us. We are sorry it happened in such case. Please ask your warehouse people to mark down the details and let me know.

(1) Are there giftboxes in the cartons?

(2) With accessories or no accessories at all?

(3) Or with poly foam to stuff the empty room in the carton?

(4) Other details.

Please describe more details to me and it could help to find out the problem happened.

I have to say that we have tied two belts on the carton to protect, and to avoid others opening the carton. And we weigh the cartons before shipment. If the belts are loose and gone, it would be easy to open and to seal again. And because of LCL shipment, the player may be gone in customs warehouse. But it is surprising that the players are missed from carton No.1-12. Anyway we are not sure and cannot judge how it caused till now.

Looking forward to your further reply.

Merry Christmas and best wishes to you and your family and to SMG.

Best regards,

Water

Dear Paola,

Happy New Year!

I would like to talk to you about the missing goods. Shall we know that if you have found out the details? If you have more information, please kindly let me know.

Looking forward to hearing from you.

Best regards,

Water

Notes

产品到港之后少货的现象也时有出现，可能是工厂漏装，在装箱和发货时没有发现，还有可能是在国内或在国外的海关仓库或者码头出现一些状况而导致少货的。出现少货的现象之后，必须向客户清楚了解情况，按要求提供相关图片说明，例如，打开货柜之后的图片，纸箱包装拆箱之前和之后的图片，包装箱内的图片等一系列图片，这样更容易分析问题到底出现在哪个环节。

同时，向客户提供出货时的图片，说明出货的做法及可能出现问题的环节。互相配合，安抚客户的情绪，积极帮助客户解决问题。

2. Making Wrong Production

Dear Oscar,

For the order PI090408, we are going to finish it and arrange for delivery on next Monday, 13th, July. Now after checking the finished products, we found something different according to the order, some mouse we have done it with USB, not with U+P.

We are sorry for this case. We would like to talk to you about this shipment for these 4 000pcs products. Listing as below.

BL-M0319 1000PCS USB

BL-M0339 1000PCS USB

BL-M0206 2000PCS USB

We believe the mouse with USB is also popularly used in your markets. We sincerely hope you could accept this discrepancy and allow for shipment. As you know if we change to the mouse with U+P, we have to change the chipset and remake the mouse, that will spend much time, and it is also not good to remake the mouse, it will ruin its appearance.

Currently, most of the goods are OK, some just need packing. And we already got the S/O from forwarder today, the vessel closing time is on 15th July. We should load it on 13th July.

Surely we must do our part to fulfill the responsibility. We agree to reduce US＄400 from the total value.

Please kindly understand and help to confirm. We have to catch the vessel closing on 15th July. Thanks in advance.

Best regards,

Cindy

Dear Cindy,

USB is OK, no problem; please send me the new PI and the commercial invoice.

Have a good day,

Sincerely,

Oscar Castillo Saldarriaga

Notes

通常客户对OEM产品都有指定的功能要求和唯一的产品包装。业务员在和工厂确认资料的过程中，可能由于客户的资料过多，漏掉一些需要确认的内容，或因疏忽造成资料确认错误。这些不符点可能在生产的过程中被发现，或者被自己的验货人员在验货时发现，甚至直到客户的验货人员验货时才发现。无论是何时发现，出现返工的情况都是极其严重的，因为这将涉及一笔返工费用，如人工费、耗材费，最主要的是时间的浪费。因为返工是很复杂、很繁琐的一个过程，特别是在产品的销售旺季，时间更显得珍贵。通常这个时候的订单生产周期都排得比较满。一旦出现错误或者产品被拒，将打乱所有的生产排期，变得很被动。

但错误已经造成，也要正确对待。追究责任是应该的，但当务之急不是追究责任，而是如何妥善地解决问题。无论对于工厂或者客户来说时间都是宝贵的。分析问题的情况，确认其是产品性能问题、包装问题，还是外观问题。这些问题是否会影响产品的正常使用，是否会有碍运输，是否会影响销售。还有工厂的解决方法。每一点都分析完毕之后，需要写一封详尽的邮件，告知客户具体的情况和解决的方法。客户有决定权，决定拒绝还是接受。但是作为销售人员，需要向客户分析发现的问题，把事情的轻重缓急向客户言明。如果不是非常严重的问题，客户也会根据具体的情况而接受不符点或者做出轻微的修改。

杜绝问题的最好方法就是认真对待工作，将工作做细致。多一双眼留意客户的要求。

资料链接 Material—link

1. Standard Model

Model 1:Lodging a Claim for Damaged Goods

Dear Sirs,

We have received your shipment covering our order No. 1121 for 200 units of electric heater, which you shipped by M/S "President", but much to our regret we have to inform you that we have found that one of the cases of your consignment is in a badly damaged condition. Among the goods, the panels of 20 heaters were broken and the mechanisms were exposed. It looks as if some heavy cargo had fallen on it.

As you see in our survey report stating twenty sets of heaters severely damaged, these goods are quite unsaleable. Therefore we would ask you to ship replacements for the broken goods as soon as possible while we will register our claim with the insurance company. We hope the matter will come to your best attention.

Yours faithfully,

Model 2: Apologizing for Mixture of Other Goods

Dear Sirs,

We are really sorry for your complaint that your goods have been mixed up with others. We have made the most searching inquires but the only explanation we could find was that the labels had been confused. How this error failed to be found out by our checking system is beyond our understanding.

We hasten to offer our sincere apologies for this mistake which is all the more unfortunate as we were so pleased that you had given our goods such splendid admiration. It goes without saying that 20 sets were on their way to New York within a week on receipt of your letter and we hope that they will reach you in time to meet the anticipated demand for this article.

To compensate you to a certain extent for the trouble we have caused you, we will grant you a special discount of 1% for your next order within the amount of USD100 000.

Yours faithfully,

Model 3 :Letter in Response to the Claim of Discrepancy of Goods

Dear Sirs,

We have read carefully your letter of complaint on the discrepancy of the goods with the original sample.

Apparently this was caused by the oversight of our production department. Please accept our apologies for your inconvenience.

We are sending you a new lot by air at once, and would ask you to return the faulty goods at your convenience with freight forward. Or you may keep them for sale at a reduced price of 30% discount.

You are perfectly correct in saying that packing and insurance are normally less for air cargo. However we remind you that your request to send the goods by air was made at very short notice. It was impossible for us to use the lighter air freight packing materials. Furthermore, our insurance is on an open policy, and depends on the value of the goods, not the method of transportation.

We look forward to receiving your remittance when due.

Yours faithfully,

2. *Writing Guide*

(1) 什么情况下写投诉和索赔信函?

When the importer finds the wrong goods delivered ,the quality below the requirements as specified in the sales contact , the discrepancy between delivered goods and samples , the arrived goods on damaged condition, and so on , he will be unhappy and disappointed and make complaints .

(2) 买家在发现货物有问题时应该怎么做?

The buyer should look into the matter, if the loss is not serious , and does not influence the sale, the buyer may just write a complaint to arouse the seller's attention to avoid the matter happening again, if the loss is serious , the buyer may find the necessity of lodging a claim against the seller.

(3) 报诉/索赔内容的信函应该包含哪些方面?

① *In the beginning of the letter , the buyer should present the problem in detail. The presentation should include : the date of the order , the date of the delivery, name and quantity of goods, the contract number or any other in formation that help the reader easily check the order.*

② *Mention the inconvenience and ask for an explanation .*

③ *Present the evidence such as the survey report issued by the local authorities.*

④ *Suggest how to deal with the matter.*

(4) 解决投诉/索赔问题的信函包含哪些方面?

① *Apologize for the inconvenience caused to the buyer as soon as receiving the complaints or claims .*

② *Decide whether the complaint is justified. If so, the seller should admit it readily and explain the reasons of the problems on the ground of investigation . There is no need for the seller to go into a long story of how the mistake was made.*

③ *Present the adjustment methods in detail and promise no mistakes happen again.*

④ *Hope to cooperate with the buyer again in the future.*

⑤ 如果拒绝索赔，卖主回复时应该注意哪些方面?

If the complaints and claims made by the buyer are not justified, the seller should point out politely and in an agreeable manner. It would be a wrong policy to reject the buyer's request without thinking. The kind of letter should begin with your regret for the trouble caused and present sufficient evidence and reasons to support your rejection . In the end of the letter, the seller should tell the buyer that you are ready to give help for the early settlement of the problem.

Section Four Selected Sentences
精选句型表达

1. I was asked to come to your company on my way home in order to settle the claim .
我顺路来你们公司是为了处理索赔问题的。

2. We have received your remittance in settlement of our claim .
我们已经收到你方解决我们索赔问题的汇款。

3. Claims for incorrect material must be made within 60 days after arrival of the goods .
有关不合格材料的索赔问题必须在货到后 60 天内予以解决。

4. We want to settle our claim on you for the 100 tons of bleached cotton waste, as per Sales Confirmation No.1254E .
我们想处理一下关于销售确认书第 1254E 号 100 吨漂白废棉的索赔问题。

5. We have already made a careful investigation of the case.
我们已经对这个索赔案件做了详细的调查研究。

6. We are not in a position to entertain your claim.
我们不能接受你们提出的索赔要求。

7. We regret our inability to accommodate your claim .
很抱歉我们不能接受你方索赔。

8. We may consider withdrawing the claim .
我们可以考虑撤回索赔要求。

9. I'11 write to our home office to waive our claim immediately .
我立即写信给我们的总公司提出放弃索赔。

10. I'm afraid you should compensate us by 5% of the total amount of the contract .
贵公司要赔偿我方合同全部金额的 5%。

11. I propose we compensate you by 3% of the total value plus inspection fee .
我想我们赔偿贵方 3%的损失，另外加上商检费。

12. We regret for the loss you have suffered and agree to compensate you by $ 500 .
我们对你方遭受的损失深表歉意，同意向你们赔偿 500 美元。

13. The Japanese Company agreed to compensate us for the defective watches by 4% of the total value .
日本一家公司同意就手表不精确向我们赔偿总价值的 4%。

14. Please give our claim your favorable consideration .
请合理考虑我们的索赔要求。

15. Please examine the matter and send us the goods to meet the shortage as soon as possible.
请调查此事，并尽快将货物发给我们以弥补数量的不足。

16. As regards inferior quality of your goods , we claim a compensation of US $ 10 000 .
至于你方产品质量低劣的问题，我方要求你方赔偿1万美元。

17. We shall lodge a claim for all the losses incurred as a consequence of your failure to ship our order in time .
由于你方未能及时交货，我方将向你方提出由此而遭受的全部损失的索赔。

18. Any complaint about the quality of the products should be lodged within 15 days after their arrival.
任何有关该产品质量问题的申诉应该在货物到达后的 15 天内提出。

19. Our customers are complaining of the inferior quality of our products .
我们的客户投诉我们的产品质量低劣。

20. This seems to be a very clear case and we hope you will see your way to make a prompt settlement.
看来情况已十分清楚，我们希望你能设法尽快解决问题。

21. We regret that your claim on shortage cannot be accepted .
很遗憾，我们无法接受你方关于货物短装的索赔。

22. Our investigation shows that improper packing caused damage . Therefore we have to refer this matter to you .
我方检验证明，货物受损是由于包装不当而造成的。因此，我们不得不将此事提交你处解决。

23. As the goods are inferior in quality, we are returning the whole of the 20 cases and must ask you to replace them.
由于这些产品质量低劣，所以我方把 20 箱全部退回，并务必请贵方更换这些产品。

24. We very much regret the mistake in article number , which resulted in your receiving the wrong goods.
因货号有误，致使到货错误，对此，我们深表歉意。

25. The goods we've received do not tally with the sample on which we ordered.
我们收到的货物与订货样品不符。

26. In view of the long business relations between us, we wish to meet you half way to settle the claim.
考虑到我们之间长期的业务关系，我们愿意各让一半解决这项索赔问题。

27. We hope this unfortunate incident will not affect the relationship between us.
我们希望这一不幸事件将不会影响到我们双方之间的关系。

28. Apparently, the shortage is due to omission in packing.
很明显，货物短缺系包装遗漏所致。

29. In view of our friendly business relations, we are prepared to meet your claim for the 25 tons shortage weight.
考虑到我们之间的业务关系，我们准备接受 25 吨短装的索赔。

30. We are sorry that the quality of our goods did not turn out to your satisfaction .
我们很抱歉你们不满意我们货物的质量。

31．We can assure you that such a thing will not happen again in future deliveries .

我们保证在以后的交货中不会出现类似的事件。

32．Enclosed is the surveyor's report on the three damaged cases .

内附有鉴定人对这破损的 3 箱货物的鉴定报告。

33．Here's a survey report by a well-known lab in Houston , whose testimony is absolutely reliable .

这是由休斯顿的一个著名实验室提供的一份检验报告，证据绝对可靠。

34．Claim on shortweight is caused by packing damage or shortloading .

短重索赔是由包装破损或装运短重引起的。

35．Claim on delayed shipment is that sellers fail to make the delivery according to time schedule.

延期索赔是对卖方没有按时装运货物而提出的索赔。

36．Claim on quality originates from inferior quality of goods or quality changes.

(质量)索赔是在货物质量低劣或是质量改变的条件下发生的。

Abstract

通过本章学习，①了解申诉与理赔的基本分类；②掌握申诉与理赔来往函电写作必须包含的基本内容；③掌握申诉与理赔来往函电写作的基本规律和注意事项；④通过熟悉标准模板掌握申诉与理赔函电写作的基本方法；⑤熟练掌握申诉与理赔函电经典句型的表达。

Useful Words & Expressions

1．types of complaints 申诉的分类
2．claim arising from a breach of the contract 因违约而向某人提出索赔
3．claim arising from defect of the goods 货物瑕疵所引起的索赔
4．claim arising on a bill of lading 有关提单引起的索赔
5．claim barred on lack of conformity of the goods 受时效限制的索赔
6．claim based on a physical loss damage 货物灭失所产生的索赔
7．claim letter 索赔信
8．claim for compensation of damage 损害索赔的诉权
9．claim for contribution in general average 要求分担共同海损
10．claim for financial loss 关于经济损失的诉权
11．claim for general average 共同海损分担的诉权
12．claim for inferior quality 由于质量低劣而索赔
13．claim for payment 要求付款的诉权
14．claim for proceeds 要求赔偿货款
15．claim for reimbursement 要求偿还；索偿
16．claim for short delivery 由于短装而索赔
17．claim on account of damage 因损坏而索赔
18．claim on the goods 对该货物提出索赔
19．entertain a claim 受理索赔

20. dismiss a claim 驳回索赔
21. reject a claim 拒绝索赔
22. relinquish a claim 撤回索赔
23. withdraw a claim 撤回索赔
24. waive a claim 放弃索赔
25. lodge a claim on sb. 向某人提出索赔
26. make a claim on sb. 向某人提出索赔
27. place a claim on sb. 向某人提出索赔
28. issue, lay, put in, raise, file, register, render, bring up a claim on sb. 向某人提出索赔
29. to claim US $ 10 000 索赔美元 1 万元
30. to claim a compensation of US $ 10 000 要求赔偿 1 万美元
31. to claim US $ 10 000 for damage 因损坏赔偿 1 万美元
32. to claim US $ 10 000 on the goods 对该货索赔 1 万美元
33. to claim US $ 10 000 from the underwriters 向保险公司索赔 1 万美元
34. to claim (a compensation of)…from sb. for sth. 因……而向某人提出索赔
35. refund the excess on a tax 归还多收的货款
36. refund the goods to the sell 把货物归还卖方
37. obtain the fund of deposit 获得保证金的退款
38. refundable 可归还的
39. short delivery 短交
40. short shipment 短装
41. short-calculated 少算
42. Short-delivered 短交
43. Short-established 少开
44. short-invoiced 发票少开
45. short-landed 短卸
46. short-shipped 短装
47. short-paid 少付
48. amicable settlement 灵活处理
49. claim 索赔；赔偿；赔偿金
50. compensate 赔偿；补偿
51. to make a (one's) claim 提出索赔
52. to register a (one's) claim 提出索赔
53. to file a (one's) claim 提出索赔
54. to lodge a (one's) claim 提出索赔
55. to raise a (one's) claim 提出索赔
56. to put in a (one's) claim 提出索赔
57. to bring up a (one's) claim 提出索赔
58. claim for damage 由于损坏而索赔

59. to make a claim for (on) sth. 就某事提出索赔
60. to settle a claim 解决索赔(问题)
61. to withdraw a claim 撤销(某项)索赔
62. to waive a claim 放弃索赔(要求)
63. claim on the goods 对某(批)货索赔
64. claim report 索赔报告
65. claim on sb. 向某人(方)提出索赔
66. claim for trade dispute 贸易纠纷(引起的)索赔
67. claim for short weight 由于短重而索赔
68. to make a claim with (against) sb . 向某方提出索赔
69. claim for loss and damage of cargo 货物损失索赔
70. claim for inferior quality 由于质量低劣而索赔
71. claim against carrier 向承运人索赔
72. claimee 被索赔人
73. claimant 索赔人
74. claimsman 损失赔偿结算人
75. claims assessor 估损人
76. claims settling agent 理赔代理人
77. claims surveying agent 理赔检验代理人
78. claiming administration 索赔局
79. claim letter 索赔书
80. claims department (commission board) 索赔委员会
81. claims documents 索赔证件
82. claims settlement 理赔
83. claim indemnity 索赔
84. insurance claim 保险索赔
85. adjusted claim 精算后请求金额
86. attendant claim 附带要求
87. baggage claim 领取行李
88. belated claims 迟索的赔款
89. complaint and claims 抗议与索赔
90. Creditor's claims 债务要求权
91. dated consumption claims 标时消费请求权
92. claims settling fee 理赔代理费
93. claims rejected 拒赔
94. accessory claim 附带权利要求
95. assigned claim 转让债权
96. bad claim 不良债权
97. barred claim 失去时效的债权

98. compensation claim 赔偿要求
99. counter claim 反索赔，反诉
100. claims statement 索赔清单

Exercises

1. Multiple choice.

(1) Fifty cases of Green Tea you sent us were found badly damaged. This was apparently attributable to ____ packing.

A. faulty B. superior C. inferior D. mistake

(2) We are sorry to find that the damage ____ the goods was caused by heavy rain during transportation.

A. on B. for C. about D. to

(3) We lodge a claim ____ you ____ the short-weight.

A. with, with B. for, for C. with, for D. for, with

(4) After unpacking the case we found the goods did not ____ with the original sample.

A. measure B. match C. compare D. agree

(5) We have lodged a claim ____ the seller for the shortage of shipment ____ S.S. DONGFENG.

A. against, ex B. with, under C. on, as per D. with, to

(6) We have to point out that the ____ of the fulfillment of the contract has caused us certain expenses.

A. guarantee B. arrival C. postponement D. advancement

(7) We lodged a claim ____ you ____ fertilizer yesterday.

A. with, on B. against, about C. on, with D. to, against

(8) After inspection of the above shipment we found 5 cases ____ .

A. losing B. missing C. lost D. missed

(9) We regret that it is necessary to complain ____ the non-delivery of the 10 000 tons of sugar under Contract BC-023.

A. concerning B. about C. regarding D. with

(10) Appearance is apt ____ lead one to misjudge the substance.

A. to B. with C. on D. above

2. Answer the questions according to the passage.

(1) What are the methods of settlement in an international trade dispute?
(2) How to make a complaint?
(3) How to reply to a reasonable complaint?

3. Put the following sentences into English.

(1) 我方要求索赔 8 000 欧元以补偿所受的损失。

(2) 经检查发现近30%的包装破烂，显示由于包装不妥所致。

(3) 很遗憾贵方到货的质量与双方商定的不符。由于该货不能出售，对我方也无用，我方向贵方索赔金额××。

(4) 经目的港复检，“维多利亚号”运来的羊毛的质量与第 3215 号合同所规定的完全不符。

(5) 我方对“东风轮”装运的1 000吨小麦水分过多提出索赔。

(6) 2 月 14 日向贵方订购的玻璃板已于昨日收到，遗憾的是，其中 18%已破，40%起泡，且大部分有划伤，因此本批货品几乎不能使用。烦请贵方指示贵方代理人进行检查，并向贵方发货人报告。我方将向贵方提出按发票金额40%的损坏索赔。

如能从速处理，将不胜感激。

Case Practice

以本章的导入案例为背景，以公司业务员 Frank 的名义回一封邮件，妥善解决此事。希望对方能接受此订单，因为已经完成了订单 85%的生产。表达自己很重视提高产品的质量，但有时候样品之间存在细微的色差是被允许的。希望客户能劝说零售商接受此批货物，如果对方确实不能接受，则自己公司只能放弃完成的产品，购买原材料重新生产，而这需要一段时间。

Chapter 11 Agency

代　理

案例导入 Case-lead-in

广州市宝爵钟表有限公司(Guangzhou Baojue Watch Co.,Ltd.)是一家拥有瑞士资本以及港资的专业手表生产企业及品牌运作企业，是瑞士亨达钟表(香港)国际集团有限公司的全权代理子机构。公司在钟表批发市场拥有多年的内单以及外单的批发经验，目前在全球各地拥有广泛的客户。代理国内外多家时尚品牌，设计生产多种类别和款式的手表，礼品类客户包括中美史克、宝洁中国、中国工商银行、农业银行、中国移动礼品合作、亚太资源、蒙牛奶业、友邦保险和百威啤酒等。公司现欲代理瑞士亨达钟表(香港)国际集团有限公司旗下的中高端瑞士品牌的专业防水手表“瑞士汉爱表-HANDLOVE”，于是给该公司去信寻求建立代理关系。

Guangzhou Baojue Watch Co.,Ltd.
120 Renmin Road, Guangzhou, 510000, China
July 28, 2005
Switzerland HendDa Watch&Clock International Group Limited
Avenue Louis-Casaï 1809
08 Geneva Switzerland

Dear Sirs,

We take the liberty to address this letter to you, asking if you are interested in extending your export of "Handlove" to our country by appointing us sole agent for the sale of your products.

There is a growing demand here for good watches, and the prospects are really excellent for good quality watches at competitive price. If you are not already represented here, we should be interested in acting as your sole agent.

As a leading importer and distributor of nearly twenty years' standing in the watch trade, we have a good knowledge of the local market and have fostered close business relations with the domestic wholesalers in this district. We feel confident that you give us any opportunity to deal in your goods.

Please let us know your quotations, the rate of our commission and payment terms if we can be allowed to be your sole agent, so that we may begin negotiating with our customer to secure their orders.

We await your affirmative reply.

Faithfully yours,
Wang Yong

Section One Essentials of Agency 代理要点

1. Definitions of some terms.

When choosing an agent, the principal should make sure that the agent has sufficient means to develop trade and has reliable connections in the designated area. The followings are the definitions of some terms about agency.

Agency: It also refers to a business or organization established to provide a particular service, typically one that involves organizing transactions between two other parties. As far as the international trade is concerned, agency means that the exporter empowers a foreign businessman to conduct business performance abroad.

As far as buying and selling are concerned, there are mainly three types of agents: General Agent, Sole Agent (exclusive agent) and Commission Agent.

A general agent may be a firm or a person who acts under some degree of instructions from his principals of sell (or buy) goods on the best terms obtainable. He charges a commission for his services under some kinds of agreement or contract.

A sole agent similar to a general agent, may be a firm or a person who acts for one foreign principal with exclusive agency rights to sell on a commission basis certain commodities in a certain area under some kinds of agreement or contract.

Other types of agency:

Broker

Who negotiates sales and purchases contracts for buyers and sellers, without rights of his own in the goods.

Factors

Who have authority to sell in their own name for the principal, to receive payment, and to sell at times and prices which they consider advisable.

Forwarding agent

Who carries out all the duties connected with collecting and delivering the goods.

2. Why is appointing foreign agent important?

In international trade, most of the business activities are negotiated between buyers and sellers directly. But when the company does not have a branch office or representative in one place, he (the principal) may authorize another person or firm (agent) to act as his behalf. Usually the seller authorize some foreign firms to sell certain goods to the customers in a particular area during a particular period of time. There are two reasons. First, it's more economical appointing an agent than sending a member of its own staff to a foreign country. Second, a native of any country knows what goods are best suited to the area and what prices the market will bear.

3. What should we know about a prospective agent?

In choosing an agent, either a firm or a person, the principal should make searching enquiries into the qualifications, experience and personal qualities of prospective agents, for example: their reliability and financial soundness; their market connections and the effectiveness of their sales organization, their technical ability to handle the goods to be marketed, the nature and extent of other agencies they may hold, and in particular, whether these are connected with the sale of competing products.

Section Two Essentials of Business Correspondence of Agency 代理商务信函要点

1. Letters concerning agency can be written in the following structure:

(1) Put forward the problem of agency in a positive way.

(2) State which kind of agency is desired and provide the reader with convincing and specific reasons.

(3) Express expectation for an early reply or cooperation.

2. What is the structure of a formal agreement?

(1) Preamble.

(2) The nature of the agreement.

(3) The name of commodity and specifications.

(4) The territory to be covered.

(5) The method of purchase and sale.

(6) Mode of payment.

(7) Details of commission and expense to be allowed.

(8) The duties of agent and principal.

(9) Arbitration and court jurisdiction in the event of disputes.

(10) The language.

(11) The governing law.

(12) Validity of the agreement.

(13) Witness clause.

3. The different types of correspondences of Agency.

1) Marketing Agency

(1) Agency solicitation.

(2) Asking to be a Sales Agent.

(3) Entrusting customer with sole agency.

(4) Decline to grant a sole agency.

2) Banking Agency

3) Forwarding Agency

Section Three Cases in Detail
具体案例分析

(一) 经典案例解析

Agency Solicitation
(寻找代理)

Dear Sirs,

Our company manufactures a range of automatic copying machines possessing exquisite workmanship and numerous styles, and available in full sizes. Our automatic copying machines, which are widely accepted and very popular in your country, are sophisticated in design, elegant in patterns and beautiful in color. They can satisfy different customers' needs for the whole world.

Our products are already being sold in North America. With the steady increase in demand for our products in new markets, we are therefore looking for any company or individual who would be willing to represent us as a sole agent.

The agent must be fully conversant with the technical side of automatic copying machines and have a comprehensive understanding of all the features of the line. Meanwhile, they should have enough experience in promoting the sale of the product and have contacts with suitable outlets. On our part, we can offer the best machines to your satisfaction.

If you are interested in representing us in New York, please contact us.

We look forward to hearing from you.

Yours faithfully,

Notes

1. a range of 一系列
2. automatic copying machines 自动复印机
3. exquisite 精美的；精致的；制作精良的
4. workmanship 手工
5. available 可以得到的
6. sophisticated 精细的；复杂的，老于世故的；高级的、先进的
7. satisfy/meet/fulfill different customers' needs 满足不同顾客的需求
8. be conversant with/in 熟悉的；精通的
9. line 产品的种类
10. outlets 渠道
11. to your satisfaction 让你满意
12. 本文是一篇出口商主动寻求代理商的信函，其写作可以遵循以下步骤：首先，介绍自己的产品优势和公司的销售优势，给人留下深刻印象；其次，表达在特定区域寻求代理的真诚愿望；再次，提出自己的代理要求；最后，希望获得代理的积极联系。

（二）一般案例表述

Marketing Agency

Asking to be a Sales Agent- Letter 1

Dear Sirs,

We are interested in your wine products and would be very happy to offer our services as your agent in Egypt.

We are one of the largest firms in the wine and spirit trade in Egypt. We have better knowledge of the market here and good and effective distributing channels. There is a growing demand here for Chinese wine since more and more Chinese visitors and businessmen have come to Egypt. We had some kind of your wine products at a banquet last week and were impressed by its unique taste and smell.

If you give us an opportunity to be your agent, we think it will be a mutual-benefit deal. When we have details of your ranges with samples and prices, we shall advise you of their suitability for this market and choose the types that are likely to sell well.

As to our financial standing and reliability, you may refer to our bank or to any of our major customers. They will offer you the first-class references that prove us agents of high integrity.

We are looking forward to your favorable reply.

Yours faithfully,

Notes

1. offer our services as your agent 作为您的代理提供服务
2. reference: 资信证明、推荐信
3. good and effective distributing channels 良好有效的分销渠道
4. financial standing 财务状况
5. refer to 参考、向……求助
6. favorable reply 肯定的答复
7. Steps of writing a letter for asking for sole agency.

(1) Identifying the reference.

(2) Stating that you are able to represent the seller.

(3) Asking for conclusion of agency agreement.

(4) Presenting the reference for your credit standing.

(5) Urging a favorable reply.

Asking to Be a Sales Agent- Letter 2

Dear Sirs,

We would like to inform you that we act on a sole agency basis for a number of manufacturers. We specialize in finished cotton goods for the Middle eastern market: Our activities cover all types of household linen. Until now, we have been working with your textiles department and our collaboration has proved to be mutually beneficial.

Please refer to them for any information regarding our company. We are very interested in an exclusive arrangement with your factory for the promotion of your products in Bahrain.

We look forward to your early reply.

Dear Sirs,

We have received your letter of August 3 and after careful consideration, have decided to entrust you with the sole agency for our iron square hinges in Canada.

The agency agreement has been drawn up for the duration of one year, automatically renewable on expiration for a similar period unless notice is given to the contrary. The terms and conditions are set forth in detail.

Enclosed is a copy of the draft. Please go over the previsions and advise us whether they meet with your approval.

We shall do all in our power to assist you in establishing a mutually beneficial trade.

Yours faithfully,

Notes

1. entrust sb. with sth. 委托某人做某事
2. agency agreement 代理协议
3. draw up 草拟
4. set forth in detail 详尽的解释

Entrusting Customer with Sole Agency-Letter 1

Dear Sirs,

We have read your letter of the 15th May and are favorably impressed with the proposal you make for us.

After a careful review of our relations and the business achievements, we have decided to entrust you with the sole agency for our "Tiantan" brand Men's Shirts in the territory of Egypt. We have drawn up a draft agreement, which we are sending herewith. Please go over the detailed terms and conditions and advise us whether they meet with your approval.

Please be assured that we are always anxious to cooperate with you closely with a view to furthering a mutually beneficial trade.

Yours faithfully,

Encl.

Notes

1. entitle *v.* 给予权利或资格

The buyers are entitled to ask for replacement of the goods which are found defective.

2. feel (or: be) inclined 倾向于(做某事)，有意(做某事)

Carelessness of this kind makes our buyers feel inclined to give their orders to your competitors.

3. with a view to 为了；为的是

We are always anxious to cooperate with you closely with a view to furthering a mutually beneficial trade.

4. entrust v. 委托；托付

In view of the fact that the rate of premium you quoted is quite reasonable, we have decided to entrust your company with the insurance of this shipment.

5. go over v. 研究；检查；审阅

In going over our accounts, we find that there is a balance of US$96.55 in our favor.

6. further v. 增进；促进

Multinational corporations grew into strong entities by reinvesting their profits prudently so as to further the access to natural resources in the host countries.

7. Steps for writing a favorable reply.

(1) Identifying the reference and informing the recipient of appointing them as your sole agent.

(2) Adding further terms and conditions of appointment.

(3) Request the recipient to confirm the terms and conditions.

Entrusting Customer with Sole Agency-Letter 2

Dear Sirs,

Thank you for your letter of April 12 proposing a sole agency for our office machines. We have examined our long and, I must say, mutually beneficial collaboration. We would be very pleased to entrust you with the sole agency for Bahrain.

From our records, we are pleased to note that you have two service engineers who took training courses at our Milan factory. The sole agency will naturally be contingent on you maintaining qualified after sales staff. We have drawn up a draft agreement that is enclosed. Please examine the detailed terms and conditions and let us know whether they meet with your approval. On a personal note, I must say that I am delighted that we are probably going to strengthen our relationship. I have very pleasant memories of my last visit to Bahrain when you entertained me so delightfully.

I look forward to reciprocating on your next visit to Milan.

My very best wishes to you and your wife.

Yours faithfully,

Decline to Grant a Sole Agency

Dear Sirs,

Thank you for your letter of September 1 suggesting that we grant you a sole agency for our household linens.

I regret to say that, at this stage, such an arrangement would be rather premature. We would, however, be willing to engage in a trial collaboration with your company to see how the arrangement works. It would be necessary for you to test the market for our products at your end. You would also have to build up a much larger turnover to justify a sole agency.

We enclose price lists covering all the products you are interested in and look forward to hearing from you soon.

Yours faithfully,

Notes

Steps for writing an unfavourable reply.

(1) Identify the reference.

(2) Stating the problem.

(3) Pointing out that the agent's obligation should be included.

(4) The closing sentence of the letter.

Banking Agency

Request for the Establishment of Agency Relationship (Request)

Dear Sirs,

As you are well aware, China and Canada recently come to open trade with each other. This development is expected to bring about a lot of direct trade transactions between our two countries in the years to come.

We are pleased to note that we have already had banking transactions with your fine bank on letters of credit, our records show that LCs in favor of beneficiaries located in your country were directed to your bank through a third bank, your correspondent bank in for there exist no agency arrangements between us.

In order to ensure the speedy handling of the relevant banking transactions along with the increasing trade volume, we would like to propose and solicit your concurrence to establish a direct correspondence banking relationship with your esteemed bank, we are confident that this step would allow us to avoid any possible delay that may occur in handling business to the benefit of clients on both sides.

We enclose herewith a copy of our Terms and Conditions together with our annual report for the fiscal year 2005 for your reference. We would highly appreciate receiving your control documents in return to accomplish our arrangements. Please let us know if you would prefer to use your Test Key or ours.

We look forward to your favorable reply.

Yours faithfully,

Agency Relationship (Reply)

Dear Sirs,

Thank you for your letter dated May 25, 2005.We fully understand your desire to set up agency relationship with us. As you are aware, the trade exchange between China and Canada is limited with a small volume at present. Since our existing correspondent banks in your city can fully meet our business requirements, we therefore do not intend to expand our agency net work in the near future. We shall, of course, consider the matter in the light of trade development and hope you will give us understanding in this respect.

We wish you a greater business volume.

Yours faithfully,

Freight Forwarding Agency

Dear Sirs,

We are one of the largest air freight forwarders in the world. Our business is to move packages and freight through the air and on the ground throughout China and around the world. We would like to open a dialogue with you to develop the possibilities of our doing business together in handling the projected air freight business which will in the years ahead increasingly occur between our two great nations.

In addition to the transportation of goods, we also provide total documentation services for both importers and exporters. All licensing, invoicing and banking requirements can be taken care of at each of our offices. We also operate our own sea forwarding company for the Customer's ocean needs.

The above is a brief summary of our air cargo services. We would like to pursue the possibilities of expanding our services, offering them to the People's Republic of China. To begin the dialogue between China and us, we cordially invite your representatives to visit us in our headquarters next month. Please let us know what time would be convenient for you.

For your information, we enclose our Annual Report and various supporting material about our services.

Very truly yours,

资料链接 Material—link

1. Standard Model

Model 1:Apply for Sole Agency

Letter 1

Dear Sirs,

_____ [company] is one of the leading companies in _____retail business. We have outlets throughout _____ [country/area]. We are interested in your _____ [products] displayed at _____ [exhibition] and would like to know whether you could offer us a sole agency to retail your products in _____ [country/area].

We are confident that there is a growing market for your products in _____ [country/area], due to the increasing demand for _____.

We operate on a _____% commission basis on net list prices, with an additional _____% commission if required. We usually pay our principals by bill of exchange on a quarterly basis.

If you are interested in the above proposal, we will send our representative to discuss further details with you. We look forward to hearing from you soon.

Yours sincerely,

_____ [name]

_____ [title]

Encl.

Model 2:Apply for Sole Agency

Letter 2

Dear Sirs,

I am replying to your company's advertisement in _____ [commercial journal] in which you indicated the need for a buying agent to represent your group in _____ [country/area].

My company specializes in buying _____ [products] and we have acted for several firms in _____ [country/area]. We have well-developed connections with leading brand manufacturers in _____ [country/area]. We are able to keep you well informed of new products from the _____ industry and purchase a wide range of products at reduced export prices. In addition, we can offer excellent terms for freight and insurance.

Our usual commission is _____% on CIF invoiced values, and we make purchases in our principals' names, sending them accounts for settlement.

I have enclosed literature providing details about our services and terms. If you are interested, please contact me at the above address. I am looking forward to hearing from you.

Sincerely yours,

_____ [name]

_____ [title]

Encl.

Model 3:Appointing a Sole Agency

Dear Sirs,

Thank you for your proposal to act as our agent for the sale of _____ [products] in _____ [country/area]. I am pleased to inform you that we have decided to accept your proposal on the basis of a _____ percent commission, payable on all orders received through you. In addition, we will refund expenses reasonably incurred in promoting our sales.

Provided that the arrangements you make with customers are favorable to our interests, we will trust your judgement such matters as discounts and the granting of credit. We trust that the orders we receive through you and the terms on which you have accepted them will justify our confidence in your ability to promote the sale of our products in _____ [country/area].

Sincerely yours,

_____ [name]

_____ [title]

Model 4:Consignee's Request for Trial Consignment

Dear Sirs,

We are a large retail chain specializing in _____ business. We have recently received a number of inquiries from our customers in _____ [area/country] for your _____ [product]. We have also learned from other sources that there are good prospects for the sale of this product. We would like to suggest that you send us a trial delivery for sale on consignment terms.

We make this proposal, hoping that we will place firm orders when we feel sure that the market is established. If you agree, we will get down to details in regard to payment, commission, and so on. You may check our standing with _____ [bank], our banker.

We look forward to your early reply.

Sincerely yours,
_____ [name]
_____ [title]

Model 5:Consignor's Instruction for Consignee

Dear Sirs,

We have shipped to you today a consignment of ten cases of _____ [goods] by _____ [ship], which is due in _____ [port] on _____ [date].

We are now enclosing the shipping documents for this consignment, a proforma invoice, and a price list of all the items are shipped.

You will of course sell at the best prices you can get. The listed prices are for guidance only and represent the limits below which the _____ [goods] may not be sold on our behalf.

We hope to hear from you soon.

Yours sincerely,
_____ [name]
_____ [title]
Encl.

Model 6:Agreement for Exclusive Agency

Agreement For Exclusive Agency

This agreement, made and entered into this day of 15 th day of2008, by and between the ABC Trading Company, Inc., of New York, N.Y. U.S.A., Party of the first part, and DEF&Co., of Tokyo, Japan, its duly appointed agent Party of the second part, witness:

1. Party of the first part (hereinafter called the Company) hereby grants to the Party of the second part (hereinafter called the Agent) the exclusive right to sell the GYROCOMPASS in Tokyo, Japan for the period of three years from the date hereof.

2. The Agent covenants that it will use every reasonable diligence in executing all orders placed with it by the Company and will not, without the consent of the Company, deviate from any instructions given by the Company in regard to its orders and shipment.

3. On all orders executed by the Agent during the continuance of this contract, the Agent shall be paid the following commission:

On an order to the total amount of $_____ or less_____ percent;

On an order amounting to $_____ more than_____ percent.

4. The amount of an invoice rendered by the Agent including its commission and its disbursements except postage and petties, shall be paid by the Company under irrevocable Letter of Credit against the delivery of shipping documents.

5. This agreement may be terminated by either party upon three months' written notice delivered or sent by registered mail to the other, and may be terminated at any time without such notice, upon breach of any of its terms and conditions.

Witness the hands and seals of the parties of this Agreement the day and year aforesaid.

For THE ABC TERADING COMPANY, INC.

(signed) __________

For DEF&Co.

(signed) __________

2. *Writing Guide*

Tips in Drafting an Agency Agreement

Generally speaking, the term of exclusive sale, selling on a consignment basis and agency is a long period of time ranging from one year to even several decades. It' s usually understood that an initial agreement is generally reached concerning the vital principles at first and then such details as specifications, quantity, packing, unit price, terms of payment, insurance and delivery time etc. of each transaction are clearly and precisely stipulated in the latter confirmation, contract and orders.

Prior to the establishment of agency, the principal should make a survey about the qualifications, experiences and qualities etc. of the potential and prospective agent. In drafting a formal agency agreement, attention should be paid to the following.

(1) Choose the agent with good credit and capability to avoid the responsibility escape of agents. Precautionary clauses are necessary. For instance, the principal enjoys the right to terminate the contract and the exclusive agent is required to fulfill the stipulated task to be in a specified period of time.

(2) The nature and term of agent.

(3) The region represented.

(4) Responsibilities of the agent and principal.

(5) The method of purchasing or selling, e.g. whether the agent makes purchase at his or her own expense or on a consignment basis.

(6) The stipulation about the total sale volume fulfilled by the agent in a specified period of time should be within a reasonable scope, without being too high or too low.

(7) In drafting the agency agreement, the rights and obligations to either party should be clear and specific.

(8) All kinds of agency agreement are subject to the ninth chapter (Contracts for Sale), the twenty-first chapter (Contracts for Commission) and twenty-second chapter (Contracts for Brokerage) of Contract Law of the People's Republic of China.

Section Four Selected Sentences
精选句型表达

申请代理的语句

1. With your excellent connection, we believe it will be possible to promote the sale of our products in your territory, and we hope your acting as our agent will be to our mutual benefit.

因为你们良好的关系网，我们认为在你们地区促销我们的产品是可能的，而且我们也希望任命你为我们的代理人符合双方的利益。

2. We have much confidence that we can play an important part as a buying agent in your overseas trade.

作为采购代理人，我们相信能在你们的海外贸易中起到重要作用。

3. If you would appoint us as your agent, we could give you a reasonable guarantee to sell

US$ 100 000 a month, because yours is a line we can handle well.

如果你们委任我们做代理人，我们可以保证每月销售 10 万美元，因为你方产品是我们善于经营的。

4．We would like to know if you wish to be represented in this market.

我们想了解贵公司是否在本地寻找代理商。

5．Should you be prepared to appoint us as your agents, we would guarantee a turnover of £100 000 each year.

如你方委任我们作为你们的代理人，我们保证每年营业额达到 10 万英镑。

6．We should be glad to know what terms you would be willing to represent us, also the terms on which business is generally conducted in your country.

我们想知道在什么条件下你方愿做我们的代理以及什么条件下可以在贵国展开贸易。

7．We are seeking a reliable representative who would undertake to buy for us on commission.

我们正在寻找一个可靠的，并保证在佣金的基础上向我方购货的代理。

8．We write to offer our services as your agents in West Africa. If, however, you are already satisfactorily represented here, please ignore this letter.

我们愿意为你们在西非提供代理服务。然而，如果你们在以上地区已有代理，请忽略这封信。

9．We would be glad if you would consider our application to act as your sole agent for the sale of your shoes.

如能考虑我们担任贵公司鞋子销售代理的申请，我们将深感荣幸。

10．Your application for sole agency is now under our careful consideration.

我们正在仔细考虑你方想要独家(经营)代理的请求。

11．Please let us know whether you now represent any suppliers in the same line.

请告知你方是否代理其他同类产品。

不同意代理的语句

1．We would suggest that we leave aside the problem of agency until circumstances necessitate doing so.

我们建议将代理一事暂且搁置，待情况发展到双方都感到满意时再谈。

2．We feel it would be better to consider the matter of agency after you have done more business with us.

我们认为在你们和我们开展更多的业务后再考虑代理问题为宜。

3．We think it premature for us to discuss the question of agency at the present stage.

我们认为目前考虑代理问题还为时尚早。

4．The time is not yet mature for discussion of agency.

考虑代理问题的时机还没成熟。

5．We wish to inform you that this particular line has already been taken by…, who has acted as our sole agent for quite some time.

我希望告诉你们的是该产品已经由……独家代理了很长一段时间了。

6．The question of agency is still under consideration and we hope that you will continue your efforts to push the sale of our products at the present stage.

代理问题正在考虑之中，我们希望你方能够继续努力促销我们的产品。

7．We have already had agency arrangement with ABC Co., Ltd. for the sale of this product in your region ,we think it would be much better for us to start business on commission basis first.

在该地区我们已经和 ABC 贸易有限公司有销售该产品的代理协议，因此，我方认为以佣金为基础来开展你我双方贸易更为妥当。

8．Referring to the question of sole agency, we are not yet prepared to take the matter into consideration for the time being. We shall revert to this subject as soon as the business between us has developed to our mutual satisfaction.

关于独家代理一事，目前我们还不打算考虑，当业务发展到你我双方都满意时，我们将再谈此事。

达成代理协议的语句

1．After giving careful consideration to your proposal and investigating your business standing, we have decided to appoint you as our sole agency in the district you defined, subject to the following terms and conditions.

经过对你方的提议及对你方商誉的调查，我们已经决定指定你方作为我们在该区域的代理，取决于以下条款。

2．We shall be pleased to learn that you are willing to accept the sole agency on these terms.

我方将欣然获悉你方接受我方独家代理条款。

3．We thank you for your letter of offering your service as our sole agent for the sale of our TVs in your district.

感谢贵方来函愿在贵地为我方提供电视机独家代理服务。

4．Thank you for your letter of your willing to be our sole agency dealing in our computers in Ningbo, China.

感谢贵方来函乐于作为我方驻中国宁波的电脑独家代理。

5．We have approved your proposal of acting as our agent in view of your past efforts in pushing the sale of our products, we have decided to accept you as our agent.

鉴于你们过去在推销我们产品上所做的努力，我们同意指定你们为我方的代理人。

6．Regarding your proposal to represent us for the sale of …, we have decided to appoint you as our agent.

就你们代理销售我们的……产品的提议，我们决定指定你为我们的代理人。

同意有条件代理的语句

1．Although we have full confidence in your sales ability, we suggest that this stage you do business with us on our usual trade terms. As soon as marked success is achieved by you, we will take your proposal to act as our sole agent into consideration.

尽管我们对你方的销售能力充满信心，我们建议你方在现阶段仍与我们按原来条款进行交易，一旦你方取得显著成绩，我们将考虑你方担任独家代理的建议。

2. We appreciate your suggestion that you sell our goods on an exclusive basis, but first of all we should like to know the approximate quantity you may sell in the coming year.

我们理解你们想要独家销售我方货物的建议，但是我们首先想要知道的是下一年你们能销售的大概数量。

3. In reply, we would like to inform you that it is rather difficult for us to consider your suggestion before we know the records of sale, the possible annual turnover, and the import license conditions.

兹复你方，我方告知你方：在我方了解你方销售记录、可能的年营业额和进口许可证条件之前，我方很难接受你方建议。

4. Your intention to do our agent has been noted. In order to enable us to make a careful study of your proposal, we should like to know your plan for promoting the sale of our products, the market consumption and the volume of business which you are able to conclude monthly or quarterly. At the same time, please let us know whether you now represent any suppliers in the same line.

我们已经注意到你们想当代理的意愿。为了使我们能仔细研究你们的建议，我们想知道你们推销我方产品的计划、市场消费量和你方每月或每季度能够成交的营业额。同时，还请告知，你们目前是否担任其他供货人的同样商品的代理。

5. When we have done more together, better mutual understanding is built up, further improvement in our business relations becomes necessary, we shall be very glad to take up the matter with you.

当你我双方已多次共同开展贸易，建立更多共同了解，有必要进一步提升贸易关系时，我方将乐于与你方洽谈此事。

6. In the meantime, we are now assorting samples suitable for your market and will airmail them to you soon under separate cover together with our price list, which we trust will make you feel much interest in doing business with us as principal.

与此同时，我方将把样品分类邮至你方市场，并随函附上我方价单，我方相信这会使你方以我方为委托人来进行交易更感兴趣。

7. We have noted your request to act as our sole agent in your district, but before going further into the matter, we should like to know your plan for promoting the sales and the annual turnover you may realize in your market.

我们已注意到你方要做我方在你处代理的要求，但在此之前，请把你们的推销计划和你地市场可能达到的营业额告知我方。

8. We suggest a trial period of one year if everything turns out satisfactory, we can renew the agency agreement on its expiry.

我们建议试做一年，如果一切令人满意，我们可以在一年代理协议期满后予以续延。

9. If you could pursue your efforts in building a larger turnover, we shall be glad to take into consideration our signing of an agency agreement.

如果你方能够继续努力获得一个较大的营业额，我们将乐意考虑签订代理协议的问题。

Abstract

通过本章学习，①了解代理的基本分类；②掌握代理来往函电和代理协议写作的基本内容；③掌握代理来往函电写作的基本规律和注意事项；④通过熟悉标准模板掌握代理函电写作的基本方法；⑤熟练掌握代理函电经典句型的表达；⑥掌握代理的基本术语。

Useful Words & Expressions

请求担任代理

offer our services as your agent

be interested in becoming/acting as your agent

apply as your agent

按独家代理条件

on an exclusive basis

act as agent on a sole commission basis

handle… (commodity) on an exclusive basis

委托某人为代理

appoint sb. (as) agent in … (place) for… (commodity)

appoint sb. (as) for the sale of … (commodity) in … (place)

avail yourself of our services as selling agents (avail oneself of… 利用……)

entrust sb. with sole agent

同意某人做代理

approve your proposal for acting as our agent

accept your proposal to act as our agent

act as a sole agent

担任独家代理

entrust sb. with the sole agency

委托某人担任独家代理

offer sb. a sole agency

提议某人担任独家代理

appoint sb. as a sole agent

指定某人担任独家代理

sole agent/exclusive agent 独家代理人

forwarding agents 货运代理

the agent carrying stock 储货代理

insurance agent 保险代理商

advertising agent 广告代理人

sales/selling agent 销售代理人

purchasing/buying agent 采购代理人

commission agent 佣金代理人
agent commission 代理佣金
agent bank/agency house 代理行
sole agency 独家代理
customs agency 报关代理行
ocean shipping agency 外轮代理公司
agency agreement 代理协议
travel agency 旅行社

Exercises

1. Multiple choice.

(1) We give you the exclusive sales____in your country.
A. representative　B. agent　C. representation　D. agency

(2) ____our general agent, you would also have to look after the advertising.
A. Being　B. For　C. As　D. To be

(3) Your proposal____transact business____this Bank is agreeable.
A. and, with　B. to, with　C. to, for　D. for, with

(4) Here is a list of our signatures and branch offices____your use.
A. for　B. to　C. in　D. of

(5) They____that the subsidiary do business with the principal and at the allocating prices.
A. propose　B. suggest　C. noted　D. announce

(6) ____on or past experience, we suggest establishing a branch office in that city.
A. Basing　B. Based　C. Relying　D. Rely

(7) We appreciate your suggestion____establish agency relationship between our banks.
A. to　B. that　C. we　D. for

(8) We confirm we agree____your suggestions made in our last letter.
A. with　B. on　C. to　D. that

(9) This agreement is applicable to transactions in____direction between the two parties.
A. both　B. two　C. either　D. one

(10) ____party shall notify the other party of the ratification by their respective authorities.
A. Each　B. One　C. Either　D. A

(11) We are pleased to note that you wish to expand our relationship, suggest that we consider the matter of agency later.
A. and　B. but　C. however　D. nevertheless

2. Answer the following questions.

(1) What is agency?
(2) Why agency business relation establishment is important to international trade?

(3) When an agent is being selected, what qualifications should be considered?

(4) What details should be attended when you are drafting an agreement of agency?

(5) What are the main categories of agents?

3. Translate the following into English.

(1) 我们愿意担任你们现行出口商品的代理，因为我们拥有一个广阔的国内市场。

(2) 我们深信，担任你们海外贸易的进口代理，能起重要作用。

(3) 代理问题尚在考虑中，希望在现阶段继续努力推销我们的产品。

(4) 我们认为讨论代理问题的时机还未成熟。

(5) 我们已委托 ABC 公司为你地区的代理。

(6) 得知你方推销瓷器很有经验，非常荣幸能和你们打交道。

(7) 对你们想担任独家代理的请求，我们正在仔细考虑。同时，我们很想了解你方推销我们产品的计划。

(8) 在产品的广告方面我们尽了很大努力，营业额仍不能令人满意。

(9) 我们所有做这类商品的代理都只拿 5%的佣金。

(10) 如果情况令双方满意，可以延长协议有效期。

4. Translate the following into Chinese.

(1) In consideration of your extensive experience in the field, we are glad to appoint you as our agent.

(2) I'm entitled to being appointed as your agent.

(3) We keep a stock in London and act as distributors as well as agents.

(4) We've decided to entrust you with the sole agency for cars.

(5) Thank you for your proposal of acting as our agent.

(6) If we come to terms, we'll appoint you as our agent.

(7) We wish to handle as an agent the goods you are exporting.

(8) We can play an important part as a buying agent in your overseas trade.

(9) We're in a position to take good care of your import business as a buying agent.

(10) Please get in touch with our agents for the supply of the goods you require.

(11) We'll leave aside the problem of agency until next week.

(12) We're not prepared to take the agency into consideration for the time being.

(13) We won't consider agency in your market at present.

(14) We have to decline your proposal of acting as our sole agency.

(15) I think it premature for us to discuss the question of agency.

(16) Unless you increase the turnover, we can hardly appoint you as our sole agent.

(17) Don't you think the annual turnover for a sole agent is rather conservative?

(18) It was two years ago that we made them our sole agent.

(19) When opportunity matures, we will consider making you as our exclusive agent for the U.K.

(20) We'll consider appointing you as our sole agent for our T-shirts for the next two years in your local market.

(21) I am here today to apply for the sole agency of your product in our local market.

(22) How can we appoint you as our sole agent for such a small quantity?

(23) I propose a sole agency agreement for bicycles for a period of 3 years.

(24) We are not yet prepared to take the question of sole agent into consideration for the time being.

(25) Your application for sole agency is now under our careful consideration.

(26) We should be interested in acting as your sole agent.

(27) When do you expect to sign the agency agreement?

(28) The agency agreement has been drawn up for the period of one year.

(29) I want to sign a sole agency agreement with you on this item for a period of 2 years.

(30) The agency agreement was made out with great care and we have found no loopholes in it.

(31) I hope we can see eye to eye about the other terms of the agency then.

(32) We wonder whether we may conclude a long term agency contract with you.

(33) Well, what annual quantity would you like to suggest for the new agreement then?

(34) Our agency agreement calls for a timely market report.

(35) Since the agency agreement was signed, your turnover has amounted to $500.

(36) I hope you'll spare no efforts to promote the sale of our products so as to pave the way for renewing the agency agreement when it expires at the end of this year.

(37) We can renew the agreement of agency on its expiry.

(38) I've come again to renew our sole agency agreement for another 3 years.

Case Practice

以本章的导入案例为背景，请以公司业务员 Smith 的名义写一封回信。信中表明乐意接受对方为本公司提供独家代理销售“瑞士汉爱表-HANDLOVE”专业防水手表的申请。条款如下。

(1) 价格：以宁波到岸价、美元报盘。

(2) 佣金：当商业发票的金额完全付清后，每次装运 5%的发票金额将会作为佣金汇至你方。

(3) 付款方式：最好保兑的，不可撤销信用证更受欢迎，但是即期付款交单也可以接受。若付款金额不超过 1 万美元或等值金额，也可以受理付款交单的付款方式。

Chapter 12 Documentation in International Trade

外贸单证

案例导入 Case-lead-in

经理要求小李跟着王师傅学着制作相关的商业单据。王师傅拿出一份以往填制的发票样张，要求小李对照资料，自己先看一看，熟悉一下格式。王师傅告诉小李，作为对商业发票的补充，还需填制装箱单，主要显示货物的包装、毛重、净重以及尺码方面的情况。那么，商业发票和装箱单是如何缮制的呢？

Section One Types of International Trading Documents 外贸单证的种类

In this section, we will discuss the types of international trading documents.

A document is a written or printed paper furnishing information or evidence, as a passport, deed, bill of sale, or bill of lading, a legal or official paper. In the international trade, the documents are the titles which the customers obtain the goods.

According to the character and usage, the documents can be classified into financial documents, commercial documents, official documents and subordinate documents, etc.

The financial document is the receiving voucher, for example, the Draft, Promissory Note, Check or other similar vouchers.

The commercial documents are Commercial Invoice, Transport Documents, Insurance Policy, Certificate of Inspection and Quarantine, Certificate of Origin (CO) or other similar documents. Among them, all kinds of transport documents are collectively called "Transport Document", bill of lading (B/L), non-negotiable maritime transport document, airway bill of lading, universal transport document, shipping note, goods declaration for exportation, etc.

The official documents are the documents and certificates issued by governmental office, for example, Export License, Customs Invoice, Consular Proof or Consular Invoice, etc.

The subordinate documents include Certificate for Dispatch of Documents, Certificate for Dispatch of Shipment Sample, Shipping Advice, etc.

Section Two Requirements of Documents Making
制 单 要 求

Generally speaking, there are five requirements in documents making. They are "Correctness", "Completeness", "Punctuality", "Conciseness" and "Tidiness".

Correctness, it is premise of all the documents making. If the documents are incorrect, we can not settle a foreign exchange account safely. Firstly, when make the documents, the points that we should pay attention to are the conformity between credit terms and documents and the conformity between the documents. Secondly, any kinds of documents should be fit for the requirements of the international trade practice, the law and the rule of all kinds of countries. Thirdly, it is consistent with the goods that it stands for.

Completeness, in a way, it mainly is the completeness of documents that a transaction refers to. We can explain as follows in details, "the completeness of contents", "the completeness of copies", and "the completeness of species". In a word, all the documents that the customer needs or the import country needs should be provided.

Punctuality, that is to say, dealing with documents should be finished in a set time. We need to learn the following points, "making documents in time", "reviewing documents in time", "handing in documents in time", "settlements in time". Besides, we also learn that the issuing date of every document should be reasonable and workable.

Conciseness, that is to say, the contents of documents should be concise, avoid unnecessary lengthiness. The conciseness can not only reduce the workload and improve work efficiency, but also improve the quality of documents and reduce the mistakes of documents.

Tidiness, that is to say, the documents should be clear, clean, and beautiful etc. Besides, the smeared appearance should not be appeared; meanwhile, amending should be avoid or reduced.

Section Three Cases in Detail
具体案例分析

(一) 经典案例解析

Commercial Invoice

1) SELLER **注释：**卖方 一般为信用证受益人 (L/C 中 59)	3) INVOICE NO. **注释：**发票号码	4) INVOICE DATE **注释：**发票日期
	5) L/C NO. **注释：**信用证编号	6) DATE **注释：**信用证开证日期
	7) ISSUED BY **注释：**开证行，通常在买方所在地	

续表

<table>
<tr><td rowspan="3">2) BUYER
注释：买方
一般为信用证开证申请人(L/C 中 50)</td><td>8) CONTRACT NO.
注释：合同编号</td><td>9) DATE
注释：合同日期</td></tr>
<tr><td>10) FROM
注释：启运地，见 L/C 中 44A</td><td>11) TO
注释：目的地，见 L/C 中 44B</td></tr>
<tr><td>12) SHIPPED BY
注释：运输工具名称
如用海运，则还要填写相应的船名、船次</td><td>13) PRICE TERM
注释：贸易术语</td></tr>
</table>

<table>
<tr><td>14) MARKS</td><td>15) DESCRIPTION OF GOODS</td><td>16) QTY.</td><td>17) UNIT PRICE</td><td>18) AMOUNT</td></tr>
<tr><td>**注释**：
唛头
也称为
运输标志
OSAKA
C/NO.A-250</td><td>**注释**：货物描述
不得使用统称、简称、必须与信用证中的货物描述保持一致，并列明不同型号(L/C 中 45A)
TOTAL
总计
对于不同型号的不同数量、不同金额，还需算出总数、总价</td><td>**注释**：数量
根据合同或者信用证中的内容进行填制
总数量</td><td>**注释**：单价
包括币别、金额、计价单位、贸易术语
(L/C 中 45A)</td><td>**注释**：总值
数量×单价
总金额</td></tr>
</table>

	19) ISSUED BY
	注释：签发人，即卖方公司名称
	20) SIGNATURE
	注释：签署，卖方公司负责人签名

Notes

商业发票关键词

1	INVOICE NO.	发票号码
2	PRICE TERM	贸易术语
3	DESCRIPTION OF GOODS	货物描述
4	QTY.	数量
5	SHIPPING MARKS	运输标志
6	FROM	启运地
7	TO	目的地
8	L/C DATE	信用证开立日期
9	ISSUED BY	签发人
10	FAX NO.	传真号码

(二) 一般案例表述

1. Bill of Lading 海运提单

1. Shipper
注释：托运人，通常填卖方公司名称及地址

2. Consignee
TO ORDER OF SHIPPER
注释：收货人
三种填写方法，参照信用证 46A 中提单的要求进行填制
① 记名式：照抄 L/C 中指定收货人名称
② 空白抬头：本栏留空或仅填入 TO BEARER
③ 指示抬头：to order of shipper 或者 to order of 开证行

3. Notify Party
注释：通知人，一般为开证申请人，信用证中 50

Pre-carriage by
注释：前程运输方式
可留空

Vessel **注释**：船名、船次 多见于补充资料中	Port of transshipment **注释**：转运港，根据相关资料填制，如果没有，可留空
Port of discharge **注释**：目的港 (44B)	Final destination **注释**：最终目的地 若与目的港相同，可留空

Container seal No. or marks and Nos.	Number and kind of packages Description of goods	Gross weight (kgs)	Measurement(M^3)
注释： 集装箱号或者唛头 填写实际集装箱号、唛头 如无唛，则填 N/M	**注释**：包装种类数量和货物描述(统称) 注意格式 ON BOARD 已装船 在货物装船后，需向船公司取得标有已装船字样的提单，才能结汇	**注释**： 货物总毛重 应与其他单据相一致	**注释**： 总尺码 指货物的体积，应与其他单据相一致

Freight and charges
注释：运费支付标注，一般留空

Prepaid at	Freight payable at **注释**：运费支付地 CIF \ CFR 时，为出口港 FOB 时，为进口港	Place and date of issue **注释**：提单签发日和签发地点 填写承运人实际装运的地点和时间
Total Prepaid	Number of original Bs/l **注释**：正本提单份数(大小写)如： THREE (3)	Signed for or on behalf of the master 注释：提单签署 1. 作为承运人的代理人签发提单时，签字栏下端一般须加注 AS AGENTS FOR THE CARRIER ××× 2. 承运人签字时，则加注 AS CARRIER 字样 3. 作为船长签字时，则加注AS MASTER 字样

Notes

海运提单关键词

1	SHIPPER	买方	6	Final destination	日期
2	Consignee	收货人	7	Number and kind of packages	包装种类和数量
3	Notify Party	通知方	8	Freight and charges	运费及费用
4	Pre-carriage by	前程运输方式	9	Place and date of issue	签发地点及日期
5	Port of discharge	卸货港	10	Signed for or on behalf of the MASTER	船长或授权人签署

2. Insurance Policy 保险单

PICC 中国人民财产保险股份有限公司

PICC Property and Casualty Company Limited

总公司设于北京　　　　一九四九年创立

Head Office: BEIJING　　　　Established in 1949

货物运输保险单 **CARGO TRANSPORTATION INSURANCE POLICY**

发票号码:　　　　保险单号次**注释：保险单号码**

INVOICE NO.　　　　POLICY NO.**此栏填写保险公司指定号码**

被保险人：**注释：即投保人，一般为出口商**

中国人民财产保险股份有限公司(以下简称本公司)要求，以被保险人向本公司缴付约定的保险费为对价，按照本保险单列明条款承保下述货物运输保险，特订立本保险单。

THIS POLICY OF INSURANCE WITNESSES THAT PICC PROPERTY AND CASUALTY COMPANY LIMITED(HEREINAFTER CALLED "THE COMPANY") AT THE REQUEST OF THE INSURED AND IN CONSIDERATION OF THE AGREED PREMIUM PAID TO THE COMPANY BY THE INSURED

UNDERTAKES TO INSURE THE UNDERMENTIONED GOODS IN TRANSPORATION SUBJECT TO THE CONDITIONS OF THIS POLICY

AS PER THE CLAUSES PRINTED BELOW.

标　记 MARKS & NO. INSURED	包装及数量 QUANTITY	保险货物项目 GOODS	保险金额 AMOUNT
注释：应与发票、提单等一致，也可只填 AS PER INVOICE NO. ×××	**注释：** 填写最大包装件数，与提单同一栏内容相同	**注释：**货物描述，与合同信用证中的货物描述一致	**注释：**保险金额=发票金额×（1+投保加成率）保留整数

总保险金额：

TOTAL AMOUNT INSURED: SAY U.S. DOLLARS SIXTY SIX THOUSAND ONE HUNDRED AND THIRTY TWO ONLY

保费 **注释：一般已由保险公司印**　　　　启运日期

PREMIUM: AS ARRANGED **注释：（如约定）字样** DATE OF COMMENCEMENT: **AS PER B/L DATE**

装载运输工具

PER CONVEYANCE: . **DALONG 03**

自：　　　　至：

FROM: SHANGHAI , CHINA　　　　TO: TORONTO , CANADA

CONDITIONS: **注释：此栏系保险单的核心内容，填写时应注意保险险别及文句与信用证严格一致**

所保货物如发生保险单项下可能引起索赔的损失，应立即通知本公司或下述代理人查勘。如有索赔，应向本公司提交正本保险单（本保险单共有____**注释：贰**份正本）及有关证件。如一份正本已用于索赔，其余正本自动失效。

IN THE EVENT OF LOSS OR DAMANGE WHICH MAY RESULT IN A CLAIM UNDER THIS POLICY, IMMEDIATE NOTICE MUST BE GIVEN TO THE COMPANY OR AGENT AS MENTIONED. CLAIMS，IF ANY，ONE OF THE ORIGINAL POLICY WHICH HAS BEEN ISSUED IN__2__ORGINALS TOGETHER WITH THE RELEVANT DOCUMENTS SHALL BE SURRENDERED TO THE COMPANY. IF ONE OF THE ORIGINAL POLICY HAS BEEN ACCOMPLISHED, THE OTHERS TO BE VOID.

SURVEY TO BE CARRIED OUT BY A LOCAL COMPETENT SURVEYOR. CLAIM DOCUMENTS TO BE MAILED TO THE UNDERWRITER, WE SHALL EFFECT PAYMENT BY REMITTANCE TO THE CLAIMANT.

赔款偿付地点：

CLAIM PAYABLE AT __TORONTO IN USD__

注释：一般将目的港作为赔付地点。赔款货币一般为投保额相同的货币。

日期：

DATE：___**注释：** __**此栏指保险单的签发日期**__

3. Generalized System of Preference 普惠制产地证明申请书

<table>
<tr><td colspan="2">1. Goods consigned from (Exporter's business name, address, country)
注释：L/C 中 59</td><td colspan="4" rowspan="2">Reference No.：**注释：**普惠制产地证编号
GENERALIZEDSYSTEMOFPREFERENCES
CERTIFICATE OF ORIGIN
(Combined declaration and certificate)
FORM A

(COUNTRY)
and that they comply with the Origin requirements specified for those goods in the Generalized System of Preference for goods exported to
注释：进口国
Issued in THE PEOPLE'S REPUBLIC OF CHINA
(country)
(importing country)
注释：出口商签署地点及日期
Place and date. Signature of authorized signatory</td></tr>
<tr><td colspan="2">2. Goods consigned to(Consignee's name, address, country) 收货人
注释：L/C 中 50</td></tr>
<tr><td colspan="2">3. Means of transport and route (as far as known)
注释：运输方式及运输路线
From…to…via…by…</td><td colspan="4">4. For official use</td></tr>
<tr><td>5. Item number
注释：项目号
按不同品种分列 1、2，以此类推。
单项商品，此栏填 1</td><td>6. Marks and numbers
注释：唛头</td><td>7. Number and kind of packages; description of goods
注释：货物描述
货物包装总件数
*****
信用证相关信息标注</td><td>8. Origin criterion(See Notes. overleaf)
注释：原产地标准
完全自产，填 P</td><td>9. Gross weight or other quantity
注释：总毛重或者总数量</td><td>10. Number and date of invoices
注释：
发票日期
发票号码</td></tr>
<tr><td colspan="3">11. Certification
It is hereby certified, on the basis of control carried out ,that the declaration by the exporter is correct.</td><td colspan="3">12. Declaration by the exporter
The undersigned hereby declares that the above details and statement are correct, that all the goods were produced in
注释：商品原产国</td></tr>
</table>

4. Shipping Advice 装船通知

SHIPPING ADVICE

INVOICE No.: **注释：见补充资料**___

L/C No.:_**注释：见 L/C**

S/C No.:_**注释：见合同**

TO:

注释：填合同中进口方公司名称与地址或 LC 申请人名称及地址

DEAR SIRS:

WE HEREBY INFORM YOU THAT THE GOODS UNDER THE ABOVE MENTIONED CREDIT HAVE BEEN SHIPPED. THE DETAILS OF THE SHIPMENT ARE STATED BELOW.

COMMODITY:__________**注释：货物的总称(与合同或 LC 一致)**__________

NUMBER OF PKGS:______**注释：填外包装总数量**__________

TOTAL G.W:__________**注释：填货物的总毛重**__________

OCEAN VESSEL:________**注释：见补充资料**__________

DATE OF DEPARTURE:___**注释：填 B/L 日期**__________

B/L No.:______________**注释：见补充资料**__________

PORT OF LOADING:______**注释：见合同或 L/C44A**__________

DESTINATION:__________**注释：见合同或 L/C44B**__________

SHIPPING MARKS:

Notes

1) 填写唛头(要与合同或 LC 中规定的一致)
2) 装船通知关键词

1	TO MESSERS	收件人名称和地址
2	S/C NO. 或 L/C NO.	合同号或信用证号
3	COMMODITY	货物名称
4	OCEAN VESSEL	船名
5	DATE PG DEPARTURE	开航日期
6	B/L NO.	提单号码
7	PORT OF LOADING	装运港口
8	DESTIDATION	目的地

5. Bill of Exchange 汇票

BILL OF EXCHANGE	
NO.___ **注释**：发票号码或者汇票号码	**注释**：出票日期、地点 一般在出口地、由受益人交单议付当天签发，但不得晚于最迟交单日
FOR **注释**：货币单位＋小写金额	
AT___**注释**：付款期限，参见 L/C 中 42C 如为即期，则填***** SIGHT OF THIS *FIRST* BILL OF EXCHANGE (*SECOND* UNPAID) PAY TO THE ORDER OF 注释：收款人通常为议付行名称，参见 L/C 中 41D THE SUM OF **注释**： 总金额英文大写	
Drawn under ___**注释**：开证行名称	
L/C No.___**注释**： 信用证编号 Dated **注释**： 开证日期	
TO: **注释**：付款行名称及地址(如果信用证没有明确规定，可以填写开证行名称及地址)	**注释**：出票人签署 在汇票右下角由出票人(L/C 中 59)填写公司名称并签署

资料链接 Material—link

1. Standard Model

Model 1: Commercial Invoice 商业发票

ISSUER WENSLI GROUP. #309 JICHANG RD, HANGZHOU,CHINA TEL: 86-25-4729178 FAX:82-25-4715619	**商业发票** COMMERCIAL INVOICE			
TO N.E.ORIENTAL TRADING CO.LTD. P.O. BOX 12345 CODE 55400 T-3456789 RIYADH KINGDOM OF SAUDI ARABIA	**NO.** 2010SDT001		**DATE** 2010.10.11	
TRANSPORT DETAILS SHIPMENT FROM SHANGHAI TO DAMMAM PORT BY SEA	**S/C NO.** NEO2010/026		**L/C NO.** DES505606	
	TERMS OF PAYMENT L/C AT SIGHT			
Marks and Numbers	**Number and kind of package** **Description of goods**	**Quantity**	**Unit Price** **USD**	**Amount**

续表

N.E OT NEO2010/026	CFR DAMMAM PORT, SAUDI ARABIA			
DAMMAM PORT B/N 1-600	400 BUNDLES TEXTILE FABRIC 200 BUNDLES LADIES' SUIT	400 BUNDLES 200 BUNDLES	USD120.00 USD50.00	USD58 000.00
	Total:	600 BUNDLES		USD58 000.00

SAY TOTAL:SAY USD FIFTY EIGHT THOUSAND ONLY.

We hereby certify that the contents of invoice herein are true and correct.

DESUNSOFT TRADING COMPANY

(出口商签字和盖单据章)

WENSLI GROUP.

Model 2: Insurance Policy 保险单

PICC 中国人民保险公司 杭州市分公司

The People's Insurance Company of China，Hangzhou Branch

货物运输保险单

CARGO TRANSPORTATION INSURANCE POLICY

发票号(INVOICE NO.) **2010SDT001**
合同号(CONTRACT NO.) **NEO2010/026**
信用证号(L/C NO.) **DES505606**

保单号次
POLICY NO 123456

被保险人:
Insured: **WENSLI GROUP.**
#309 JICHANG RD,
HANGZHOU, CHINA

TEL: 86-25-4729178 FAX: 82-25-4715619

中国人民保险公司(以下简称本公司)根据被保险人的要求，由被保险人向本公司缴付约定的保险费，按照本保险单承保险别和背面所列条款与下列特款承保下述货物运输保险，特立本保险单。

THIS POLICY OF INSURANCE WITNESSES THAT THE PEOPLE'S INSURANCE COMPANY OF CHINA (HEREINAFTER CALLED “THE COMPANY”) AT THE REQUEST OF INSURED AND IN CONSIDERATION OF THE AGREED PREMIUM PAID TO THE COMPANY BY THE INSURED UNDERTAKES TO INSURE THE UNDERMENTIONED GOODS IN TRANSPORTATION SUBJECT TO THE CONDITIONS OF THIS POLICY AS PER THE CLAUSES PRINTED OVERLEAF AND OTHER SPECIAL CLAUSES ATTACHED HEREON

标　记 MARKS & NOS.	数量及包装 QUANTITY	保险货物项目 DESCRIPTION OF GOODS	保险金额 AMOUNT INSURED
AS PER INVOICE NO. 2010SDT001	**400 BUNDLES 200 BUNDLES**	**TEXTILE FABRIC LADIES' SUIT**	**USD63 800.00**

总保险金额

TOTAL AMOUNT INSURED: **SAY US DOLLARS SIXTY-THREE THOUSAND EIGHT HUNDRED ONLY**

保费　　启运日期：　　装载运输工具：

PREMIUM **USD319** DATE OF COMMENCEMENT **25th OCT, 2010** PER CONVEYANCE **SKY BRIGHT V.047A**

自　　经　　至

FROM **SHANGHAI PORT** VIA TO **DAMMAM PORT, SAUDI ARABIA**

承保险别：

CONDITIONS: **WPA AND WAR RISKS FOR 110% OF THE INVOICE VALUE AS PER THE RELEVANT OCEAN MARINE CARGO OF PICC DATED 1/1/1981**

所保货物，如发生保险单项下可能引起索赔的损失或损坏，应立即通知本公司下述代理人查勘。如有索赔应向本公司提交保险单正本(共 2 份正本)及有关文件。如一份正本已用于索赔，其余正本自动失效。

IN THE EVENT OF LOSS DAMAGE WHICH MAY RESULT IN A CLAIM UNDER THIS POLICY, IMMEDIATE NOTICE MUST BE GIVEN TO THE COMPANY AGENT AS MENTIONED HEREUNDER CLAIMS IF ANY, ONE OF THE ORIGINAL POLICY WHICH HAS BEEN ISSUED IN 2 ORIGINAL TOGETHER WITH RELEVANT DOCUMENTS SHALL BE SURRENDERED TO THE COMPANY IF THE ORIGINAL POLICY HAS BEEN ACCOMPLISHED, THE OTHERS TO BE VOID .

赔款偿付地点

CLAIM PAYABLE AT **SAUDI ARABIA**　　中国人民保险公司杭州市分公司

出单日期　　The People's Insurance Company of China

ISSUING DATE **25th OCT，2010**　　Hangzhou Branch

Model 3 : Certificate of Origin 原产地证书

1. Exporter WENSLI GROUP. #309 JICHANG RD,HANGZHOU,CHINA TEL:86-25-4729178 FAX:82-25-4715619	Certificate No. **CERTIFICATE OF ORIGIN** **OF** THE PEOPLE'S REPUBLIC OF CHINA
2. Consignee TO ORDER OR SHIPPER	
3. Means of transport and route SHIPMENT FROM SHANGHAI, CHINA To : DAMMAM PORT, SAUDI ARABIA BY SEA	5. For certifying authority use only
4. Country / region of destination SAUDI ARABIA	

6. Marks and numbers	7. Number and kind of packages; description of goods	8. H.S.Code	9. Quantity	10. Number and date of invoices
N/M	400 BUNDLES TEXTILE FABRIC 200 BUNDLES LADIES' SUIT	6001920000 6110.300090	600 BUNDLES	2001SDT001 Sep. 30, 2010
SAYT OTAL:SIX HUNDRED BUNDLES ONLY. CERTIFICATE OF CHINESE ORIGIN ISSUED BY C.C.P.I.T. STATING THE NAME AND ADDRESS OF MANUFACTURER OR PRODUCERS AND STATING THAT GOODS EXPORTED ARE WHOLLY OF DOMESTIC ORIGIN.				

续表

11. Declaration by the exporter	12. Certification
The undersigned hereby declares that the above details and statements are correct, that all the goods were produced in China and that they comply with the Rules of Origin of the People's Republic of China. WENSLI GROUP. CHINA Sep. 30, 2010 ------------------------------ Place and date, signature and stamp of authorized signatory	It is hereby certified that the declaration by the exporter is correct. China Council for the Promotion of International Trade Sep. 30, 2010 ------------------------------ Place and date, signature and stamp of certifying authority

Model 4 : Shipping Advice 装船通知

SHIPPING ADVICE

DEAR SIR，

WE ARE PLEASED TO INFORM YOUR ESTEEMED COMPANY THAT THE FOLLOWING MENTIONED GOODS WILL BE SHIPPED OUT ON THE 25th OCT， FULL DETAILS WERE SHOWN AS FOLLOWS:

1. INVOICE: 2010SDT001
2. BILL OF LADING NUMBER: TMSH5247
3. OCEAN VESSEL: SKY BRIGHT V.047A
4. PORT OF LOADING: SHANGHAI PORT
5. DATE OF SHIPMENT: OCT. 25, 2010
6. PORT OF DESTINATION: DAMMAM PORT
7. ESTIMATED DATE OF ARRIVAL: NOV. 20, 2010
8. DESCRIPTION OF PACKAGES AND GOODS:
   400 BUNDLES TEXTILE FABRIC
   200 BUNDLES LADIES' SUIT 9. MARKS AND NUMBER ON B/L: N.E OT
   NEO2010/026
   DAMMAM PORT
   B/N 1-600
   TMSH5247
9. CONTAINER/SEAL NUMBER: EMCU2862697/JBF2222
   UGMU8734320/JBF2211
10. L/C NUMBER: DES505606

WE WILL FAX THE ORIGINAL BILL OF LADING TO YOUR COMPANY UPON RECEIPT OF IT FROM SHIPPING COMPANY.

(出口商签字和盖单据章)

BEST REGARDS,

WENSLI GROUP.

Model 5 :Bill of Exchange 汇票

Drawn under ROYAL BANK OF NEW YORK

L/C No. DES505606

DATE Nov 20,2010

PAYABLE WITH INTEREST@ %PER ANUM

NO. **2010SDT001** EXCHANGE **USD26840.00** FOR HANGHZOU,CHINA Oct 20, 2010

AT XXX SIGHT OF THIS FIRST OF EXCHANGE(SECOND OF EXCHANGE BEING UNPAID)

PAY TO THE ORDER OF ROYAL BANK OF NEW YORK

TO **N.E.ORIENTAL TRADING CO. LTD.**

2. *Writing Guide*

1) 单证制作“五要求”

(1) 正确/准确(CORRECTNESS)要做到单、单一致，证、货一致，单、货一致，单、证一致。

(2) 完整(COMPLETENESS)单证在通过银行议付或托收时，一般都是成套、齐全而不是单一的。 单据的本身内容必须完备齐全。出口人所提供的各种单据的份数要如数交齐，不能短缺。

(3) 及时(PROMPTNESS)。

(4) 简明(CONCISENESS)。

(5) 整洁(TIDINESS)。

2) 制单的一般程序

(1) “核”：首先应将货物的原始资料，如出仓单或装箱单与信用证或合同核对，查清证、货是否相符。

(2) “算”：单据有很多数据需要计算，都必须在制单前算好。

(3) “配”：根据信用证要求把本批出口货物所需的各种单据的空白格式按需要的份数(包括送交银行结汇所需的份数、留底及其他所需要的份数)逐一配妥备用。

(4) “制”：制单可以先从发票入手，因为发票是一切单据的中心，发票制妥后，再参照其内容缮制其他单据。

(5) “审”：单据制好后，制单人应自审，如有差错应立即更正，再将单据交有关人员进一步审核。

Section Four Selected Sentences
精选句型表达

1．离岸价条款 Terms of FOB Delivery:

(1) 装运本合同货物的船只，由买方或买方运输代理人中国租船公司租订舱位。卖方负担货物的一切费用风险到货物装到船面为止。

For the goods ordered in this Contract, the carrying vessel shall be arranged by the Buyers or the Buyers’ Shipping Agent China National Chartering Corporation. The Sellers shall bear all the charges and risks until the goods are effectively loaded on board the carrying vessel.

(2) 卖方必须在合同规定的交货期限30天前，将合同号码、货物名称、数量、装运口岸及预计货物运达装运口岸日期，以电报通知买方以便买方安排舱位，并同时通知买方在装港的船代理。倘在规定期内买方未接到前述通知，即作为卖方同意在合同规定期内任何日期交货，并由买方主动租订舱位。

30 days before the contracted time of shipment, the Sellers shall advise the Buyers by cable,

and simultaneously advise the Buyers' shipping agent of the contract number, name of commodity, quantity, loading port and expected date of arrival of the goods at the loading port, enabling the Buyers to arrange for shipping space. Absence of such advice within the time specified above shall be considered as Sellers' readiness to deliver the goods during the time of shipment contracted and the Buyers shall arrange for shipping space accordingly.

(3) 买方应在船只受载期 12 天前将船名、预计受载日期、装载数量、合同号码、船舶代理人，以电报通知卖方。卖方应联系船舶代理人配合船期备货装船。如买方因故需要变更船只或更改船期时，买方或船舶代理人应及时通知卖方。

12 days before the expected loading date, the Buyers shall advise the Sellers by cable, of the estimated laydays, contract number, name of vessel, quantity to be loaded and shipping agent. The Sellers shall then arrange with the shipping agent for loading accordingly. In case of necessity for substitution of vessel or alteration of shipping schedule, the Buyers or the shipping agent shall duly advise the Sellers to the same effect.

(4) 买方所租船只按期到达装运口岸后，如卖方不能按时备货装船，买方因而遭受的一切损失包括空舱费、延期费及/或罚款等将由卖方负担。如船只不能于船舶代理人所确定的受载期内到达，在港口免费堆存期满后第 16 天起发生的仓库租费，保险费由买方负担，但卖方仍负有载货船只到达装运口岸后立即将货物装船的义务并负担费用及风险。前述各种损失均凭原始单据核实支付。

In the event of the Sellers' failure in effecting shipment upon arrival of the vessel at the loading port, all losses, including dead freight, demurrage fines etc. thus incurred shall be for Sellers' account. If the vessel fails to arrive at the loading port within the laydays, previously declared by the shipping agent, the storage charges and insurance premium from the 16th day after expiration of the free storage time at the port shall be borne by the Buyers. However, the Sellers shall be still under the obligation to load the goods on board the carrying vessel immediately after the arrival at the loading port, at their own expenses and risks. The expenses and losses mentioned above shall be reimbursed against original receipts or invoices.

2．装运通知：卖方在货物装船后，立即将合同号、品名、件数、毛重、净重、发票金额、载货船名及装船日期以电报通知买方。

Advice of Shipment：The Sellers shall upon competition of loading, advise immediately the Buyers by cable of the contract number, name of commodity, number of packages, gross and net weights, invoice value, name of vessel and loading date.

3．保险：自装船起由买方自理，但卖方应按本合同第(11)条通知买方。如卖方未能按此办理，买方因而遭受的一切损失全由卖方负担。

Insurance：To be covered by the Buyers from shipment, for this purpose the Sellers shall advise the Buyers by cable of the particulars as called for in Clause(11) of this Contract, In the event of the Buyers being unable to arrange for insurance in consequence of the Sellers' failure to send the above advice, the Sellers shall be held responsible for all the losses thus sustained by the Buyers.

4．检验和索赔：货卸目的口岸，买方有权申请中华人民共和国国家质量监督检验检疫总局进行检验。如发现货物的品质及/或数量/重量与合同或发票不符：除属于保险公司及/或船公司的责任外，买方有权在货卸目的口岸后90天内，根据中华人民共和国国家质量监督检验检疫总局出具的证明书向卖方提出索赔，因索赔所发生的一切费用(包括检验费用)均由卖方负担。FOB价格条件时，如重量短缺，买方有权同时索赔短重部分的运费。

Inspection and Claim：The Buyers shall have the right to apply to the General Administration of Quality Supervision, Inspection and Quarantine of the People's Republic of China (AQSIQ) for inspection after discharge of the goods at the port of destination. Should the quality and/or quantity/weight be found not in conformity with the contract or invoice the Buyers shall be entitled to lodge claims with the Sellers on the basis of AQSIQ's Survey Report, within 90 days after discharge of the goods at the port of destination, with the exception, however, of those claims for which the shipping company and/or the insurance company are to be held responsible. All expenses incurred on the claim including the inspection fee as per the AQSIQ inspection certificate are to be borne by the Sellers. In case of FOB terms, the buyers shall also be entitled to claim freight for short weight if any.

5. 不可抗力：由于人力不可抗拒事故，使卖方不能在合同规定期限内交货或者不能交货，卖方不负责任。但卖方必须立即通知买方，并以挂号函向买方提出有关政府机关或者商会所出具的证明，以证明事故的存在。由于人力不可抗拒事故致使交货期限延期一个月以上时，买方有权撤销合同。卖方不能取得出口许可证不得作为不可抗力。

Force Majeure：In case of Force Majeure the Sellers shall not held responsible for delay in delivery or non-delivery of the goods but shall notify immediately the Buyers and deliver to the Buyers by registered mail a certificate issued by government authorities or Chamber of Commerce as evidence thereof. If the shipment is delayed over one month as the consequence of the said Force Majeure, the Buyers shall have the right to cancel this Contract. Sellers' inability in obtaining export licence shall not be considered as Force Majeure.

6. 延期交货及罚款：除本合同第(14)条人力不可抗拒原因外，如卖方不能如期交货，买方有权撤销该部分的合同，或经买方同意在卖方缴纳罚款的条件下延期交货。买方可同意给予卖方15天优惠期。罚款率为每10天按货款总额的1%。不足10天者按10天计算。罚款自第16天起计算。最多不超过延期货款总额的5%。

Delayed Delivery and Penalty：Should the Sellers fail to effect delivery on time as stipulated in this Contract owing to causes other than Force Majeure as provided for in Clause (14) of this Contract, the Buyers shall have the right to cancel the relative quantity of the contract, Or alternatively, the Sellers may, with the Buyers' consent, postpone delivery on payment of penalty to the Buyers. The Buyers may agree to grant the Sellers a grace period of 15 days. Penalty shall be calculated from the 16th day and shall not exceed 5% of the total value of the goods involved.

7. 仲裁：一切因执行本合同或与本合同有关的争执，应由双方通过友好方式协商解决。如经协商不能得到解决时，应提交北京中国国际贸易促进委员会对外经济贸易仲裁委员会。按照中国国际贸易促进委员会对外经济贸易仲裁委员会仲裁程序暂行规定进行仲裁。仲裁委员会的裁决为终局裁决，对双方均有约束力。仲裁费用除非仲裁委员会另有决定外，由败诉一方负担。

Arbitration：All disputes in connection with this Contract or the execution thereof shall be friendly negotiation. If no settlement can be reached, the case in dispute shall then be submitted for arbitration to the Foreign Economic and Trade Arbitration Commission of the China Council for the Promotion of International Trade in accordance with the Provisional Rules of Procedure of the Foreign Economic and Trade Arbitration Commission of the China Council for the Promotion of International Trade. The Award made by the Commission shall be accepted as final and binding upon both parties. The fees for arbitration shall be borne by the losing party unless otherwise awarded by the Commission.

8．附加条款：以上任何条款如与以下附加条款有抵触时，以以下附加条款为准。

Additional Clause ：If any of the above-mentioned Clauses is inconsistent with the following Additional Clause(s), the latter to be taken as authentic.

Abstract

通过本章学习，①了解外贸单证的基本分类；②掌握单证制作的要求；③掌握各类单证的基本规律和注意事项；④通过熟悉标准模板掌握外贸单证填写的基本方法。

Useful Words & Expressions

1．documents 单据
2．documentation 单据的制作或使用
3．take delivery of 提货
4．commission 佣金
5．discount 折扣
6．shipping marks 唛头；运输标记
7．bill of lading 提(货)单
8．carrier 承运人: The shipping company
9．shipper 货主、托运人、发货人
10．consignor 托运人
11．carriage 运输；运费
12．consignee 收货人
13．notify party 到货通知人；被通知人
14．payable 应支付的；可支付的
15．airway bill 空运(提)单
16．railway bill 收货单(铁路)
17．insurance policy 保险单(大保单)
18．insurance certificate 保险单(小保单)
19．cargo receipt 铁路运单；货运收据
20．commercial invoice 商业发票
21．legal holder 合法持有人
22．customs invoice 海关发票

23．consular invoice 领事发票
24．consular visa 领事签证
25．shipping advice 装船通知
26．certificate of quality 质量证书
27．certificate of weight 重量证书
28．certificate of quantity 数量证书
29．certificate of health 健康证书
30．certificate of disinfection 消毒证书
31．certificate of origin 产地证书
32．veterinary certificate 兽医证书
33．packing list 装箱单
34．straight bill of lading 记名提单: It is made out so that only the named consignee is entitled to take delivery of the goods under the bill.
35．port of shipment 发货港；装运港；起运港

References
参考文献

[1] 阿里巴巴(中国)网络技术有限公司. e时代外贸英语[M]. 北京：世界图书出版公司北京公司，2007.

[2] 曹元寿. 外贸英语函电读写译[M]. 北京：北京理工大学出版社，2000.

[3] 蔡惠伟. 外经贸函电教程(A Course of English for the International Business Communication) [M]. 上海：华东理工大学出版社，2007.

[4] 董金玲，等. 国际商务函电双语教程[M]. 北京：机械工业出版社，2011.

[5] 陈岩. 国际商务制单[M]. 北京：对外经贸大学出版社，2007.

[6] 陈祥国. 国际商务函电[M]. 北京：中国商务出版社，2004.

[7] 方春祥，外贸函电[M]. 北京：中国人民大学出版社，2005.

[8] 方宁，王维平. 商务英语函电[M]. 杭州：浙江大学出版社，2004.

[9] 冯祥春，隋思忠. 新编大学国际商务英语函电教程[M]. 北京：中国商务出版社，2008.

[10] 侯方淼. 外贸英语函电[M]. 北京：电子工业出版社，2010.

[11] 黄水乞. 外贸英文信函范例与常用精句[M]. 广州：广东经济出版社，2006.

[12] 胡鉴明. 商务英语函电[M]. 北京：中国商务出版社，2008.

[13] 胡鉴明. 商务英语函电自学手册[M]. 北京：中国商务出版社，2008.

[14] 胡庚申. 国际商务合同起草与翻译[M]. 北京：外文出版社，2001.

[15] 简新亚. 英文合同协议“快易通”[M]. 北京：清华大学出版社，2003.

[16] 蒋磊. 国际商务英语函电[M]. 北京：北京大学出版社，2007.

[17] 金双玉，钦寅. 外贸英语——函电与单证[M]. 上海：同济大学出版社，2006.

[18] 兰天，时敏，叶富国. 外贸英语函电[M]. 北京：科学出版社，2010.

[19] 李国平，程艳红. 外贸英语函电[M]. 北京：北京大学出版社 2009.

[20] 李蕾. 商务英语函电[M]. 北京：对外经济贸易大学出版社，2011.

[21] 李文彪. 国际商务函电[M]. 北京：北京理工大学出版社，2009.

[22] 李文彪，张丽红，鄢华平. 国际商务函电学习指导[M]. 北京：北京理工大学出版社，2009.

[23] 刘超先. 外贸英语单证与函电[M]. 上海：复旦大学出版社，2008 年.

[24] 刘慧侠，贾钊. 外贸函电[M]. 北京：科学出版社，2004.

[25] 苏丽萍. 国际金融英文函电[M]. 厦门：厦门大学出版社，2007.

[26] 谈芳. 外经贸英语函电[M]. 上海：学林出版社，2005.

[27] 田运银. 国际贸易单证精讲[M]. 北京：中国海关出版社，2008.

[28] 滕美荣，许楠. 外贸英语函电[M]. 3 版. 北京：首都经济贸易大学出版社，2011.

[29] 王虹，耿伟. 外贸英语函电[M]. 北京：清华大学出版社，2009.

[30] 王慧敏. 外贸函电[M]. 北京：北京大学出版社，2005.

[31] 王俊，商务英语函电[M]. 北京：对外经济贸易大学出版社，2011.

[32] 王俐俐. 外贸英语函电与单证[M]. 北京：机械工业出版社，2010.

[33] 王美玲. 商务英语函电[M]. 北京：中国商务出版社，2007.

[34] 魏莉霞，张逸. 国际商务函电[M]. 北京：北京大学出版社，2004.

[35] 吴文劲. 外经贸函电. 湖北经济学院经贸学院教师授课教案.

[36] 冼燕华．国际商务英语函电[M]．广州：暨南大学出版社，2008．
[37] 徐良霞．实用英语教你写合同[M]．北京：北京航空航天大学出版社，2004．
[38] 杨文惠．现代商务英语写作集萃[M]．广州：中山大学出版社，2005．
[39] 姚克勤．外贸英语函电[M]．西安：西北工业大学出版社，2008．
[40] 毅冰．外贸高手客户成交技巧[M]．北京：中国海关出版社，2012．
[41] 易露露，王娜娜，陈原．外贸英语函电[M]．北京：清华大学出版社，2008．
[42] 尹小莹．外贸英语函电—商务英语应用文写作[M]．西安：西安交通大学出版社，2004．
[43] 郑敏．商务英语函电与合同[M]．北京：清华大学出版社/北京交通大学出版社，2005．
[44] 诸葛霖．外贸英文书信[M]．北京：对外经济贸易大学出版社，2000．
[45] 实惠网外贸论坛：http://bbs.sfyh.com
[46] 中国采购经理人论坛：http://home.purchasingbbs.com/archiver/?tid-898138.html

北京大学出版社本科财经管理类实用规划教材（已出版）

财务会计类

序号	书 名	标 准 书 号	主 编	定价	序号	书 名	标 准 书 号	主 编	定价
1	基础会计（第2版）	7-301-17478-4	李秀莲	38.00	21	财务管理学	7-5038-4897-1	盛均全	34.00
2	基础会计学	7-301-19403-4	窦亚芹	33.00	22	财务管理学	7-301-21887-7	陈 玮	44.00
3	会计学	7-81117-533-2	马丽莹	44.00	23	基础会计学学习指导与习题集	7-301-16309-2	裴 玉	28.00
4	会计学原理（第2版）	7-301-18515-5	刘爱香	30.00	24	财务管理理论与实务	7-301-20042-1	成 兵	40.00
5	会计学原理习题与实验（第2版）	7-301-19449-2	王保忠	30.00	25	税法与税务会计实用教程（第2版）	7-301-21422-0	张巧良	45.00
6	会计学原理与实务（第2版）	7-301-18653-4	周慧滨	33.00	26	财务管理理论与实务（第2版）	7-301-20407-8	张思强	42.00
7	会计学原理与实务模拟实验教程	7-5038-5013-4	周慧滨	20.00	27	公司理财原理与实务	7-81117-800-5	廖东声	36.00
8	会计实务	7-81117-677-3	王远利	40.00	28	审计学	7-81117-828-9	王翠琳	46.00
9	高级财务会计	7-81117-545-5	程明娥	46.00	29	审计学	7-301-20906-6	赵晓波	38.00
10	高级财务会计	7-5655-0061-9	王奇杰	44.00	30	审计理论与实务	7-81117-955-2	宋传联	36.00
11	成本会计学	7-301-19400-3	杨尚军	38.00	31	会计综合实训模拟教程	7-301-20730-7	章洁倩	33.00
12	成本会计学	7-5655-0482-2	张红漫	30.00	32	财务分析学	7-301-20275-3	张献英	30.00
13	成本会计学	7-301-20473-3	刘建中	38.00	33	银行会计	7-301-21155-7	宗国恩	40.00
14	管理会计	7-81117-943-9	齐殿伟	27.00	34	税收筹划	7-301-21238-7	都新英	38.00
15	管理会计	7-301-21057-4	彤芳珍	36.00	35	基础会计学	7-301-16308-5	晋晓琴	39.00
16	会计规范专题	7-81117-887-6	谢万健	35.00	36	公司财务管理	7-301-21423-7	胡振兴	48.00
17	企业财务会计模拟实习教程	7-5655-0404-4	董晓平	25.00	37	财务管理学实用教程（第2版）	7-301-21060-4	骆永菊	42.00
18	税法与税务会计	7-81117-497-7	吕孝侠	45.00	38	政府与非营利组织会计	7-301-21504-3	张 丹	40.00
19	初级财务管理	7-301-20019-3	胡淑姣	42.00	39	预算会计	7-301-22203-4	王筱萍	32.00
20	财务管理学原理与实务	7-81117-544-8	严复海	40.00	40	统计学实验教程	7-301-22450-2	裘雨明	24.00

工商管理、市场营销、人力资源管理、服务营销类

序号	书 名	标 准 书 号	主 编	定价	序号	书 名	标 准 书 号	主 编	定价
1	管理学基础	7-5038-4872-8	于干千	35.00	28	市场营销学	7-301-21056-7	马慧敏	42.00
2	管理学基础学习指南与习题集	7-5038-4891-9	王 珍	26.00	29	市场营销学：理论、案例与实训	7-301-21165-6	袁连升	42.00
3	管理学	7-81117-494-6	曾 旗	44.00	30	市场营销学	7-5655-0064-0	王槐林	33.00
4	管理学	7-301-21167-0	陈文汉	35.00	31	国际市场营销学	7-301-21888-4	董 飞	45.00
5	管理学	7-301-17452-4	王慧娟	42.00	32	市场营销学（第2版）	7-301-19855-1	陈 阳	45.00
6	管理学原理	7-5655-0078-7	尹少华	42.00	33	市场营销学	7-301-21166-3	杨 楠	40.00
7	管理学原理与实务（第2版）	7-301-18536-0	陈嘉莉	42.00	34	国际市场营销学	7-5038-5021-9	范应仁	38.00
8	管理学实用教程	7-5655-0063-3	邵喜武	37.00	35	现代市场营销学	7-81117-599-8	邓德胜	40.00
9	管理学实用教程	7-301-21059-8	高爱霞	42.00	36	市场营销学新论	7-5038-4879-7	郑玉香	40.00
10	管理学实用教程	7-301-22218-8	张润兴	43.00	37	市场营销理论与实务（第2版）	7-301-20628-7	那 薇	40.00
11	通用管理知识概论	7-5038-4997-8	王丽平	36.00	38	市场营销学实用教程	7-5655-0081-7	李晨耘	40.00
12	管理学原理	7-301-21178-6	雷金荣	39.00	39	市场营销学	7-81117-676-6	戴秀英	32.00
13	管理运筹学（第2版）	7-301-19351-8	关文忠	39.00	40	消费者行为学	7-81117-824-1	甘瑁琴	35.00
14	统计学原理	7-301-21061-1	韩 宇	38.00	41	商务谈判（第2版）	7-301-20048-3	郭秀君	49.00
15	统计学原理	7-5038-4888-9	刘晓利	28.00	42	商务谈判实用教程	7-81117-597-4	陈建明	24.00
16	统计学	7-5038-4898-8	曲 岩	42.00	43	消费者行为学	7-5655-0057-2	肖 立	37.00
17	应用统计学（第2版）	7-301-19295-5	王淑芬	48.00	44	客户关系管理实务	7-301-09956-8	周贺来	44.00
18	统计学原理与实务	7-5655-0505-8	徐静霞	40.00	45	公共关系学	7-5038-5022-6	于朝晖	40.00
19	管理定量分析方法	7-301-13552-5	赵光华	28.00	46	非营利组织	7-301-20726-0	王智慧	33.00
20	新编市场营销学	7-81117-972-9	刘丽霞	30.00	47	公共关系理论与实务	7-5038-4889-6	王 玫	32.00
21	公共关系理论与实务	7-5655-0155-5	李泓欣	45.00	48	公共关系学实用教程	7-81117-660-5	周 华	35.00
22	质量管理	7-5655-0069-5	陈国华	36.00	49	跨文化管理	7-301-20027-8	晏 雄	35.00
23	企业文化理论与实务	7-81117-663-6	王水嫩	30.00	50	企业战略管理	7-5655-0370-2	代海涛	36.00
24	企业战略管理	7-81117-801-2	陈英梅	34.00	51	员工招聘	7-301-20089-6	王 挺	30.00
25	企业战略管理实用教程	7-81117-853-1	刘松先	35.00	52	服务营销理论与实务	7-81117-826-5	杨丽华	39.00
26	产品与品牌管理	7-81117-492-2	胡 梅	35.00	53	服务企业经营管理学	7-5038-4890-2	于干千	36.00
27	东方哲学与企业文化	7-5655-0433-4	刘峰涛	34.00	54	服务营销	7-301-15834-0	周 明	40.00

序号	书　名	标准书号	主　编	定价	序号	书　名	标准书号	主　编	定价
55	运营管理	7-5038-4878-0	冯根尧	35.00	67	会展服务管理	7-301-16661-1	许传宏	36.00
56	生产运作管理（第2版）	7-301-18934-4	李全喜	48.00	68	现代服务业管理原理、方法与案例	7-301-17817-1	马　勇	49.00
57	运作管理	7-5655-0472-3	周建亨	25.00	69	服务性企业战略管理	7-301-20043-8	黄其新	28.00
58	组织行为学	7-5038-5014-1	安世民	33.00	70	服务型政府管理概论	7-301-20099-5	于干千	32.00
59	组织行为学实用教程	7-301-20466-5	冀　鸿	32.00	71	新编现代企业管理	7-301-21121-2	姚丽娜	48.00
60	现代组织理论	7-5655-0077-0	岳　澍	32.00	72	创业学	7-301-15915-6	刘沁玲	38.00
61	人力资源管理（第2版）	7-301-19098-2	颜爱民	60.00	73	公共关系学实用教程	7-301-17472-2	任焕琴	42.00
62	人力资源管理经济分析	7-301-16084-8	颜爱民	38.00	74	现场管理	7-301-21528-9	陈国华	38.00
63	人力资源管理原理与实务	7-81117-496-0	邹　华	32.00	75	现代企业管理理论与应用（第2版）	7-301-21603-3	邸彦彪	38.00
64	人力资源管理实用教程（第2版）	7-301-20281-4	吴宝华	45.00	76	服务营销	7-301-21889-1	熊　凯	45.00
65	人力资源管理：理论、实务与艺术	7-5655-0193-7	李长江	48.00	77	企业经营ERP沙盘应用教程	7-301-20728-4	董红杰	32.00
66	政府与非营利组织会计	7-301-21504-3	张　丹	40.00	78	项目管理	7-301-21448-0	程　敏	39.00

经济、国贸、金融类

序号	书　名	标准书号	主　编	定价	序号	书　名	标准书号	主　编	定价
1	宏观经济学原理与实务（第2版）	7-301-18787-6	崔东红	57.00	21	国际贸易规则与进出口业务操作实务（第2版）	7-301-19384-6	李　平	54.00
2	宏观经济学（第2版）	7-301-19038-8	蹇令香	39.00	22	金融市场学	7-81117-595-0	黄解宇	24.00
3	微观经济学原理与实务	7-81117-818-0	崔东红	48.00	23	财政学	7-5038-4965-7	盖　锐	34.00
4	微观经济学	7-81117-568-4	梁瑞华	35.00	24	保险学原理与实务	7-5038-4871-1	曹时军	37.00
5	西方经济学实用教程	7-5038-4886-5	陈孝胜	40.00	25	东南亚南亚商务环境概论	7-81117-956-9	韩　越	38.00
6	西方经济学实用教程	7-5655-0302-3	杨仁发	49.00	26	证券投资学	7-301-19967-1	陈汉平	45.00
7	西方经济学	7-81117-851-7	于丽敏	40.00	27	证券投资学	7-301-21236-3	王　毅	45.00
8	现代经济学基础	7-81117-549-3	张士军	25.00	28	货币银行学	7-301-15062-7	杜小伟	38.00
9	国际经济学	7-81117-594-3	吴红梅	39.00	29	货币银行学	7-301-21345-2	李　冰	42.00
10	发展经济学	7-81117-674-2	赵邦宏	48.00	30	国际结算（第2版）	7-301-17420-3	张晓芬	35.00
11	管理经济学	7-81117-536-3	姜保雨	34.00	31	国际结算	7-301-21092-5	张　慧	42.00
12	计量经济学	7-5038-3915-3	刘艳春	28.00	32	金融风险管理	7-301-20090-2	朱淑珍	38.00
13	外贸函电（第2版）	7-301-18786-9	王　妍	30.00	33	金融工程学	7-301-18273-4	李淑锦	30.00
14	国际贸易理论与实务（第2版）	7-301-18798-2	缪东玲	54.00	34	国际贸易理论、政策与案例分析	7-301-20978-3	冯　跃	42.00
15	国际贸易（第2版）	7-301-19404-1	朱廷珺	45.00	35	金融工程学理论与实务（第2版）	7-301-21280-6	谭春枝	42.00
16	国际贸易实务（第2版）	7-301-20486-3	夏合群	45.00	36	金融学理论与实务	7-5655-0405-1	战玉峰	42.00
17	国际贸易结算及其单证实务	7-5655-0268-2	卓乃坚	35.00	37	国际金融实用教程	7-81117-593-6	周　影	32.00
18	政治经济学原理与实务（第2版）	7-301-22204-1	沈爱华	31.00	38	跨国公司经营与管理（第2版）	7-301-21333-9	冯雷鸣	35.00
19	国际商务	7-5655-0093-0	安占然	30.00	39	国际金融	7-5038-4893-3	韩博印	30.00
20	国际贸易实务	7-301-20919-6	张　肃	28.00	40	国际商务函电	7-301-22388-8	金泽虎	35.00

法律类

序号	书　名	标准书号	主　编	定价	序号	书　名	标准书号	主　编	定价
1	经济法原理与实务(第2版)	7-301-21527-2	杨士富	39.00	5	劳动法和社会保障法(第2版)	7-301-21206-6	李　瑞	38.00
2	经济法实用教程	7-81117-547-9	陈亚平	44.00	6	金融法学理论与实务	7-81117-958-3	战玉锋	34.00
3	国际商法理论与实务	7-81117-852-4	杨士富	38.00	7	国际商法	7-301-20071-1	丁孟春	37.00
4	商法总论	7-5038-4887-2	任先行	40.00	8	商法学	7-301-21478-7	周龙杰	43.00

电子商务与信息管理类

序号	书　名	标准书号	主　编	定价	序号	书　名	标准书号	主　编	定价
1	网络营销	7-301-12349-2	谷宝华	30.00	8	电子商务概论（第2版）	7-301-17475-3	庞大莲	42.00
2	数据库技术及应用教程（SQL Server版）	7-301-12351-5	郭建校	34.00	9	网络营销	7-301-16556-0	王宏伟	26.00
3	网络信息采集与编辑	7-301-16557-7	范生万	24.00	10	电子商务概论	7-301-16717-5	杨雪雁	32.00
4	电子商务案例分析	7-301-16596-6	曹彩杰	28.00	11	电子商务英语	7-301-05364-5	覃　正	30.00
5	管理信息系统	7-301-12348-5	张彩虹	36.00	12	网络支付与结算	7-301-16911-7	徐　勇	34.00
6	电子商务概论	7-301-13633-1	李洪心	30.00	13	网上支付与安全	7-301-17044-1	帅青红	32.00
7	管理信息系统实用教程	7-301-12323-2	李　松	35.00	14	企业信息化实务	7-301-16621-5	张志荣	42.00

序号	书　名	标准书号	主　编	定价	序号	书　名	标准书号	主　编	定价
15	电子商务法	7-301-14306-3	李　瑞	26.00	28	电子化国际贸易	7-301-17246-9	李辉作	28.00
16	数据仓库与数据挖掘	7-301-14313-1	廖开际	28.00	29	商务智能与数据挖掘	7-301-17671-9	张公让	38.00
17	电子商务模拟与实验	7-301-12350-8	喻光继	22.00	30	管理信息系统教程	7-301-19472-0	赵天唯	42.00
18	ERP 原理与应用教程	7-301-14455-8	温雅丽	34.00	31	电子政务	7-301-15163-1	原忠虎	38.00
19	电子商务原理及应用	7-301-14080-2	孙　睿	36.00	32	商务智能	7-301-19899-5	汪　楠	40.00
20	管理信息系统理论与应用	7-301-15212-6	吴　忠	30.00	33	电子商务与现代企业管理	7-301-19978-7	吴菊华	40.00
21	网络营销实务	7-301-15284-3	李蔚田	42.00	34	电子商务物流管理	7-301-20098-8	王小宁	42.00
22	电子商务实务	7-301-15474-8	仲　岩	28.00	35	管理信息系统实用教程	7-301-20485-6	周贺来	42.00
23	电子商务网站建设	7-301-15480-9	臧良运	32.00	36	电子商务概论	7-301-21044-4	苗　森	28.00
24	网络金融与电子支付	7-301-15694-0	李蔚田	30.00	37	管理信息系统实务教程	7-301-21245-5	魏厚清	34.00
25	网络营销	7-301-22125-9	程　虹	38.00	38	电子商务安全	7-301-22350-5	蔡志文	49.00
26	电子证券与投资分析	7-301-22122-8	张德存	38.00	39	电子商务法	7-301-22121-1	郭　鹏	38.00
27	数字图书馆	7-301-22118-1	奉国和	30.00	40	ERP 沙盘模拟教程	7-301-22393-2	周　菁	26.00

物流类

序号	书　名	书号	编著者	定价	序号	书　名	书号	编著者	定价
1	物流工程	7-301-15045-0	林丽华	30.00	28	物流项目管理	7-301-18801-9	周晓晔	35.00
2	现代物流决策技术	7-301-15868-5	王道平	30.00	29	物流工程与管理	7-301-18960-3	高举红	39.00
3	物流管理信息系统	7-301-16564-5	杜彦华	33.00	30	交通运输工程学	7-301-19405-8	于　英	43.00
4	物流信息管理	7-301-16699-4	王汉新	38.00	31	国际物流管理	7-301-19431-7	柴庆春	40.00
5	现代物流学	7-301-16662-8	吴　健	42.00	32	商品检验与质量认证	7-301-10563-4	陈红丽	32.00
6	物流英语	7-301-16807-3	阚功俭	28.00	33	供应链管理	7-301-19734-9	刘永胜	49.00
7	第三方物流	7-301-16663-5	张旭辉	35.00	34	逆向物流	7-301-19809-4	甘卫华	33.00
8	物流运作管理	7-301-16913-1	董千里	28.00	35	供应链设计理论与方法	7-301-20018-6	王道平	32.00
9	采购管理与库存控制	7-301-16921-6	张　浩	30.00	36	物流管理概论	7-301-20095-7	李传荣	44.00
10	物流管理基础	7-301-16906-3	李蔚田	36.00	37	供应链管理	7-301-20094-0	高举红	38.00
11	供应链管理	7-301-16714-4	曹翠珍	40.00	38	企业物流管理	7-301-20818-2	孔继利	45.00
12	物流技术装备	7-301-16808-0	于　英	38.00	39	物流项目管理	7-301-20851-9	王道平	30.00
13	现代物流信息技术	7-301-16049-7	王道平	30.00	40	供应链管理	7-301-20901-1	王道平	35.00
14	现代物流仿真技术	7-301-17571-2	王道平	34.00	41	现代仓储管理与实务	7-301-21043-7	周兴建	45.00
15	物流信息系统应用实例教程	7-301-17581-1	徐　琪	32.00	42	物流学概论	7-301-21098-7	李　创	44.00
16	物流项目招投标管理	7-301-17615-3	孟祥茹	30.00	43	航空物流管理	7-301-21118-2	刘元洪	32.00
17	物流运筹学实用教程	7-301-17610-8	赵丽君	33.00	44	物流管理实验教程	7-301-21094-9	李晓龙	25.00
18	现代物流基础	7-301-17611-5	王　侃	37.00	45	物流系统仿真案例	7-301-21072-7	赵　宁	25.00
19	现代企业物流管理实用教程	7-301-17612-2	乔志强	40.00	46	物流与供应链金融	7-301-21135-9	李向文	30.00
20	现代物流管理学	7-301-17672-6	丁小龙	42.00	47	物流信息系统	7-301-20989-9	王道平	28.00
21	物流运筹学	7-301-17674-0	郝　海	36.00	48	物料学	7-301-17476-0	肖生苓	44.00
22	供应链库存管理与控制	7-301-17929-1	王道平	28.00	49	智能物流	7-301-22036-8	李蔚田	45.00
23	物流信息系统	7-301-18500-1	修桂华	32.00	50	物流项目管理	7-301-21676-7	张旭辉	38.00
24	城市物流	7-301-18523-0	张　潜	24.00	51	新物流概论	7-301-22114-3	李向文	34.00
25	营销物流管理	7-301-18658-9	李学工	45.00	52	物流决策技术	7-301-21965-2	王道平	38.00
26	物流信息技术概论	7-301-18670-1	张　磊	28.00	53	物流系统优化建模与求解	7-301-22115-0	李向文	32.00
27	物流配送中心运作管理	7-301-18671-8	陈　虎	40.00	54	集装箱运输实务	7-301-16644-4	孙家庆	34.00

相关教学资源如电子课件、电子教材、习题答案等可以登录 www.pup6.com 下载或在线阅读。

扑六知识网(www.pup6.com)有海量的相关教学资源和电子教材供阅读及下载(包括北京大学出版社第六事业部的相关资源)，同时欢迎您将教学课件、视频、教案、素材、习题、试卷、辅导材料、课改成果、设计作品、论文等教学资源上传到 pup6.com，与全国高校师生分享您的教学成就与经验，并可自由设定价格，知识也能创造财富。具体情况请登录网站查询。

如您需要免费纸质样书用于教学，欢迎登录第六事业部门户网(www.pup6.com)填表申请，并欢迎在线登记选题以到北京大学出版社来出版您的大作，也可下载相关表格填写后发到我们的邮箱，我们将及时与您取得联系并做好全方位的服务。

扑六知识网将打造成全国最大的教育资源共享平台，欢迎您的加入——让知识有价值，让教学无界限，让学习更轻松。联系方式：010-62750667，wangxc02@163.com，lihu80@163.com，欢迎来电来信。